cousin Francis came over today for the
day! C. and 6 women! I tremble
at every lawn-cutting and blow of a
hammer - and C. saying it is "just
like Englewood". I think each time -
"We will never come again - this will
finish it."

Of course there always were those
days at North Haven - weeks - when
we waited breathless - and said staunchly
this is the last batch of visitors - n
this is the last noisy week - after
this - no more mowing - or hammering -
"a war to end wars" kind of talk -
next week - it will be the quiet blissful

C. A. LINDBERGH

Cover MASID 10743

LOCKED ROOMS AND
OPEN DOORS

Books by Anne Morrow Lindbergh

LOCKED ROOMS
AND
OPEN DOORS

*Diaries
and Letters
of
Anne Morrow Lindbergh*

1933-1935

*A Helen and Kurt Wolff Book
Harcourt Brace Jovanovich
New York and London*

Copyright © 1974 by Anne Morrow Lindbergh

All rights reserved.
No part of this publication may be reproduced
or transmitted in any form
or by any means, electronic or mechanical,
including photocopy, recording,
or any information storage and retrieval system,
without permission in writing
from the publisher.

Printed in the United States of America

Library of Congress Cataloging in Publication Data

Lindbergh, Anne (Morrow) 1906–
  Locked rooms and open doors: 1933–1935.
  "A Helen and Kurt Wolff book."

  1. Lindbergh, Anne (Morrow) 1906–   I. Title.
PS3523.I516Z52   818'.5'209 [B]   73–16152
ISBN 0-15-152958-2

B   C   D   E

John Masefield's lines on page 229 are from "The Passing Strange" and are
reprinted with the permission of The Macmillan Company, New York, and
The Society of Authors as the literary representative of the Estate of John
Masefield, from *Poems* by John Masefield, copyright 1920 by John Masefield,
renewed 1948 by John Masefield. Edna St. Vincent Millay's lines on page 322
are from Sonnet 36 in *Fatal Interview* and are reprinted with the permission of
Norma Millay Ellis, from *Collected Poems,* copyright 1931–1959 by Edna
St. Vincent Millay and Norma Millay Ellis, published by Harper & Row.

Editorial Note

The diary and letter material in this book has been cut for repetition and corrected for readability. Since this is a personal rather than a historical record, the footnotes were kept, in general, contemporary with the diary and purposely brief, confined to information essential to understanding the text.

The following abbreviations have been used throughout:

D. W. M.—Dwight Whitney Morrow

E. C. M.—Elizabeth Cutter Morrow

E. R. M. M.—Elisabeth Reeve Morrow Morgan

D. W. M., Jr.—Dwight Whitney Morrow, Jr.

C. C. M.—Constance Cutter Morrow

E. L. L. L.—Evangeline Lodge Land Lindbergh

A. M. L.—Anne Morrow Lindbergh

C. A. L.—Charles A. Lindbergh

ILLUSTRATIONS

Illustrations

Landing among icebergs at Angmagssalik, Greenland
Eskimo women at Angmagssalik
Julianehaab bridge
Iceland's plateaus
Approaching the Faeroe Islands
Boats surrounding plane after landing in the Faeroes
Leaving the Shetland Islands

Between pages 198 and 199

Kayaks following the Sirius at Copenhagen
Flying over Stockholm
The farms of Skåne
The Lindberghs arriving at Moscow, September 25, 1933
Portrait of Elisabeth Morrow Morgan
The Morgans' sitting room at Tynewydd, Wales
The Lindberghs with Theodore Marriner in Paris, 1933
The Sirius tied to a bank of the Rio Minho, Portugal
Spanish fort and Moorish camp at Villa Cisneros
French flying boat base at Porto Praia
Anne Lindbergh at Porto Praia
Doping down fabric edges on the Sirius wing
The Lindbergh plane circling S.S. *Westfalen*
The Lindberghs arrive at Miami, December, 1933

Between pages 262 and 263

Anne Lindbergh with Jon, 1934
Charles Lindbergh with Jon, July, 1934
Aerial view of Next Day Hill
The Lindberghs at Lambert Field, Saint Louis

Illustrations

INTRODUCTION

"A traveler is to be reverenced . . . going from—toward; it is the history of every one of us." Thoreau's *Journal*, July 2, 1851.

The early part of this volume is given over to a long journey— the Atlantic air-route survey flight on which my husband studied the geographical terrain, the weather conditions, and possible landing sites for air service between America and Europe, still in the future in 1933. The volume ends on our sea voyage to England with our three-year-old son, in December of 1935, to start a new life in another country. But both trips were part of the same journey in Thoreau's sense—"going from—toward."

What were we "going from"? For the reader who has not read the first two volumes of my *Diaries and Letters*, I should explain that I came from a sheltered bringing-up in a close and affectionate family circle. The first volume, *Bring Me a Unicorn*, takes me through a super-shy adolescence and follows me into the broadening community of Smith College under President Neilson, where I discovered an interest in writing. The story continues with the dramatic expansion into the new and fascinating world of Mexico, where my father, Dwight Morrow, became Ambassador in 1927, and where, on a Christmas visit, I met the hero of the time, Charles Lindbergh, with whom I fell in love and whom eventually—to my surprise—I married in 1929.

In the second volume, *Hour of Gold, Hour of Lead*, I was catapulted into an even wider and newer world of aviation, then in its pioneer stages. For us this was a period of ground contact flying—often hedge-hopping—across the country in single-engine planes, poorly equipped for instrument flying. Our longer flights included the opening of a transcontinental air route and a survey flight to South America and around the Caribbean.

The bookish schoolgirl with no technical aptitude or training learned to fly a plane, to operate radio, and to navigate. We came to earth long enough for me to have a first baby, Charles A. Lindbergh, Jr., and to buy some land near Hopewell, New Jersey, where we planned to build. For a short period we rented a first home, a little farmhouse in Rosedale, not far from Princeton, where we stayed until our own house was ready. But these events did not interrupt for long our flying expeditions. The first half of the second volume ("Hour of Gold") terminates after our *North to the Orient* survey flight over Canada and Alaska to Japan and China, in 1931. In China we received word of my father's death—the first break in the family circle. We returned immediately by boat and plane to my mother's home in Englewood, New Jersey.

That winter, we moved into our newly built house near Hopewell, where a few months later our life was shattered by the kidnapping on March 1st of our first child—an ordeal which ended only, after weeks of suspense and negotiation, in the discovery of his dead body not far from our home. This was the "Hour of Lead" my diary covers in the latter half of the second volume. For security purposes and for protection against the overwhelming pressure of reporters and crowds, we returned to my mother's home, Next Day Hill, in Englewood while waiting for the birth of our second son, Jon, on August 16, 1932. Happiness returned to the whole family with the arrival of the new baby and also with the marriage of my older sister, Elisabeth, to Aubrey Morgan, of Wales. That volume ends with my description of their wedding in December, 1934.

This is where we were when this third volume begins: living with my mother at Next Day Hill. My older sister had just been married; my younger sister, Constance, and my brother, Dwight, were both away at college.

It is easier to explain where we were than where we were going. As in Thoreau's phrase, we were "going from—toward." Toward what? Toward the new life we were trying to find. The period of 1933–35 was an interim between two lives. It is the story of our recovery from the disruption of an old life and an account of our attempts to find a new one.

But before we could start the new, the old had to be dissolved. We still had to deal with the problems of security, publicity, and privacy. We continued to be the object of press pressure and threatening letters which usually follow an excess of publicity. A constant armed guard was necessary to assure our son's safety. There was the burden of recovery from a grief, the horror and mystery of which were still unsolved. There was the question of what to do with our property at Hopewell. Could we ever stay there again? If not, where could we go when we left my mother's home?

Next Day Hill was not the simple, sprawling, clapboard house on Palisade Avenue in which I had been brought up and in which I lived until the time of my marriage. That first home had been replaced in 1928 by an enormous Georgian mansion set in wooded slopes on the outskirts of Englewood. A long-postponed dream of my mother, the house was reminiscent of the big Long Island estates of an era just coming to an end in a booming America. It was built at the height of my father's career. He was Ambassador to Mexico, and soon to run for Senator from New Jersey. My mother looked forward to and was preparing for a political career that my father was apparently just entering. The kind of public life she envisioned was mirrored in the spacious halls, large reception rooms and dining room, the huge "new wing," added after their return from Mexico—a library with offices over it—and another long wing given over to the staff needed to run such an estate. Unhappily, my father, for whom it had been planned, lived in this house a bare three years. When his sudden death cut short his career, the need for such an establishment vanished, but the house continued to serve my mother and her vast circle of family and friends for two more decades.[1]

To the grown children who from time to time took shelter in its walls, during the years of depression, the "New Deal" of Franklin Roosevelt, and the socialist undercurrents of the time, the house seemed an anachronism. I would cringe, under a plush lap robe, being driven into New York by a uniformed chauffeur in a limousine, anticipating over-dramatically that at any moment a brick might come crashing through a window.

For my mother, the large organization of secretaries and staff must have been a burden, but one that helped to fill the sudden vacuum in her life. The halls of Next Day Hill were busy with goings and comings of family, guests, social occasions, and philanthropic meetings. For my husband (who enjoyed simple living and who had had enough of crowds in 1927 and 1928 to fill several lifetimes) it was an exacerbating situation. And it was an atmosphere to which, once emancipated, I found it difficult to adjust. However, in the interim years between the kidnapping and our departure to England, it was a haven for us and our boy. Here we could remain safely and in privacy in suburban country until we found a new home.

In 1933, as we started to pick up the threads of our old life, there were fortunately some good firm lines to grasp. Most important, there was our five-months-old baby, growing strong, active, and responsive, filling our immediate present and opening a vista to the future. There was my unfinished manuscript. I began again to write the story of our flight of two years before, *North to the Orient*. My husband's work in biological research with Dr. Alexis Carrel[2] at the Rockefeller Institute was becoming increasingly absorbing. And there were always the unsolved

[1] Next Day Hill now houses The Elisabeth Morrow School.

[2] French surgeon and biologist who was awarded the Nobel Prize in physiology and medicine in 1912.

challenges of new air routes, especially across the oceans. The summer of 1933 saw us setting out on an exploratory flight around the Atlantic.

The decision to make the Atlantic survey flight was a natural one for my husband. Since his flight to Paris in 1927, he had been interested in the development of transoceanic air routes. Who was better fitted than he to study such routes, weather conditions, and terrain? Flying was normal life for us, and the project lifted us out of the aftermath of crime and turned the publicity that surrounded us to a constructive end—the advance of air travel. For my husband there was the eternal fascination of adventure and exploration. For me, the trip was the nearest approximation to "a life of our own" that could then be found. It meant more freedom, more privacy with my husband, and more contact with people in natural surroundings. In addition, there was the satisfaction of taking a practical part in the work of the expedition as radio operator and copilot-navigator. I carried my part in the project and shared in the triumphs of successful accomplishment. I also learned the invaluable lesson—the gift of all travel but particularly travel on which one works one's way: the necessity of living in the moment.

All these factors were restoring. But on the other hand, the trip, especially as it was prolonged for five and a half months, separated me from my child, the most healing and nourishing element in my life. It also crowded out any possibility of a quiet contemplative coming to terms with grief, for me a necessary inner process, and it meant a long interruption in the work I had just restarted of writing my book.

The rigorous daily routine, I can now see, was also enormously taxing physically and nervously. The demands made on me of long hours, hard work, concentrated attention—and often, under emergency conditions, fear in the back cockpit—would have been a challenge to most men. I was no longer a page, as I had romantically pictured myself just after our marriage. I was a crew member on an extraordinarily difficult survey mission, which was in fact one of the best prepared and executed of all exploratory flights.

The feminist in me longed passionately to prove that I could hold my own and take the place of a man. And in the radio operation, I succeeded to a large degree. My work was indispensable to the success of the flight; and over the southern Atlantic I established a long-distance record for communication between an airplane and a ground station. I was amused but also inordinately proud to hear about the comment of a Pan American radio operator who, after sending me a one-hundred-and-fifty-word message in code through heavy static, made the astonished remark, "My God, she got it!"

The price of my successful efforts to fit myself into a new profession was a temporary eclipse of my normal responses. There was neither time nor place for them. My head was down in the cockpit, my fingers on the transmitter key; and my ears, clamped by earphones, heard only radio code, maddeningly interrupted by crashes. There was little chance to observe the beauty of sea, sky, and mountains, or to think about my lost child or the new baby at home ("He is there, a hidden treasure," I wrote). My diary, written in odd moments between flights and ground duties, became a clipped radio log. Occasionally, when radio was not needed, I could lift my head up in the cockpit and see the flamelike peaks of Greenland mountains, or dazzling icebergs in an arctic sea below, or a bright Eskimo village on a rocky coast. From time to time, the inner process of reconciliation with the past broke through painfully in vivid dreams, or with the sound of a howling wind at night, or at the sight of a curly-headed child.

On the whole, however, the time in Greenland was invigorating as a plunge in a northern sea. The wild beauty of that rocky coast, the cordiality of the Danish settlers and explorers, and the warm friendliness of the Eskimos, in their bright hoods and boots, washed us clear of memories. In those tiny, isolated outposts of the North the burden of fame fell from us and we achieved a measure of anonymity. We were strangers; we were guests; but we were not celebrities set apart from the human race. The daily round of the northern outposts flowed on regardless of our presence, and we enjoyed both watching it and sharing in its rhythm.

But after Greenland, as the flight continued for months and we touched in swift succession Iceland, Denmark, Sweden, Finland, Russia, Norway, England, Ireland, Scotland, France, Switzerland, Spain, Portugal, Africa, and South America, it became for me somewhat unreal and arid. In the more populated cities of Europe, with the usual pressure of newspapers and crowds, our privacy vanished. With each new place my ability to absorb new impressions decreased and my longing to be home with my boy mounted. A sense of reality returned only during a long-anticipated visit to my newly married sister in Wales.

At last, after a hard-worked-for crossing of the South Atlantic from Bathurst, Gambia, to Natal, Brazil, we arrived in the United States just before Christmas, 1933. We were alone in Next Day Hill, my mother having gone to California to help my sister Elisabeth settle in Pasadena.

On our return there were, of course, problems of readjustment, but I became once more the absorbed mother of an engaging little boy and started immediately to look for a home of our own. We rented an apartment in New York City as the best immediate answer to our need for privacy and security. The year 1934 began auspiciously in our new city base. Every morning I walked our son—with two dogs straining on the leash—around the corner to nursery school. The diary notations in these early months are few, as I turned again to writing *North to the Orient,* and also a long article for the *National Geographic* Magazine on our recent trip around the North Atlantic. Any extra writing time went into letters to my sisters.

The letters to Elisabeth show a new closeness after my now forgotten adolescent years of competition and jealousy. We were both married and could meet on the same level. She had early been a prime mover in the project to find a biographer to write the life of our father. Harold Nicolson[1] was approached and had agreed to undertake the biography, planning to spend the following winter in Next Day Hill gathering material. Elisabeth was also writing her own recollections of our childhood, partly to help Nicolson understand the atmosphere of our family setting, but more to preserve certain early memories which she felt would never be carried in a formal biography.

The winter passed swiftly with weekends in Englewood, and in the summer we returned to my mother's home on North Haven, Maine. In September we flew to Saint Louis to pick up a new plane being built for us there, and continued to the West Coast for a visit with Elisabeth and Aubrey Morgan. After three idyllic days, the visit was cut short by a long-distance telephone call to my husband from Colonel Norman Schwarzkopf, head of the New Jersey State Police, telling us he thought the kidnapping case had been broken and the criminal apprehended.

We flew back immediately to the East Coast and moved into Next Day Hill with my mother, preparing ourselves for the winter of the trial in Flemington, New Jersey.

This new development brought a sudden reversal in our lives. The morbid and intense press pressures that had surrounded us at the time of the kidnapping returned with added force. The newspapers were full of details of the crime and the case as it unfolded from day to day. Again, the familiar crowd of reporters gathered at the entrance of our driveway. As usual with increased publicity, threatening letters increased in our mail, some criminal, but chiefly from unbalanced minds invariably triggered by headlines. An armed guard roamed the grounds and watched our son day and night. My husband, following every detail of evidence and testimony to be given, plunged again into long conferences with police, lawyers, and advisers who were preparing the case.

Our attempts to find a life of our own (in a flying trip) or a

[1] See note p. 8.

home of our own (the New York apartment) had to be temporarily abandoned. With the renewed pressure on our privacy and security caused by the trial, we needed the protection of my mother's home for our child and for ourselves. My mother welcomed us with the utmost generosity, understanding, and patience. She gave us a wing of her big house and she scrupulously respected my husband's privacy and desire for independence. But I, as a daughter, was inevitably drawn into her activities, and torn between my loyalty to her and to my husband.

When a married daughter goes back to live at home, a curious unconscious regression seems to occur. Despite the best intentions on both sides, the old patterns for mother and daughter tend to take over. Willy-nilly, one falls into the trap and begins acting the outworn role. My mother's interests were quite different from ours, and her way of meeting grief, although gallant, was the opposite of mine. She threw herself unremittingly into activity of all kinds. Next Day Hill churned with people and projects.

Harold Nicolson had arrived from England to start collecting material for the biography of my father. A constant stream of friends, relatives, and business associates came to the house to be interviewed by him—or, I fear, as with most biographers, to give him gratuitous advice about how to write his book.

It was not an atmosphere in which two young people could lead a life of their own or start a new one. All the major events that took place during the winter of 1934-35 pointed to the past: another premature death in the family; the need to focus on past history for a biography; the trial at Flemington, which recapitulated a crime now three years behind us; and last of all, for me, the retreat into an adolescent role in my mother's house.

Even today, I can see no other solution to the situation in which we were caught. We had to be in the vicinity because of the trial. As a second daughter, and the only child at home, I wanted to support my mother during this difficult year and to uphold her in some of the prickly decisions which arose in connection with the biography of my father. I also knew that my little boy brought her almost the only unshadowed joy of those days. Because of our frequent flying trips, when her home had been our base, a very close and direct bond had developed between grandmother and grandson. It was, I felt, the one real comfort I could give her.

In the "Hour of Lead," I wrote prophetically in my diary of 1931, "It isn't for the moment you are struck that you need courage, but for the long uphill climb back to sanity and faith and security." The year 1935 was for me the long uphill climb. There was little solitude for the absorption of the new sorrow. The stoic tradition of hiding grief was strong and observed in both my mother and my husband. I cried silently at night or sitting on a stump in the scrubby woods outside the fenced grounds. The suppression of my natural feelings created terrible inner tensions, distorted fears and sensibilities. I regressed to the adolescent I had once been and found rising in me all the demons I thought I had left behind: resentment, despair, self-consciousness, and oversensitivity. With my Puritan sense of sin, I beat down fiercely my rebellious feelings, only to have them balloon at night like monstrous toadstools. Since it was unacceptable for me to resent my mother, her environment, or the outward circumstances around me, I turned my negative feelings inward on myself. I was convinced I was a total failure and felt trapped in a hopeless situation. All this inner turmoil was, of course, hidden. Between my face-to-the-world and the inner pits of despair, there was no bridge of expression. Lying awake at night, I began to understand Thoreau's phrase, "The mass of men lead lives of quiet desperation."

My reaction was familiar psychodynamic behavior as understood today, but unrecognizable to someone meeting it for the first time with no insight or help. I had reached, rather late, that painful point in the process of growing up when one realizes that one's adored parent is not perfect, or—at any rate—that one's own point of view, values, and tastes are not identical with hers. What is painful is not so much the realization but how to implement it. How to free oneself of the outgrown patterns without inflicting hurt on a loved person and without suffering oneself pangs of disloyalty and guilt?

Looking back with the insight of forty years, I realize today that the period of our living together must have been equally difficult for my mother. How it must have baffled her, my reluctance to enter her activities. What a mystery to her must have been my rejection of those interests, social, charitable, or political, I could have joined. What opportunities, in her eyes, I turned down; what invitations I refused, to speak, to sit on committees, to take part in public life or even—what was to her—normal social life. She was, I am sure, perplexed and often disappointed, but I do not remember her ever reproaching me for my refusal to take a different path.

Incomprehensible as it now seems, it never occurred to me to see a doctor for my problems. At that time—at least in my family —one saw a doctor for physical illness, and I was well, even if sleepless. Psychiatry was for those who had nervous breakdowns, and I did not break down. Even a modicum of counseling from doctor, minister, or wise friend would have helped me to realize that contrary to what I thought, most of my feelings were normal and valid and it was the circumstances surrounding me that were abnormal. It was normal to grieve over a family tragedy; normal to want a home of my own, independent of my mother; normal to wish to express my talents. It was abnormal to be recapitulating a crime, to sustain another major loss in three years, to be living in my mother's house as a married woman with a husband and child.

There was no doctor to whom to talk freely even had I dared. And in those days, modern psychiatry had not seeped down into women's magazines, parents' meetings at school, or advice-to-the-lovelorn columns in daily newspapers. I struggled to find wisdom in books—Rilke's *Letters to a Young Poet* ("Be patient towards all that is unsolved in your heart and try to love the *questions themselves* like locked rooms and like books that are written in a very foreign tongue"). I repeated that desperate prayer of Baudelaire: *"Mécontent de tous et mécontent de moi . . ."* I copied out advice given to characters in novels ("For freedom is not to be found in any accident or adjustment of the circumstances of life, but only in willing realization and acceptance of the conditions under which life is carried on").

There were, of course, many moments of joy. For happiness one needs security, but joy can spring like a flower even from the cliffs of despair. Communication with my boy, sometimes in words—with his growing perception and vocabulary—sometimes wordlessly in walks or games, was a constant nourishment, and again enforced the lesson of the flights—to live from day to day. The ever renewing face of nature was an unfailing refreshment. I invented games of acute surface observation which drew me from the dark inner pits to the outer landscape. "Well, what *do* you like?" I would ask myself, and make lists of the unnoticed joys around me. I walked around the paths of Next Day Hill under the bare beech trees, praying myself out through their branches to the clear sky above.

The rare peaceful periods of 1935 should have enlightened me about what was wrong with our situation. Whenever my husband, my child, and I were left alone in Next Day Hill or North Haven, our days suddenly smoothed out and seemed normal. My family became my own again. I could rejoice in my little boy. There was no conflict between opposing loyalties. I could make my own decisions and look forward to work and life.

The habit of writing almost daily in my diary also helped me and probably saved my sanity. If I could write out moods which could be admitted to no one, they became more manageable, as though neatly stacked on a high shelf. Brought to the aseptic light of the diary's white page, the giant toadstools withered.

Many pages of these depressed diaries were destroyed long ago, and of what remained, I have cut still more. But some entries are still there, left in this volume. For after all, this is part of the story, as it is part of many people's hidden lives. It

explains the abnormal peaks and lows of my emotional barometer
and was one of the many factors that led to our abrupt departure
for England at Christmas of that year. My depressions were the
inner counterpart of the outer frustration of our lives. A final
incident convinced us of the impossibility of giving our son a
normal life in this country. The car that was carrying him
home from school in Englewood was chased by newspaper photographers and forced in to the curb, where one of the men
jumped out and took photographs of the terrified child.

Despite the difficulties of 1935, I finished writing my first book,
North to the Orient, an account of our 1931 survey flight. In
many ways it is a rather restrained account. The stress of the
winter does not show in its pages and even the stresses of the
trip are politely smoothed out. At the time I felt that conflicts,
weakness, fears, and the general "nitty gritty" of life were a kind
of indecent exposure, not only for myself but especially for my
husband, who strictly guarded his privacy. So that my first book
now seems to me a somewhat glazed account of our adventures.

When one has processed and packaged part of one's life in
books, as I have, it is fair to ask, Why not leave it in that form?
Why go back to the imperfect raw material of the diaries? Why
publish the grimy minutiae of preparing for a trip; the tedium
of long hours of work, the reluctant early risings; the exaspera-
tions of cold feet and dusty clothes; the irrational night terrors,
lost tempers, and depressions?

Because, after sixty, I think, one knows the ups and downs
that life holds for everyone, and would like—a last chance—to
see and present, truthfully and not glamorized, what happened.
This is what life is, one feels; these are the conditions, the terms
on which one accepts or rejects it—and one loses too much in the
rejection. Besides the satisfactions, the joys, the gaiety, there are
always the sorrows, the trials, and confusions; the contradictions
and frustrations one runs into, trying to find one's way on this
journey "going from—toward." This is what life is, in one form
or another. It is sitting frightened to death in a back cockpit

in stormy weather and deciding rebelliously that one can't stand it a moment longer, only ironically to find oneself that same evening praised by a stranger for being a good and fortunate wife! It is also life to think one has failed and wasted a year producing nothing, when one has actually finished the job one undertook—for me, writing a book—simply by plugging along blindly and stubbornly from day to day, until one suddenly realizes that the door to a new life has opened.

But I did not have any of this foresight when I wrote in my 1935 diary. I did not know what was beyond the open door.

1933

DIARY   *Sunday, January 1, 1933*
Charles, of Princeton and the Rosedale farmhouse:[1] "A dreadful
house"—and I thinking with sudden heartsickness that I will
never never be as happy again as I was in that house.

All my life I will be looking back to that winter as the winter
of my life. We had him.

Tuesday, January 3, 1933
This will be fun anyway, I thought, the one party Elisabeth and
Aubrey said they wanted to go to. We will all be there. Mr. Bliss,
Tom Cochran, and Bubby Bliss,[2] to provide a dark rich background of tweed and smoke and a pine-paneled room. All security
and warmth, kindness and dependability. Tom's rich stories like
grand old prints. M. Monnet's[3] wit and wisdom ready to flash
when Elisabeth's humor lights on it. C. there, like a friendly arm
behind my back. Zaidie [Bliss] to mix it all together deftly,
sweetly, merrily. Mother's sharp hard wisdom, a foil to M. Monnet. Dwight and Con and I to watch.

But there in the middle Elisabeth, lovely and gay, darting one
moment, recoiling, teasing, letting herself be teased, and all of us
turning to her, lighting her up with a word here, a joke there, on
different sides. How I love being a foil to Elisabeth! Con and I
sitting back in the warmth, behind the lights and talk, to watch
and taste and talk about it afterward. For we would taste it to the

[1] House the Lindberghs rented and lived in while building their home near
Hopewell.

[2] Mr. and Mrs. Cornelius Bliss, their son, Thomas Cochran, all friends of
the Morrow family.

[3] Jean Monnet, French political economist. Worked with D. W. M. on the
Allied Maritime Shipping Council. Later responsible for the Monnet Plan
and the European Common Market.

full, that personality we have as a family, that round lovely circle that gives one light, another, shadow.

Oh, it would be a lovely evening. Zaidie would look enchanting and fragile, like a delicate and rather rare flower with a scent not too strong—delicate and passing. Candlesticks, and the table would be sparkling with Waterford glass, lots of glasses too, to catch the candlelight—goblets with facets to stroke with one's thumb. There would be flowers, delicate—like Zaidie—and delicious food one didn't have to eat and crested china and good coffee by the fire afterwards and thin chocolate peppermints. Elisabeth standing by the fire holding my hand.

Dinner at eight. We arrived. Mother was at the telephone: "Elisabeth says she is just too tired to come but she wants Aubrey to come. He doesn't feel he should. You talk to her."

I felt peeved and wanted to say, "Why didn't you say so last week, if you felt it—that you were going to be on your honeymoon and wanted to stay home with Aubrey."

The party was like a room made ready for guests, chairs drawn up, flowers arranged, canapés set out, all the guests standing around the fireplace—and no fire.

I found the next day she had a high temperature and flu. I felt compunctious.

Friday

Wrote a little. Elisabeth can't sail. Down in the subway express, trying not to cry, terrified of a smashup. All these people—listless, tired, already dead. The pale fish-faced boy poking his mother, who read the *Mirror*. Horrible horrible-looking people. I wanted to say, "And which one of you killed my boy?" I spoke to a nice Swede next to me: "Where do I get off for 39 Broadway?" She spoke slowly and kindly and I felt delivered from my terrors. Late out to Englewood; one of those nights you show everything in your face.

Saturday

Mother in Northampton. Funeral for Coolidge. With the baby all day, gay and sweet, crows out loud.

When someone dies in your family you don't accept it as *Death*. It isn't death at all but something else—terrible and shaking and personal, something no one else ever suffered.

Tuesday, January 10, 1933

Miss Sullivan[1] typewrites beginning of manuscript [*North to the Orient*]. In to see Elisabeth in afternoon. A blue transparent look under her eyes. I don't feel as though she could get well in New York.

Thursday, January 12, 1933

I am waiting for the year to strike—getting near and nearer.

Friday, January 13, 1933

Roumanian Presentation Dinner.[2] Amelia Earhart, a shaft of white coming out of a blue room. Lots of people. Nice Esther [Stevens]—perfectly real and natural. "I knew your father very well."—"Do you remember me?" Lovely room, never been to River Club before. Conscious of my pajama slippers—do they show? Amelia Earhart's husband hovering. Beautiful woman eying me, green velvet gloves, plucked eyebrows, artificially white hair. After dinner, C. and Mrs. Cornelius Vanderbilt (blue sequins and a waterfall of white curls). "I knew your father . . ." Presentation. C. misses the joke, isn't listening, bows, smiles stiffly—rotogravure Charles.

That glazed and beautiful moment when the man sings. All the women are still and unreal, all the men are still and real. Beautiful Mrs. Lawrence—English beauty. Beautiful Roumanian

[1] Katherine Sullivan, E. C. M.'s secretary.

[2] C. A. L. received a decoration from the Roumanian Government.

girl. Sad real eyes of men. My realization: This moment is of value. It has no roots, no meaning, no moral, no end. But it has value. It is a glazed and perfect moment of its kind. Let me not look beneath. Let me skim it off the surface. Let me preserve it. To itself it is consistent and true. Now I understand Proust. But how I wish I had a mask. Naked, with an unclothed emotion that embarrassed them.

Monday, January 16, 1933

Telephone call. President Hibben:[1] "I haven't very good news, I'm afraid . . . his life is spared . . . cut as deep as they could . . . imbedded . . . cannot take tumor out . . . nothing now but X-ray . . . telling you in a crude way."

Went to a Saks sale as a man to drink something—pale and horrible—ratty-looking hat, short coat, dress hem out, uneven, petticoat showing—and people eying me, passing, repassing, nudging—my fierce anger. The nice girl who waited for my clerk and hardly looked at me. Miss Sullivan types "Barrow,"[2] very poor, poor writing, can't read, my mind just like a frayed piece of paper. C. not home yet. Where is he, what is the matter? That boy—". . . cut as deep as they could." There is no happiness in the world, except Jon's soft hand against my cheek.

Tuesday, January 17, 1933

Bad night. C. home at two. In to hospital to visit the Hibbens. They feel the relief from the tenseness of the day before. Not as bad as I thought, except that you feel as though something were sucking in their faces. Life and hope being sucked out. I felt almost that they had reached a numb stage thinking about death, a stage of familiarity and recklessness, the way I have sometimes felt about someone's leaving. In the middle of sick heartache, you

[1] John Grier Hibben, President of Princeton University 1912–32. His grandson was operated on for a brain tumor.

[2] Chapter in *North to the Orient*.

6

suddenly wish them gone. You wish this terrible period over. You know it *will* be inevitably over. You cannot stay it. And the fact that you cannot stop the person's going makes it—by its very inevitability—as though it were already past. Already they are gone—already you miss them—already the blow has fallen. Quick, let us dispense with this futile handshaking, these cheap tricks of the moment. Let us take up the new relationship—accept it as we must. No more of this fawning upon the garments of the past. Then—with a shock—God! What am I doing? This precious thing is still here—let me hold it while I can!

Supper with Anna Fay[1] and Dan [Caulkins]: a fire, quiet humor, and comfortable give-and-take—and pleasure that your husband is pleasantly surprised. I want a home.

Wednesday, January 18, 1933

Bad night: long, low whistle, dogs bark. The Terror—it goes and is unbelievable in morning light. Lunch with Elisabeth and Aubrey. Charles comes in. Charles and Aubrey get on surprisingly, in a man's way. Elisabeth and I draw bated breath and watch delighted. Men kick friendship around like a football, but it doesn't seem to crack. Women treat it like glass and it goes to pieces.

Excited by *The Waves*.[2] Should one judge it as one judges a book or as one judges life? If the latter, it is glorious. It really cuts through to reality at points. Percival's death. I hate those labored in-between descriptive passages of the sun's rays and birds cheeping, etc. When I see those italics coming at me I rage.

[1] Anna Fay Prosser Caulkins, old Englewood friend; later Mrs. Leighton Stevens.

[2] Virginia Woolf's novel.

Thursday, January 19, 1933

I take care of Baby; has his first bath in big tub. Crows and laughs, pulls the bedclothes while having sun bath, can lift up his shoulders and head while on his back; likes to be held up near the shelf of little animals. Smiles at "Miaow."

Saturday, January 21, 1933

Out to Amelia Earhart Putnam's for dinner with Professor Piccard.[1] What color is the earth from that height (ten miles)? *"Gris."* (I jumped, remembering a dream in which he had replied, "Bright green.") His desire to go down in depths of ocean like Beebe, "But I think it is better to go up in the stratosphere, for I knew I would come down again. However, in the sea I fear I might not come up."

Amelia Earhart—lovely hands, long, delicate, and strong. She is *amazing.* "Have you read *A Room of One's Own?"!* She has poise, equanimity. Slightly prickly evening. I felt I was trying to swing it, with my hard-fought and earned poise, and probably just put it out of key, with my lipstick and my open sandals and my evening bag and my small quips. I had no chance to talk to her—or anyone.

[January 24th]

Darling Con,

I should be writing about the trip [*North to the Orient*]. But I hate writing that book—anything to escape it. Then I think about all kinds of things I want to tell you, so I'm writing on top of all the scribbled sheets.

I must tell you about the Nicolsons[2]—that dinner—such a

---

[1] Jean Felix Piccard, Swiss-born aeronautical engineer, made stratosphere ascent in balloon in 1934.

[2] Harold Nicolson, English diplomatist, M.P., and writer, who later wrote a biography of A. M. L.'s father, *Dwight Morrow,* published in 1935. His wife, Vita Sackville-West, was a novelist and poet.

strange collection of society people, except for Henry James,[1] who has a grand eye and mind. Awfully "nice" conservative people with "broad full lives," who enjoy *society* as well as charity balls, Stock Exchange, big-game hunting, reading popular biography, etc. None of them, I thought, as nice as slow, honest, *infinitely* kind and cultured Copley.[2] Don't you think Vita Sackville-West has a fascinating face—that long, pronounced-featured face (so English) and those beautiful eyes that see and do not appear to be seeing. What *is* there about the English? You seem to be talking openly with perfect naturalness when—*snap*—the blind goes up (or down, actually) in your face and they have shut themselves in for good. I sit in terror waiting for the moment —no warning—just *snap!* And you're left staring at the shutters.

As for him, I thought he was perfectly delightful to talk to, though when I found Copley had put me next to him I had a sudden uncontrollable wave of shyness. You know that feeling: you are twenty-six, poised and mature, with the glistening, impermeable shellac of thirty years on you—and suddenly it melts off and there you are left shivering, a girl of sixteen. Once stripped of your covering, there is nothing to do but become *more* shy and humble and seek shelter that way. Oh, it is dreadful. Will I *never* get over it?

Well, we tried all kinds of subjects: diplomatic life, big cities in America, "my wife's sinus," traveling over the country, etc. (He brilliant and facile on all.) Finally I took the bull by the horns and said, "I often think I haven't really traveled as much as Emily Dickinson." (After all, she really experienced "Pizarro's golden shores.") And on that toboggan we did very well. Her house in Amherst (I wonder if he went?). People who really lived in their houses—Jane Welsh Carlyle. They apparently did not like Katherine Mansfield. At least, when I spoke of her letters

[1] Lawyer and Pulitzer Prize-winning biographer. Son of William James, American philosopher, and nephew of the novelist Henry James.

[2] Copley Amory, member of the U. S. diplomatic corps, 1920–1929; friend of Harold Nicolson.

and Jane Carlyle's—Were they alike? I asked—H. N. said, "Oh no, not as *conscious.*" The story of Jane's death. H. N.'s conversation with a woman who as a little girl had seen Carlyle and in her embarrassment said, "Look at the pretty little dog!" (a picture on the wall), and Carlyle said, "Ah, that's the little dog that killed my poor Janie." (Now, Constance, go and look up the story—I'm not going to tell it to you.)

H. N. was fascinating to watch as he talked. His eyes seemed to flower in his face when he came to the point in his story. They were nice eyes too, kind and quick, but also the eyes of a person who has once been shy. His voice was very expressive, imitating Carlyle, and later he said, "It is a shame we haven't their voices preserved. I know what Browning's voice was like because I know someone who knew him, and Tennyson's voice, but (his eyes flowered) no one—no one knows what Edgar Allan Poe's voice was like!"

I asked him about Proust's voice. He replied, *"Mais, Monsieur, croyez-vous . . . ,"* a compressed, mincing voice—a careful voice. He told me the story (it is in *Some People*) about Proust wanting to introduce him to some grand swell. H. N.: "But it is unnecessary, I already know the Comte de ——." Proust: "Don't be stupid, my dear fellow. Imagine the pleasure it will give me to bring up a friend and be able to introduce him to le Comte de —!"

Anne, wide-eyed: "And how *did* you proceed from there?"

H. N.: "Well, it was rather difficult—I'm not very good at private theatricals."

H. N. thinks, though, that all those contacts are very important, personal contacts, casual contacts with great men, that they are very significant.

I disagreed. "But so many things get in the way when you're talking to a person—a cold in the head, his necktie, your permanent wave—you don't get to them at all. It's *so* much easier to write to a person than to speak to them."

"Ah (he pigeonholed me), that's like my wife." (Long explanation of that kind of mind.) "You write quickly?"

"No, I do nothing quickly, but it is easier." Then, thinking I was—like all women—veering to the personal, I turned the conversation to Wales, via Elisabeth's letter-writing, etc. There we got stranded on the rock of Vaughan ("I saw eternity the other night") whom *he* did not know, and bumped off to another rock —a poet, Morgan—whom *I* did not know; bump! bump! back to Proust!

H. N.: "Do you read him in English or in French?"

Anne (going into the hole of shyness): "I don't read French well enough to read him in French."

H. N.: "Good! Better to read him in English. Those long involved sentences are out of place in the French language, much more appropriate to the Anglo-Saxon. The Scott Moncrieff translation is excellent. Very difficult to read in French." Argument about Proust not being difficult.

Anne: "He may spend three pages talking about the hawthorn, but the hawthorn *is* there shining all through it, you see it the whole time, whereas with the modern writers . . ."

H. N.: "You know Virginia Woolf?" Oh, what a grand slide that was, like slipping into a smooth waltz out, out, over the floor. *To the Lighthouse, The Waves, Orlando, A Room of One's Own. To the Lighthouse* again! He said he did not understand *The Waves* (after I confessed the same). He had read it three times, even then couldn't understand, but he liked the stuff (rubbing his fingers together) out of which it was made. He said quite simply, "If you are telling a story it must be understood— that is your purpose—but if you are telling your associations, it will of necessity be incomprehensible." (Don't think I've got that quite straight, do you? Sounds too simple!) When we came to *To the Lighthouse,* we simply sat back into the complete abandon of "oh, lovely, lovely, lovely—and that part . . . and *that* part— oh, lovely, too lovely" (lahvly). And just as we were about to rise from this lethargy to the come-back of argument . . .

Copley rose: "Will . . . ah . . . the . . . ah . . . gentlemen please

. . . ah . . . rise . . . ah . . . and . . . ah . . . move . . . two seats down!"

And he said something nice about "just getting started" and moved on. And the man next to me, a smart Harvard graduate—Stock Exchange, with a mind full, rich, efficient like a cash register—started pumping me about biography. I seem to have read none of the classics. He was rather cruel. "Well, you're not interested in biography—what *are* you interested in?" I play mouse-hole!

Well, Con, I feel like the woman in Thurber's drawing, on the ice-pond: "Stop me!"

DIARY   *Friday, January 27, 1933*

I resent in a clipping, "Father of the dead child." Dead child—a waxen child stretched out. No—the child who died.

I resent, "They lost a child too"—as though that were the same. It is never the same. Death to you is not death, not obituary notices and quiet and mourning, sermons and elegies and prayers, coffins and graves and wordy platitudes. It is not the most common experience in life—the only certainty. It is not the oldest thing we know. It is not what happened to Caesar and Dante and Milton and Mary Queen of Scots, to the soldiers in all the wars, to the sick in the plagues, to public men yesterday. It never happened before—what happened today to you. It has only happened to your little boy. . . .

Monday, January 30, 1933

Terrible night. "Do you think about it so much, Anne?" All the time—it never stops—I never meet it. It happens every night —every night of my life. *It did not happen* and *It happened.* For I go over the possibilities of its not happening—so close, so narrow they are. So hard do I think about it that almost I make it unhappen. That terrible feeling, that pushing against a stone wall, that insisting "No, it didn't happen, it didn't happen"—and then always, like a bell tolling, like a clock striking, inevitable: "It happened." Then, at last, back to the only comfort—Death: We will all have it. In a century this distance between him and me will be nothing.

And then: He did not suffer, he did not know, a blow on the head.

But I want to know—to know just what he suffered—I want to see it, to feel it even.

Wednesday, February 1, 1933

My last month of him—and the shortest one of the year.

Sunday, February 5, 1933

To Hopewell. I make an excuse of it to ask C. questions; weak of me. "I went through it last spring—I can't go through it again."

There is the difference between men and women. I never went through it really then. I never accepted it. I never experienced it and I will *never* be through with it. I feel sometimes frantic, battling against time—this strange time that I thought marched along in orderly fashion to the tick of the clock. And now it does not move, it stays frozen inside of me.

Monday, February 6, 1933

Out to supper [with a couple that had lost their child]. "That was when Little Mary was alive."—"Little Mary is twenty-three now." Little Mary's picture over the mantel—"That was done from a photograph, of course." "She always sent her pennies to . . ." "She used to . . ."

I feel shocked and understand C. "I went through it last spring —I can't go through it again." God keep me from it. I don't want to glory in my sorrow, to say, "I have suffered more than any of you." I do not want to talk of him to people who never knew him. Let the sorrow be wiped out, the horror wiped out, in a vital living good—a home for children.[1] And I saw in a ghoulish

[1] The Lindberghs were planning to give their property near Hopewell to be used as a home for children, without regard to race, color, or creed.

heaven "Little Mary" shaking hands with "little Charles" and some ghoulish parents above saying, "I'm sure you're going to like each other—you know you both died young." Lord preserve me from committing such a sin!

And that lovely straight stalk of a woman, like a little bright zinnia. She didn't even let me know that she had lost an only daughter.

Sunday, February 12, 1933

"What time does it get dark at Nome?" [Chapter in *North to the Orient*] Wrote feverishly.

Monday, February 13, 1933

The lovely smooth junket-surfaced snow—life stands out on it in vivid relief, as on a beach. The tracks of birds, delicate pattern, penciled like a trailing vine. The messy jumping-off footmarks of squirrels, regular rabbit prints, the sculptured shadow of grass, where it has been pressed down in the snow.

Tuesday, February 14, 1933

What has happened to the straight pole inside of me that was *me*. I want to feel it sticking up into my chest hard and bristling. I am like a sack that's all fallen together. Where is that pole?

The unhappily married have it—lean on it. Can't one be happily married and still have it?

Thursday, February 16, 1933

It isn't the sorrow of last winter that stabs, it is those moments of hope—remembering those moments of hope is unbearable.

I planned to have him sleep in my bed the first night he came back.

It is not hard looking back at sorrow but at happiness.

To E. L. L. L.   *Englewood, Friday, February 17*

Again long delays about writing. But things are going quite well here. The baby gains. He is very jolly and alive. When C. comes home at night he plays with him when there's no one around, tossing Jon in the air (Jon always laughs), making faces at him (Jon loves it!), putting Jon on Thor's[1] back (no one enjoys that except C.!).

C. is well. I am very anxious to get him away from New York. He is too, but says we can't leave until about middle of March (after the publicity has died down).[2] Then he says we will take a rest, perhaps after we get to California, perhaps before. However, he is quite happy in his work. I went to the Institute the other day and Dr. Carrel told me, "It is really excellent, what he has done here. This (experiment with cells) has not been done before."

That work is a joy and stimulus to C.

DIARY   *Thursday, February 23, 1933*
Clearing out the boxes from Hopewell. Boxes and boxes full of papers and lists and letters and samples and advertisements and clippings—for the house, for the nursery, for the dining room; shopping lists, clothes—oh, the clothes.

All that happy drivel—all to come to this. The triviality of it in the face of such a precipice. Am I facing something else now just as much a fool?

Friday, February 24, 1933
I am doing it right over again. I am sick of clothes and gewgaws and bags and advertisements and newspaper clippings and society pages and the new *Vogue* and fittings and the main floors of department stores and the radio—jazz and magazines and hairdressers. I am sick sick to death of them. But I clutch at them madly, like smoking or drinking—anything to keep from thinking.

[1] The Lindberghs' police dog.

[2] March 1, the anniversary of the kidnapping of Charles Lindbergh, Jr., was used by the newspapers for renewed sensationalism.

Mother darling—

I am glad you are going, and Elisabeth is so happy about it.[1] She is so secure. Isn't it thrilling—like putting your hand on it— "There, that is settled."

We are going away too. The dentist says I can't go Monday but perhaps, as it is delayed, we *may* all go together—to Nassau. You have made it easy.

The baby is well and beautiful. I am perfectly happy rocking him on my shoulder.

I will write to Beauvallon.

Mrs. Aubrey Morgan   *February*
(First time I've written it!)   *The night before Mother sails.*
Mother has just ordered the car to go down to see Mrs. Loomis.[2] "Just a minute, Banks[3]—I have a few telephone calls to make first."

Your letter was lovely—so K. M. [Katherine Mansfield]. I shall read over her letters and imagine those little *"bonnes"* running in with hot water. I am glad there is sun and mimosa. Aubrey's letter (you must warn him of this passing-on-letters habit) was wonderful. It gave the most complete picture—his against yours —yours, slightly lyrical in spots, and his, terribly amusing.

As for the reporters, I simply relish his rage against them, as against the usual attitude of outsiders: "There, there, you must take all this philosophically. If you are going to be famous, what can you expect? After all, it's their living; they have to do it," and the rest of the gags. Oh, I'm glad he was angry. But I am so sorry for you two. That dreadful feeling of having your freedom taken out from under you. And we did it to you. There was a

---

[1] E. C. M. was on her way to France, to visit Aubrey and Elisabeth Morgan, then on their honeymoon in Beauvallon.

[2] Friend of E. C. M.

[3] The Morrows' butler.

frightful lot of publicity here about a so-called friend of C.'s in Denver, in all of which the press used our name to exaggerate headlines—very bad for our lives, of course. It brought us tentatively to the decision to try living in an apartment next winter. If that doesn't work, there is still abroad. And England is the best place.

So "Mrs. Lingrin" in her spectacles has been looking at apartments, penthouses, etc.

I am glad Mother is off. She needs it terribly—more the feeling of *no ties* than anything else, the feeling you get in a train or in a new place.

I am reading *Mrs. Dalloway,* in a nice small edition. I love small, thin books. Tell Mother to bring me back all of V. Woolf's in that edition (Hogarth Press).

Darling, this letter hasn't got *underneath* at all; sometimes they don't. Your letter was so happy—I'm glad.

DIARY   *Sunday, February 26, 1933*
Finish *Mrs. Dalloway.* Perfect.

"That network of visiting . . . being kind to people; . . . little presents; So and So is going to France—must have an air cushion."

Monday, February 27, 1933
It isn't that the anniversary is so terrible in itself. It is the recall of that eternal baffling mystery of death, the knife edge that one cannot understand—so fine, so sharp, so invisible, and so definite. The knife edge of "Yesterday I had him—today I have not." "A year ago I had him—soon I will not be able to say it any longer."

Yesterday, today, tomorrow—in the clamor of those three words are all the unbearables.

The punctuation of anniversaries is terrible, like the closing of doors, one after another between you and what you want to hold on to.

Somehow I feel as if this year that is over for me was just beginning its eternal round, like those cheap trick round-stories. How angry I was as a child when they would begin again: "It was a dark and stormy night and a band of robbers were sitting around the fire. The captain spoke up, 'Antonio, tell us a story,' and Antonio continued as follows: "It was a dark and, etc."

To E. L. L. L.   *Englewood, March 1st*
Dear M.
I write to you tonight because I know you are thinking about the same thing. Perhaps we do very often. Your lovely, lovely roses, reminding me of your thoughts of little Charles. Not that I make, or that you make, an anniversary of this day but I did dread it in that—a year gone—it took me further away from him. But to feel your message and thoughts counteracts that feeling, as though to say: We both know that we will never forget him, that he will never be any further away.

Thank you, and my love.

To E. L. L. L.   *[Englewood], March 2nd*
You simply must come on and see Jon—and us. We are all alone here now. Mother abroad, Con and Dwight away, Elisabeth gone. I am sending some photographs of Jon to tempt you. They were taken about a month ago but there was some delay about them. However, they look *just* like him. He is a little fatter now, and his hair is longer and beginning to curl. He is so active—shouting and talking and laughing. I *love* his laugh, I think, because it is like little Charles's, it bubbles out in an infectious wholehearted way as little Charles's did running round the room at night.

When you come into his room at night if you've forgotten something he lifts his head and smiles gently and coquettishly at you, as though you had a secret understanding. Oh, please come and see him! I feel as though I *must* share this happiness of Jon with you. I want to have you admire him and watch him and say what a grand boy he is.

We are planning to get away for a short time—perhaps Monday— *absolutely* incognito. I have some unpermanent black wash for C.'s light hair (you can shampoo it right out) and a curly bang for my prominent forehead. Also glasses for both; high high heels and a high hat for me, to make him look shorter. We would take the Ford and motor south. C. says it's the only kind of vacation he wants, away from himself, that is, the publicity self. The trip west will not give that, and when you are tired, publicity and reporters and crowds just rub salt in the sore place. The trip would only be for a week or ten days. We would not even tell anyone we had left; however, I will write you.

We have been thinking—worrying—*where* we can leave the baby, not feeling that Englewood or any suburb is safe except at huge expense, guards, etc. C. says the safest place right now in the U. S., "the only place where I'd feel content leaving a baby," is in an apartment. You have twenty-four-hour duty of doormen. You give orders not to let anyone up. You bolt your doors and no one can get in the windows. You have police protection at a moment's notice.

Of course if we ever did that—a small apartment—we would have to combine it with some spot in the country because we would *never* be happy in the city for any length of time. But oh, I do so long for a place of my own, where we are *independent*. Please come and talk this all over with us.

Thursday, March 2nd

Mother darling—

Your cable yesterday gave me that feeling both of wanting to cry and happiness, because we were both thinking of the same thing. It is not that the day was so terrible, or that I would go through it again especially then—not that at all. But that the tick of the year going by makes him seem so far away (that is foolish, of course), not being able to say any more, "This time last year I still had him."

C. and I went out last night; I with a Helen Morgan bang and *high* heels and glasses, he with hat and glasses, etc. We walked down Broadway together and went to a show—entirely without stares. It was perfectly thrilling! I felt as though we were thieves about to be nabbed any moment. But the excitement of having passersby look at you and *look away* was too exhilarating. C. was terribly happy and relieved. Don't repeat our disguises, as we want to keep them very secret.

Monday, March 6th

Last night I went in to the Coffee House to hear Amey's nephew [Putnam Aldrich] play on the harpsichord and someone else on the viola da gamba. Mrs. Norton and Garry [Norton],[1] were there—a lovely group of people. It was *heavenly*. I was in an ecstasy. They played Bach. I felt: If one can sometimes be in that restrained, ordered, precise world the other doesn't matter. Henry James was there and took me down to the door and I took him home. He agreed that it was perfect and said how much we needed it now. He was extremely nice.

Mother, you would have *loved* it. We could do so much of it next year. I keep forgetting how precious those moments are —when art puts a glaze over life and arrests it and you can stop and look at it and sink into it without being pulled off the edge of the picture by the strings that lead to daily life. How can you ever see life unless you see it that way?

Englewood, March 17th, '33

Mother darling—

I have just come back from our "trip"—a ten days' motor trip to Detroit, via Cleveland, incognito by Ford. We decided to go to Detroit at an hour's notice. In that hour I wrote Aunt Annie,[2] called on Aunt Edith,[2] planned to move Jon and Betty[3] over to

[1] The Nortons were family friends, from North Haven summers.

[2] Miss Annie Cutter, who lived in Cleveland with her mother, and Mrs. Sheldon Yates, who lived in Englewood, sisters of E. C. M.

[3] Betty Gow, nurse for the Lindberghs' baby.

the main house; spoke to Betty, Tom, Ida, Emily;[1] packed, fastened on my curly bang which completely disguises me, put on my schoolmarm hat and high-heeled shoes and lipstick, and we were ready! Aunt Edith came up every morning to see Jon, and Banks slept in the room opposite Betty and Jon. I thought it would work all right as no one knew we were going and therefore there'd be no publicity danger (to Jon).

We spent the first night in a little town outside Scranton, Pennsylvania. The hotel looked like an old saloon: a lighted sign and a few rubber plants and an old man in a purple wrapper behind the plate-glass window. He led C. and me (C. in overcoat, cap, darkened eyebrows, glasses, slicked hair, etc.) up the steep old red-carpeted stairs, for miles and miles past rooms—41, 43, 20, 26, 18, 13, 17, 12, 6, etc., etc. (They *couldn't* all be full. Why do hotelkeepers *always* do that—to impress you? Or to tire you out so that finally, when he rattles the key to room 5, at the end of the long rabbit hole you are exhausted and simply collapse on the chaste thin-looking beds!)

Well, we went right on, stopping for meals, gas, etc., getting bolder and bolder as no one recognized us. We said we were from Hackensack and gave a false name. The second day we got to Cleveland in the evening and were let in the back door. It was such fun. Grandma really was so delighted and gay. She seemed much better than at the time of the wedding. C. enjoyed looking at all the pictures, thought Jon looked like the early pictures of Dwight, Jr., but *more* like the early pictures of me!

We left after lunch the next day and got to Detroit in time for supper. Mrs. Lindbergh had been busy all day getting the house ready for us, when she needn't have. She could hardly be lieve we were there. Then C. proceeded to throw the house up-side down—rooting out old clothes, boxes, letters, photos, toys, etc., and doing them up again in brown paper parcels (introduc-

[1] Members of staff at Next Day Hill.

ing the Englewood brown-paper-wooden-locker method!). Of course when he got all of Mrs. Lindbergh's and his treasures unlocked and sorted, there wasn't time to lock it up again and get back when we had planned, so we stayed longer tidying up. Don't think *you* keep things, Mother—the tin soldiers and stones from Yosemite and shells from Redondo Beach and candy rabbits and Washington Monument souvenir paperweights of Charles that I wrapped up!

We stopped again in Cleveland, for lunch, on the way back. C. teased Aunt Annie and poor dear Grandma about their canary: "a bird in a cage—you who are so kindhearted," and shocked Grandma by telling her about my using lipstick. Grandma *was* shocked but when I came downstairs "made up" for my part she tried hard to understand and said sweetly as if to make up for her being behind the times, "*You* put it on so *nicely,* Anne!"

When we left Detroit Mrs. Lindbergh's dining room and garage were entirely blocked with huge wooden crates and the living room still strewn with little piles of knickknacks. These we threw hastily into cardboard boxes the last night. We would *never* have got away but Mrs. Lindbergh surreptitiously removed boxes and trays and trunks full of letters she had brought down hopefully to sort, *back* into her bedroom and hid them, probably under the bed, out of C.'s scouring eye. She said a little wearily the last day, "I know I *should* feel cleaned up but at this point I feel rather snowed under!"

Going back, we stopped at one of those old raggedy "Rooms for Tourists" places. Yes, really. Not bad either—a very good meal, outside of Bellefonte. "Stop by again, folks," called the man as we left. He looked at our car filled with cartons and bags (C.'s accumulation from Detroit): "You moving?"!

The whole trip did us both so much good. C. felt entirely free for the first time in six years, his freedom handed back to him. And to feel it is always there now, a hidden reserve. We *can* get away!

And oh Jon! I walked into his room and he lifted his sleek soft head from the bed and looked up at me with his big wide eyes and then just smiled quietly, as if to say, "You back again? Oh, yes. . . ." He looked strangely like little Charles, perhaps because he looks more of a real person, bigger. I've had him all day today. I came in early this morning and he was lying on his back with a lump in the bedclothes where he was pushing up his feet, and he was playing intently with your white wool rabbit. He smiled that quiet unsurprised-secret-understanding smile of a child—like little Charles again—when he saw me.

I was very happy today. It was a beautiful day, like spring; there were red and green points of tulips coming up and the maples look red. I walked through the woods and sat on a log in the sun. I realized that I hadn't felt that way for a long time, relieved of some great pain and heaviness. Wanting to live, and believing things were good, as though with the spring I could shake off the terrible winter preoccupation with the crime and think of little Charles as belonging to spring—as he did that day, the spring before, when I wheeled him over the brook and we sat in the sunshine and I thought, "This is pure joy—nothing else matters." As if spring could bring back that essence. I felt a wonderful stream flowing through me that was this life —all this eternal life—going on, and it was joyful.

DIARY   *Saturday* [*March 18th*]
Saw too many people, planned too much, telephoned too much.
Caught in the net again.

Why do I get caught? Mostly because I am weak, cowardly, and slow to think, hate to hurt people's feelings, don't like people to criticize me. I must slough off people—too many connections, too many people, too many entanglements. But it will take *all* the time just saying *no*. I don't help them, they don't help me. It's just bitter useless waste of lives, time, soul—everything.

Flying again. The things I had forgotten—things going under that still suspended wheel. How slow the cars. The pattern of houses doubled with their shadows, boxlike houses. How still the water—a boat cutting the water like shears—the heavy satin rippling back, falling away on either side. Frozen waterfalls. Woven cloth fields, rows, stripes, checks, cavalry twill, corduroy, tweed, homespun. Suddenly an arrow and a circle on a field— an air sign. The excitement of a secret language. That huge orange arrow meant nothing to the people down there—only to me. It spoke to me: "Airport this way," and I understood, and felt like God.

And over the earth a clear calm light, quiet. One could sit still and look at life—that was it. The glaze on life again, the glaze that art puts on life. Is that the fascination of flying?

Monday
Late for supper

I said, this time I will do it well. I will not be hurried. I will rest for half an hour with cold cream on my face. I will get out my things first. Then—

Ting-a-ling. "Yes?" "Colonel L." "Can you bring in my things? I'll dress at the B.s'."

"All right—if I don't call you back I'll meet you at 7:30 at the B.s'."

"All right, if it really *is* 7:30."

Bang—there goes my half hour. "Emily—Emily! Banks, I'll have to have a car after all—6:45."

Have to have a bath. No time for my nails—I'll do them while C.'s dressing—leave my hair as is.

Ting-a-ling. Ting—*"Yes?"* "Mr. M. He called before. I had to put him off."—"Hello? Yes—yes. Oh, I am so sorry. Yes, yes, yes—well, I'm sorry." Bang. Quarter of! No coat. Elisabeth's old one. The baby. The plug for C.'s razor. At last—Banks at the door. "The B.s', Henry."

We slide out. I look at the watch: four minutes of seven—I will be late.

"Again? Anne, how *could* you. You mustn't *always* be late, and tonight of all nights." He'll be waiting at the door—tight-lipped. "Really, Anne." "I can't possibly—in this time—get there."

I am sitting straight up. All the times I've ever been late climb up before me.

We stop dead with a light—in formation. We start again, crosstown. Two taxies turning in the street, breaking our tempo. Two minutes left—we can't possibly get there. The Plaza—Schwarz—down 56—turn on Madison. Left on 57—art galleries —not late yet—7:30. Now—"You're late."—"Only five minutes."

Approach—throw robe off—grab bag.

He isn't there yet!

Good Friday [April 14th]

Mother darling—

I hope this will catch you as I—alas—will not. The long postponed trip to California is due now and we leave probably Monday or Tuesday and will be away three weeks or a month, getting back about two weeks after you do. I am crushed that it works this way, but still . . . Jon will be there to greet you. He is staying in Englewood the whole time with a detail of the State Police watching him (by Governor Moore's orders) and Mrs. Graeme[1] there and perhaps also Mrs. Lindbergh for a little while. I'll move him to the guest room or perhaps my old room so he'll be right next to you and you can run in and see him often. He is awake so much more now—from twelve to two he has a real sunbath in his sunsuit and he crawls around, pulling one leg under him, hitching himself forward, quite successfully. Dr. Van Ingen says he is doing well. He is—if anything—too long!

I wanted this trip to California, but now I shall only hanker to get back to you and Jon and spring at home.

[1] Mrs. Cecil Graeme, E. C. M.'s personal house secretary.

DIARY   *Wednesday, April 19, 1933*

Newark—pre-reporter panic—towers in the distance. The long wait in the hangar while C. talks to officials. "Plenty good enough [weather] in the East?"—"Well, no—plenty good to Camden." Laughs. The stiff self-conscious walk out to the ship —snap snap snap. The wall of men doubled, each with two faces, his own and his camera's. "No, thank you, no steps." The slow rumble down to the end of the runway. The roar at the take-off —how she climbs! Terribly bumpy—keep the belt on. We're in the mist immediately—fuzzzz. This is going to be bad. The towers of Newark; we drop a little out of fog—the river—the Princeton road—New Brunswick—the steeple of the old state house—the bridge; missed Princeton, hills on right not visible.

Camden—how nice to be on ground again, how secure, how warm.

The weather report: 200 [foot ceiling] on mountains, mail not yet through, 400 at Baltimore. "We'll start and see where we get."—"Where are we going, Charles?"—"Well, if we don't get to Baltimore we'll go to Harrisburg." The river—low fog. Wilmington—very low. I stop reading poetry.

Thursday, April 26, 1933
Baltimore—Washington—Pittsburgh—Columbus

We leave Baltimore in hard rain. The man flagging us off drops the flag as we wave and shakes both hands clasped in a gesture of good luck—fervently—in the air. Small farms cut up with pine forests, gently rolling country. Hoover Airport, Washington, overcast.

Leave Washington, unsymmetrical green and plowed fields, patches of forest, gently rolling, small farms. The ridges are long lines ahead. We begin to go over them. Follow beacon into Harrisburg, small field, one runway. The Susquehanna—big, flat and curling. Leave Harrisburg 3:19. Hear Bellefonte. The ridges are long bony fingers stretching as far as one can see.

Rivers and roads run through green valleys. Johnstown and the split river. Cement roads look like ticker tape spilled over the earth. Pass eastbound plane. Coal mines. Pittsburgh airport, smooth as sidewalk, 4:55.

Leave Pittsburgh 5:45. Get up 800 feet, turn, hesitate—was the engine stopping?! Putter putter, small fields below us; I wait for it to pick up. It doesn't. The ground comes up fast. The airport is on a hill, falls off sharply—can't make it. I put my pencil up and fasten belt. Now you're up against it. No, we'll make it. Safe on the runway right up to blocks. That caved-in trembling feeling. "Motor cut?" I nod. "Not so good, this country." Bar Pete, lean and tough and nice.

We take off at 9:45. Cold. I feel scared. Night flying. At first, thrown into a bowl of darkness, starred top and bottom—the same consistency all around. Stars over and under you. Gradually two darknesses appear, a black bowl of velvet, brightly spangled below—the earth; a dark blue bowl, lightly pricked with stars above—the sky. These bright patches of stars below us are cities, all in rows and patterns, like spangles on a dress. As you look at them the lights twinkle, the whole thing shimmers, as though a woman in spangles moved and her dress rippled, catching the light.

Reaching out for one beacon as you let go of the one behind —steppingstones, signals just for us, as the lighted cities were too. The sense that the world was made for us, flying. White mist; C. flies lower, throttles down. I catch my breath. We land safely at Columbus at 10:50.

Friday, arrive Saint Louis 2:22

Leave Columbus 10:52. Nice friendly crowd; a child gives me a present, "a beret." Clear—light haze. The country has flattened out since we saw it last at Pittsburgh. It looks no longer like patchwork but a checkerboard. Fewer wooded patches—can see for miles—haze on the horizon making a second horizon, as though we were under water. Floods near Wabash River. The Missouri River, a long pale streak ahead of us. The juncture of the Mississippi and Missouri—two massive rivers joining with dignity—not a ripple of disagreement. The airport, smoothed out, new buildings, runways. We land.

A casual friendly crowd welcoming us "home." I feel at ease. I am hungry. We walk over the field, to hangars, offices, plants, see shops, airplanes, people. I want to drop with exhaustion. Frank Robertson always agreeable.[1] Phil [Love][2] grinning. Out to his house; [his wife] "Cookie." He is proud of her. She is pretty and has good taste. A little shy with us. I feel as if I could understand her. To the [Harry] Knights'[3] for supper. Irwin [his wife] very changed, tired-looking, and sad. I like her very much and feel sorry. C. and Phil steal off like bad boys on a lark.

Saturday, April 22, 1933

Late supper. Cookie and I talk and talk. I like her very much and think we have many of the same problems. Always that great temptation to unfold her—but you have to do it by unfolding yourself too. A man for a man, like a game of checkers. I feel much older emotionally, yet I could not run a house as well. The whole thing is fascinating. C. so like Phil, she like me; our lives totally different, and yet I can imagine so easily their being alike. C. comes in and bullies me up to bed—enjoys it, and I do too in a way. She understands, as Elisabeth and I might understand and smile tolerantly at our childish husbands—smile secretly.

[1] Frank H. Robertson, Vice President of the Robertson Aircraft Corporation, and a member of *The Spirit of St. Louis* organization.

[2] A classmate of C. A. L. at the army flying schools. Later a fellow air-mail pilot on the Saint Louis–Chicago route.

[3] President of the St. Louis Flying Club in 1927, Knight was one of the main backers of Lindbergh's 1927 flight.

Sunday, April 23rd

Two very smartly dressed women at airport. Why can I *never* look that way? Cookie is thinking the same thing (I guess). Does it mean a great deal of time or a great deal of money or a great deal of care? None of which I'm willing to give. Good-by to everyone.

Leave at 5:50. Flying into setting sun, quite low, an evening haze over the ground. The earth glows softly, shimmers a little, takes on an idyllic expression—towns tufted with elms, orchards, hills gently rolling covered with bushy trees—rounded shapes— looks like an English countryside.

The sun sets, the haze is gone. I can see west to the blue horizon and the pink glow above. We follow the river, which curls off in smooth circles to our right, gleaming ahead in patches on the curves, like a skipping stone.

The earth darkens. All the little pools catch the light, like bright pennies. The river glinting far off—a line, a curve of silver—glinting, disappearing, glinting—a satin ribbon in my hand, leading us.

Beacons flashing from all sides. The smoke of Kansas City ahead, ten minutes more. Lights twinkling on, towns in evening mist—the curve of the river holding the airport. We circle. Arrive 7:30. Big crowd—wild—we go into the office—they bang on the windows, shout. We drive out to country. Milk and buns and a fire and sleep.

Monday and Tuesday in Kansas City
Wednesday, April 26th

Leave Kansas City 11:32—high overcast. Going southeast—fairly big square farms. 12:10 Osage River. Arrive Springfield, Missouri, 12:43. We slide-slip into field. I think the wing isn't coming up; hot and tingly and weak in the back as we land. Large crowd. Very pressing reporter. C. tight-lipped. Leave Springfield 1:26 and head for Wichita. Flatter, bigger farms. First bare buttes—

strata show like contour lines on a map. Oil wells. Black plumes on the ground—burning the earth. Leave Wichita 3:56. The shuttle of the plow moves back and forth across a field slowly. I feel as if I could take up the loose thread, here, and unravel the whole piece of woven cloth, the plowed field. Arrive Tulsa 6:20.

Thursday

Leave Tulsa 8:59. Broken clouds. Gently rolling wooded country.

Arrive Oklahoma City 9:47. Pass TWA mailplane. Leave Oklahoma City 10:31—very hot. Big cattle farms. Outcrops of hard rock like islands in midst of green field. Over Elk City 11:20; small muddy-looking strip, the field. We drag the field innumerable times, once touching with wheels—climb up—circle again. C. afraid of soft places, makes trial landing to see how far the wheels sink in.

Small-town crowd—landed 11:40—left 12:05. Country getting very wild—sandy plains, sparsely covered. Oil wells, no more big green fields. Following Red River, shallow and sandy, many-streamed—the feathered serpent.

Arrive Amarillo 1:12—very hot, and dry and flat. Leave 1:40. Bare mesas, small dust cyclones ahead. First Indian corrals. Climbing up from one plateau to another, snow-capped mountains just visible ahead.

The Rockies rise from the plain. Ears popping. Try to fix camera. Climbing the pine-treed slopes of the Albuquerque mountains—a long climb—look down the range. On the other side, the flat golden plains of the Rio Grande valley; the sandy river and flat-topped pueblos. We've crossed into the Southwest. Arrive Albuquerque 4:18.

Leave Albuquerque 5:01, climbing mesas toward a new set of peaks. Dry river beds. Volcanic cones to north. Cross mountains to left of Mount Taylor. Lava flow and desert. Isolated peaks and mesas stand up out of the great plain ahead of us; Zuñi territory.

Storms to south. Pink walls of a canyon to right. Round mud Indian houses. The tracks of man show up on bare plains.

Arrive Winslow 6:50, right over smokestacks, telegraph wires, railroad tracks. Leave Winslow 7:13. Meteor Crater 7:20. Rough and mountainous coming into Kingman valley, jagged purple mountains on horizon. Arrive Kingman 8:26. "I want you to meet one of the nicest girls in this part of the country—my wife" (about sixty!).

Friday, April 28, 1933

Leave Kingman 11:20. Overcast, head wind, cold. Cross jagged mountains to sunny valley ahead. Colorado River. Now in California, crossing second range into second desert valley. Arrive Goffs Field 11:51. Leave Goffs 12:42. Up to another range. Fog right down on peaks—jagged white granite needles—running along them looking for a pass. Have skirted range, flying into another desert valley.

Dry desert seems to flow; molten rocks, streams of sand running down sides, dry river beds, thousands of little runnels, threads, alive as hair or flames.

Arrive Baldy Mesa 2:18, leave 2:34. "Very low over pass." How low is very low? "We'll see if there isn't a hole somewhere." Fog on mountains—trying to get through. The Terror—steep banking —still a hole behind. Turning back, following up the range. Fog sitting still and bright in the gullies, dark and heavy on tops of mountains. Spiraling up—back into the gullies. On a level with the snowy peaks, headed for them. Up—up—over—one gap. Can still see the plain on the left—one gap ahead—diving into it. Now we are in midst of mountains, no going back. Through another gap, going lower, following a valley, going for the light part in the fog. Green fields below—through another gap—mountains. Following a river and fields and road.

C. turns around and smiles, reassuring. It looks black ahead but the river is still there. We are following the valley. Very low

ceiling, poor visibility. But those lovely fields below to land on
—keep your eye on them. Even the slopes of the mountains are
greener on this side. We've left the river, cutting south over the
sides of mountains toward another hole—just sliced over. There
—the broad valley, green and beautiful below us, neat orchards,
big highways, towns, a dam—a promised land. Crossing the
crinkly, unreal, movie-set mountains just behind the airport.
Down over the telegraph wires to that long narrow field. Arrive
Los Angeles 3:31.

The house without Helen. Jack[1] very thin. It is strange and
familiar, this house where I lived when I was carrying little
Charles. Since I was here (and it seems not very long ago) he was
born, lived his life—and died. He seems more real on this trip
than Jon.

Sunday, April 30th

The beach, the sound of the waves. The head of land to the
south, fields and cliffs and houses, lit by the setting sun—idyllic,
peaceful. The line of mountains to the west, purple and unreal.
The little girl on roller skates who looked like little Charles.
"How old is she?" "A little more than two and a half."

Los Angeles, [early] May

Darling Elisabeth,
There were two fat letters here from you when I arrived last
week, one from Paris and one from Wales. "Your" house sounds
very nice to me. I like homely houses better than "pretty" ones.
They represent a period anyway and are amusing in that people
once thought them pretty. Do you think I might see it this
summer? I really think (still a dead deep secret) we will try this
summer, going very leisurely—Newfoundland, Greenland, Ice-

[1] Jack Maddux, president of Maddux Airlines; his wife Helen had died
since the Lindberghs' last visit.

land, the Faroe Islands and Denmark, Sweden, etc.—and see you somewhere! Think of seeing you so soon—so soon! Right now it is about time for you to come home. Mother is back and you should be. But if I only have to wait till August or July, that isn't bad. Then next summer, when I'm having a baby, you can come over here, and the summer after, Pan American will be jumping the Azores regularly (I hope PAA is aware of my plans for them!).

We had a good trip out, only one bad patch of weather coming into Los Angeles. We've been here almost a week with Jack Maddux. It is very strange without her, and that the last time I was here I was carrying little Charles.

Jack has a little cabin on the beach where we are now. I have not been on a beach since Nassau with you, when we sat at our desks facing each other with pink conch shells curling on the window sill and sand on the blotters and red hibiscus in a vase on the wicker table.

I have the same feeling of being absorbed by this beach life: the trails of seaweed, the tracks of birds, like a little vine over the sand, the high-tide line of stones, little crabs, things that hop, seaweed that pops under your heel, the sand sinking away under your feet as the wave goes out. The petallike waves unfolding flatly up the sand, the foam that's left when they slide back.

It is quite cold, though—not like Nassau swimming. But there is a big concrete walk here and I've been roller skating! It is really exciting except when "the big boys" come by at full tilt and I have to clump out of the way in a hurry. However, in beach pajamas and smoked glasses "Mrs. Lingrin" is quite inconspicuous and looks like all the other girls.

I dreamt very hard about you last night. We had all moved to an apartment in the Grand Central Station and I had just come back from this trip and you were showing me around. But Betty and the baby were across the Grand Central under one of the arches where you go to see what time the train is due. (Nice quiet place for a baby!) As you led me around a lot of men collected. You were sparkling beautifully and I thought as in the old days, "Nobody will dance with me." Then I thought, "What difference does it make? It's such fun to be with Elisabeth."

DIARY   *Saturday, May 6, 1933*

Left Los Angeles 9:32. Clear and sunny, a light haze over the mountains. It feels good to be in the ship[1] again, the parachute fitting snugly, the belt snapped to, the maps and things in the pouch. "That's where the key was, that's where the transmitter was, that's where the receiver was, there is the hole for the antenna, there's the cushioned headguard I clung to often!" I feel comfortable and safe, that lovely red wing below me.

We climb mountains easily. Tail wind; we are borne along swiftly. I have a wonderful feeling as though I had a life belt on, buoyed up in the sea—never feel that in a closed ship. Winslow to Albuquerque very rough but fun, like a bucking horse. I have my feet crossed on one side of the stick, in the sun, to warm them. But sometimes the bumps get too much for me and I leave my side-saddle position. I feel safer astride.

1:45 Albuquerque. Field, a shifting cross of sand, a blizzard blotting out the station at times. A car riding through it to us. 2:35, leave Albuquerque. 2:48, take picture of Albuquerque mountains. The thrill as you come right up face to face with the giants.

3:11, Las Vegas. Terrible dust storm. First a veil over the earth, then big thunderheads rolling up, the plumes of dust running along the plowed fields. We try to detour. It surrounds us. We climb and lose sight of the earth. We circle down and can't see. We turn south. The sun is a dim moon, the earth yellow—dust in your throat, your eyes, your lungs, lips parched. Burning wind.

---

[1] The Lockheed Sirius in which the Lindberghs had flown over the great-circle route from New York to Tokyo in 1931, and which had been reconditioned in the Lockheed factory at Burbank, California, after turning over in the Yangtze River.

We get up—the sun and the sky appear, one can breathe. It is like cool water, but the earth disappears.

We go down—will he see the earth before he hits it? We go so fast. We wheel on that red wing. The Terror again. Fog, he knows—but this is a strange thing, perhaps he does not know. He hasn't had experience in dust storms. We wheel—we turn—it is on all sides of us. There is no light spot. I think we will be killed. I will never fly again, I think in anger, and then, terrified, I say, you will never fly again—no—you will be killed. "Death playing hide-and-go-seek with us."

But no, I must have faith in C. "You ought to have more faith in me," he said. "I have faith in you, but I have no faith in life." I will close my eyes. I will not strain so—I will not meet this till I have to. I will not watch every moment. I don't have to live through this fear. I will deny living for this moment. I shut my eyes, and open them again and cry out. It is dark, muddy colored, on all sides. "Oh, it is so much worse!" I cry in terror. I touch the stick lightly.

If he would only smile or look at me to reassure me. But he does not move from his post; he is now on one side, now on the other, looking out, wheeling, turning. We are very near the ground. It is not as flat as I thought—mesas, canyons. We are completely enclosed now. Then a second wind. I feel that we are about to meet it—Death—and something flows into me. I feel stronger, I prepare for it, I put the things away, fasten my goggles, take off my parachute. It won't help me now.

I notice, with a new awareness, that we have passed the same strip of mesa twice. He is circling it. Oh, he is going to land! Joy! Relief! Good man! He plays safe. He knows what's best—good for him! We land—I brace for a ground loop, but am not terrified. We bounce, we roll, we stop. Thank God.

He turns and smiles at me. "We might have gotten through but it's getting dark." "Where are we? Texas?" No houses. An oil line and hut seen from the air, now downhill out of sight. We try to start the engine—starter broken. Now we are stuck— have to walk out. Will they look for us? Food? Plenty. Water? Well, enough, and two ginger ale bottles. I must have some, this wind burns you up. We try to find the oil line—too thick. We lay out the luggage, in the compartment. The wind whistles in cowling. I am very thirsty. "Don't guzzle it."

Well, we're safe, but I'm not happy as I was at Ketoi[1] when I got in touch with JOC [the Japanese radio station at Nemuro]. I knew they would let everyone know. No radio. I look at the empty springs. Will Mother worry? "Mother Mother Mother, I'm all right." If only I could let her know. "They won't worry." But they will. When one is struck one waits for the next blow. One has no confidence.

It was strange to lie there still of the world, yet out of touch. I wonder if it is like that when one is dead—seeing them worry and not being able to say it's all right. That would be agony.

We eat Jackson's sandwiches. She put in a whole loaf of salt rising bread! If only my hands were not so gritty. I get out the tiny tube of cold cream and clean my face; it helps—on my lips. But perhaps I am squandering it—we may be days. "A little more ginger ale, please." I could even drink beer! The wind shakes the ship. It is hard to breathe. C. very restless. I look out through the window at the cool stars—tell them we're all right.

Sunday

Clear. "Look out and see if you can see a house."

"No, but I can see a telephone line and a road!"

"There's a house—way off there—and there."

"All right, you can drink all you want now."

My fingers are splitting with dryness. I comb my hair (how silly the curls seem matted in my neck!) and clean off with cold cream. C. takes the cowl off, finds nut slipped.

---

[1] The reference is to the Lindberghs' forced landing on their trip to the Orient, off Ketoi Island, Chishimas, August 19, 1931.

A car comes up—two weathered ranchers and a little boy. "Have a forced landing?"

"Lindbergh's my name."

"Well, I swear! My wife has cried over you folks—cried and cried . . . How is the new baby? . . . Oh, this is a pitiful country round here—just desert."

We take off—and head for Kansas City, 7:42 A.M. (Los Angeles time). Land in Kansas City 10:40. People excited. C. taciturn and a little cross. They'd been up all night. *"Your* folks were awful worried." Three planes out looking for us. Leave Kansas City 2:10, arrive Saint Louis 3:58. Leave Saint Louis 4:20. Richmond and the first beacon 6:40. Hazy. Will the light last thirty minutes more? We follow the road and see lighted cars and beacons and towns.

Columbus—sparkling and bright—spread out. But what a gulf between us—the gulf of a safe landing at night. I remember my old nightmare, as a child, being a giant and the earth below me very small. The labor one had to go through to get back to one's right size, to fit down in that little world. And I wanted so much to get down.

Very bumpy landing, 7:34. "You might as well get out till we see what the weather's like." I prayed it was bad. "Well, I don't think we'll go any further." Joy and relief! Bread and milk and sleep—and a *hot bath!*

Monday

We get set to leave but weather closes down over the mountains. Hear a plane being guided in at Pittsburgh—300 feet!

Leave Columbus 2:55—low ceiling, good visibility till 4:35. Then bright white fog sitting down on the mountains. A lake of fog with definite borders—feathers and foam and smoke and cotton and milkweed fluff—frozen still—so bright and calm. And a beautiful blue sky above. I take pictures. We detour and fly under; it gets bad up the Potomac. Arrive Washington 5:37.

And it's such a lovely day on top! I suppose it's always a lovely day "on top"!

[To] Mrs. McLean[1] for supper. Car sent for us, high powered. We drive into big gates; a huge rambling old-fashioned house—an old monastery.

She is a bird of Paradise, absolutely no fear, no inhibitions, great zest for life, adventure, mystery. Warmhearted, impulsive, but uncompromising. "Don't you hate people without nerve! . . . I said I'll take a look at this stone, there's been so much history about it. I began to get fascinated by it—I've *got* to have that stone. . . . Sitting up in a haunted house with a gun across my knees." That raucous voice, the perfume, body like a board. Her room, the radio, the Crucifix, the mystery books, the gun on the bedside table, pink satin sheets. "Death is your best friend. . . . Life is a pretty harrowing thing at best. . . . But I want it to get better for my children."

Englewood, May 12th and 13th

Darling Elisabeth,

It is grand to get home to find Mother and Jon, and the place very lovely. The daffodils and narcissus on the hill are gone but there were glass-y tulips all through the house, cool and formal and statuesque. I thought Mother looked wonderful, though she said she was (temporarily) tired with the impact of homecoming and its responsibilities. She was full of news of you, showed me the pictures, air view first. I don't think the house is homely (couldn't you shave it clean in front someday?). And the way it is set in trees and fields is *lovely*. I am so glad to see it. Now I can imagine you there—the magnolia tree, the garden, and the hedges. It is so funny and nice to think of you planning the colors of the walls and interviewing servants. I laughed at Aubrey's comment on your picking the house for the magnolia

---

[1] Evalyn Walsh McLean, owner of the Hope diamond.

tree that only blooms two weeks, and read that to Charles. I always picked out houses for the "lovely *old* trees."

I had so much to tell you and now in this hectic rush for the boat[1]—like saying good-by—it melts. Only that it is lovely to be home, that the garden turf is very green and the box is darker green and there are white and red tulips growing around the box. The apple blossoms are out and falling, wet on the paths. It is May *13th*. A year ago you were with us in Hopewell. Doesn't it seem to you like that verse of George Herbert:

> "I once more smell the dew and rain,
>   And relish versing. O my only Light,
>   It cannot be
>   That I am he
>   On whom Thy tempests fell all night."

Isabel[2] stopped me in the hall to tell me "how well Mrs. Morgan looked, and what a wonderful man she has!"

TO E. L. L. L.   *Englewood, Thursday [May 25th]*
Dear M.

You must know by the papers what has been happening. Whateley[3] was taken suddenly ill Friday and operated on that night. It turned out to be a leaking ulcer and developed into peritonitis. He had very little hope from the beginning but he did hold his own remarkably for four days giving us hope that he might pull through or at least live until Elsie arrived from Europe Tuesday night. But he died Tuesday morning. It seems such a cruel chance with always the feeling that if he had had more warning or acted more quickly he might have been saved.

---

[1] Before the days of transatlantic airmail one planned and addressed letters to catch a particular steamship at sailing time.

[2] Isabel MacDonald, Mrs. Morrow's personal maid.

[3] Oliver and Elsie Whateley were the English couple who took care of the Hopewell house.

Charles went down to see Whateley and the doctor the day after the operation. And we both met the boat.

Elsie has been quite wonderful—quiet and calm and sane—though, poor woman, she is completely dazed and lost as to what to do. She says she must stay here and work as she cannot go home to England and be dependent on them. She has no one here, not even a close friend as they were very happy together and did not go out much. We are keeping her here, of course. I want so much to keep her in the family though there is not much for her to do now; there *would* be next winter, if we have a home somewhere. In the meantime she is doing odd jobs for the baby, whom she adores, and altogether is a lovely person to have around.

Our plans are going along and C. thinks we will leave by the first of July. Do you think you could be with Jon from the middle of July to the end of August? Or will that break into things too much? It is a long time but the family is scattered this summer and we would like you. There will also be some kind of guard.

I feel as if there were more to say. Oh, yes—Jon. He is getting a good tan, out in the sun crawling, pulling himself up and down on chairs. He is active all day and happy and gay and *hates* to go to bed, putting his arms around your neck when you go to put him down.

TO E. L. L. L.   *Englewood, Monday* [*June 12th*]
Dear M—

What a long silence! And only from a rush of things—

We have been trying to get ready for the trip[1]—clothes, equipment, food, hundreds of details. (I am always trying to get *heavy* clothes in hot weather!) Then we have been working to

---

[1] The Lindberghs were to survey possible transatlantic air routes and bases. They spent five and a half months on the trip, and flew the same single-engine monoplane seaplane that they used for their far northern flight from New York to Tokyo in 1931.

find out if Hopewell could be used for children sometime. Also trying to move our things out of Hopewell, now that Elsie and Whateley aren't there any longer to look after them. That meant packing—what packing! China, glass, excelsior, newspapers, etc.

Then I do radio every day and try to finish my account of our last trip. How hard it is to write description, isn't it? Also one wisdom tooth out, quite painlessly. All this has kept me from Jon and there is a constant pull there, for I *hate* to leave him. However, we have taken him into the swimming pool and he loved it; also, he paddles around in the little pool in the garden, good wading for him. C. teases and splashes him.

I think we will take two or three weeks more. Won't you come on before we go? There is so much to talk over. This summer Mother is going abroad, Mrs. Graeme on a vacation, and if you do not come I should feel I must get a trained nurse. I really and honestly would rather have you there. They none of them understand the way we feel about the baby, and I think you do.

TO E. L. L. L.   *Englewood, June 20th*

I was glad to get your wire and letter. I shall try to answer the questions, though we *are* vague. It depends so much on our plans. For instance, the *time*. I wanted to keep Jon here while we were here and just send him up the last moment, then stop and see him again in North Haven on our way north.

We live on a point of land right on the water and not in or near the town—in fact, it takes twenty minutes from the town of North Haven to our house. There are no houses near us, except Mr. Grant's, the farmer and his family whom we bought the land from. He is very nice, has worked hard all his life. He has three girls, but last year his wife had a son and Mr. Grant got himself a pair of false teeth and he looks years younger and prouder! I think it's rather insulting to the girls. The boy is a little older than Jon. Mr. Grant has some nephews who sometimes help him with the work on the place. I like those Maine people very much.

They are nice self-respecting people. They don't gawk at you and they mind their own business; on the other hand, they are friendly and kind. I always remember when C. and I went up there on the boat the Maine people at the ports where we stopped were perfectly natural and they made such fun of the reporters!

You won't need formal clothes of any kind. We never wear anything but a sweater and skirt. It is cool—like September. I am afraid it is going to be dull for you. Isn't there someone you would like to give a vacation to and have with you? I love it because I am perfectly happy to be on that place with my family and never move off it. But with no one there it might be quite different.

There will be a guard, C. says. He will be up all night so you won't have to worry. We don't leave the baby alone outside at any time—the dogs and somebody sit near enough to watch. Emily can take care of the baby on Betty's days off if you don't want to. But I would like to have you with him a good deal.

There is a swimming pool where little Charles went swimming two summers ago, but he spent most of the time on the stony beach playing with sunny stones. We vary in our treatment of Jon, C. saying he should be left alone, let get hurt, let cry, etc. As a rule I suppose you should "just let them cry." But I have found, with Jon, that when he cries he usually has a reason. If you fix it, he is satisfied and stops crying and does *not* cry for more attention afterwards. If he does *that* of course he should be left alone. I do agree that a certain part of each day he should be left to play alone (always watched of course) perhaps in his pen, to encourage independence, but on the other hand I like him to play with people, and children too.

Yes, *please* write me about him. And will you take some pictures of him regularly? There seem to be millions of things to tell you—much more to say about our trip. Something has turned up which eases my mind *tremendously*. Pan American is sending a boat up there [Greenland], as a kind of base. That means a radio, mechanics, repair shop, etc., right at hand and help if we need it. They will go ahead (I imagine) and report weather and guide us across the water jumps. This is all quite tentative and a secret. But I feel much safer and happier about the trip.

With you taking care of Jon, and the boat taking care of us, my summer has smoothed out beautifully!

Did you notice that President and Mrs. Hibben of Princeton were in a terrible motor accident? He died immediately; she, just lately. It makes me sad. I was fond of both of them, and they made that one winter at Rosedale very happy for me.

Englewood, June 24th

Darling Elisabeth,

We have had the letters so fast that Mother has hardly had time to be worried.[1] She was extremely grateful and felt such confidence in Aubrey and Mrs. Morgan for the first two letters, even though they brought bad news—she had a feeling of security in their care of you and in their sincerity. Then the splendid cable and now today your own letter. She feels much better. I do feel that this must be due to Christmas and the flu and all that—a cumulative thing rather than a result of Wales. And heaven knows the adjustments of the first year of marriage are enough of a strain, no matter how happy one is (in spite of C.'s saying naively that marriage isn't an effort!). Somehow, Mother and all of us feel convinced that Wales and Aubrey and Tynewydd are the right life for you and that the good results will show soon, and that this is a good-by present of the old life.

C. says we may be two months in Greenland and Iceland and we expect to start around July 4th. So you can see how you feel by the end of August. If having guests in the house is too much

---

[1] Elisabeth Morgan had suffered another heart attack and her health had deteriorated in Wales. British doctors recommended a year in a mild climate.

bother we could stay at a hotel in Cardiff (don't snort!) or visit you from London. You can let us know later—probably when we arrive in Copenhagen.

It was so lovely to hear from my old friend "Grace Irving"[1] on my birthday. It was a lovely day and we had lunch and supper out under the trees—the round table and the pink china! I gave Jon a present for little Charles [It was his birthday also]—some gay Swedish glass. He had some prune juice from the glass, though most of it went on his bib!

Isabel says wistfully, "Why does anyone want to go abroad? Nothing abroad is as lovely as North Haven."

We have moved out of Hopewell; everything is packed. We are giving the place to a Corporation of Trustees—only five so far—Col. Henry [Breckinridge], Mr. Lovejoy, head of the Children's Aid Society, Abraham Flexner,[2] and C. and I. Mother will join later. We have called the place *High Fields,* in which there is a secret second meaning. It pleases me very much.

DIARY   *Sunday, June 25, 1933*

B.'s article in a magazine waking me suddenly to the fact that in a rush of moving from Hopewell, finishing book [*North to the Orient*], Children's Aid Society, radio, clothes, dentist, etc., all preparation for the trip, I haven't stopped to breathe or think or live consciously or write in the last two months. And it wakes me to the fact that with all my talking I've never got a thing published, and I could do it—I *could,* but I haven't got the guts. Oh, I want the recognition. You can't just write and write and put things in a drawer. They wither without the warm sun of someone else's appreciation.

I feel wretched, doomed never to be anything but amateur, never in earnest, never professional.

---

1 Childhood name for Elisabeth Morgan. See *Bring Me a Unicorn,* p. 32n.

2 Director of Institute for Advanced Studies, Princeton (1930–39); educator, author.

Darling Elisabeth,

I have just had your letter and am writing immediately because I am so anxious to tell you something before you decide definitely on your place for a long vacation. Of course I haven't talked with you, I don't know all the factors—whether Aubrey can be with you all the time, the distance you can go, etc. But if you are going to be in *one* place for eighteen months I would not choose Bermuda. I think it would be heavenly for one summer or one winter.

You mention California and so I write about it. I had no idea you would go that far away so I never considered it, but if I had my choice between Bermuda and California I would certainly take California *if it was to be for a long time.* Of course the climate is perfect—all year round (as Bermuda is too). But to me it has several advantages. One is: if you get tired of Santa Barbara, a few hours' motor trip will take you to the desert (really more alluring than that sounds!) or down the coast to tropical weather, or up in the mountains for a cool change, or over to that island off Los Angeles which is semitropical—a twenty minute plane flight—regular schedules. If you get sick of Bermuda, what *can* you do? You can't motor—it is a rough trip off the island—and you are more or less imprisoned there.

If you need medical attention, you can get the best from Los Angeles. If you are north, from San Francisco. I should think much better attention than you could get anywhere except New York, London, and Paris.

Of course I think that the most beautiful coast in the world (not excepting Maine) is south of San Francisco, near Monterey. It is wild and rocky, with cypresses growing down to the water's edge. I'm afraid it might be foggy in the winter but we were there in the early spring and it was beautiful.

Also I think we might spend part of the winter there! So if you consider going as far away as that, do think seriously about California.

We are in the last throes of departure, sometime this week, and I feel desperately—you know—"Just why *am* I going to Greenland?" But I cheer myself on by thinking I shall see you [in Wales].

DIARY   *Saturday, July 8*

I want to write down before I go on this trip what I want most for Jon. I want him to be kind and appreciative and independent. I think he will be kind and appreciative if he is not spoiled, is not made to feel that he is privileged. For he is an affectionate, responsive child and will be easily led to be generous.

But I think there is quite a chance that he will be too much guarded and cared for, partly because we have him well supplied with comforts. And also because of the experience of the other baby he may be too carefully watched. Also, because of his name, things will be done for him. I want him to be left alone to fight out even his early troubles, to sleep alone, to play by himself or with other children his own age, to fight out his own quarrels, so that he will grow into an independent, courageous man—so that he will not be afraid of life but will meet it with optimism and courage and zest like his father and his grandfather.

July 9th

Left North Beach at 3:37. Thunderstorms. The red plane in a circle of cars, the movie men. Winters giving me last [radio] instructions. Good-by to Mr. Post, to Winters. Aida, Harry, and Carol, waving.[1] The ship pushed down on rollers. "This one will make it!" Splash! We're off! Quite a long take-off. Other planes in the air. We circle and circle over the river, the barges, the dump island—wheeling and turning to avoid camera planes. I reel out radio antenna. Little white sailboats in the Sound.

[1] Aida, wife of Henry Breckinridge who was C. A. L.'s friend and lawyer. Harry and Carol Guggenheim, close friends of the Lindberghs. Harry Guggenheim had been president of the Daniel Guggenheim Fund for the Promotion of Aeronautics, and Ambassador to Cuba.

Storms. Static. Hartford, New Haven, then absorbed by radio. Lowell, Massachusetts. Hit the coast and low fogs. Pass Apple-dore, clear at Portland, then we hit fog, go inland. Try to get to Rockland two or three times.

C. shakes his head, finally lands on a long lake. Raining. Motorboats surround us. We anchor to seagrass island, pull the ship around, tie ropes, put stones on anchor. We pole in to the beach—a cottage camp; a nice man and three fat children. "Well, I guess these folks are the Lindberghs," as we climb up the steps of camp.

July 10th

We take off, fly over Rockland. The islands are pale today, no color, like a gray Japanese wash. Fly over the house—little figures running out onto the green lawn. It catches my breath—the beauty and the frailty of it. Land in The Thoroughfare. A lot of boys rowing little boats. Mr. Hopkins takes us off to the *Mouette*.[1] The drive home—the baby still up. C. goes back to work on the plane, I walk around with Mother, take her to the dock.[2] That dreadful ache; can't say anything.

The drive back alone, the smell of wood burning in the house. Jon smiling at me as I blow on his whistle cup, burying his head in my lap, playing hide-and-go-seek with me behind chairs in the library. I hide and say "Where's Mum mum?" and then he smiles, starts off on all fours and says "Da!" with a broad smile when he finds me.

North Haven [*July 11th*]
After you left

Darling Mother,

Those times are always so dreadful, and if I even try to say anything, I cry, so it is better not, and I know the pat on the back and the squeeze of the arm mean what we are both feeling.

[1] A small motor yacht of the Morrow family.

[2] E. C. M. was leaving for New York and Europe.

I have such a wonderfully solid feeling having seen you here, you and Jon and Mrs. Lindbergh, all happy in North Haven. North Haven does stand for something very permanent. Do you remember

> "Yet these are things invested in my mood
> With constancy and peace and fortitude"

I shall take your sweet note with me for a "rampart."

Flying through the fog was not bad yesterday. I was not afraid so perhaps I shall not be as frightened of it as I expect. C. is careful and thorough, and we are on a flying boat and following the coast and can land anywhere.

I shall write you often and that will make it fun—to put a point to the experience. You have always done that with your life, and I hope I can.

Give my dearest love and a kiss to Elisabeth. Do you remember —is it in Katherine Mansfield's letters?—the threads that spin out after a person leaves, always connecting you, so that you are following, following them all the time? That is mixed up and sentimental. Where was it? But I follow you in the boat to Rockland and down in the truck to Portland and then to Europe. Don't you know that feeling?

Anyway, it is very nice and I feel it.

DIARY   *July 11th*

Left North Haven 9:12 GMT [Greenwich Mean Time]—3:12 daylight. "All set?"—"All right." Our backs to the mountains. We start—the roar, the spray, all arms up in the little rowboats. I hold my arms straight up—for courage. We pass the *Mouette* and Mrs. Lindbergh. Then up. The little boats in the harbor look like a scattering of pebbles now that all Penobscot Bay is thrown into the Thoroughfare: the docks, the boats, the pine-treed islands, as though floating on top of this great expanse of water. The settlement looks doubly precious—so small a part of the world.

Fly over the house: white house, green lawn, very neat and

clean and fresh. Betty in white running out, Banks with a dish towel. And then we turn back over North Haven town and head out over the fat lady-dowager lighthouse, the red brick asylum, out toward Isle au Haut.

I look back at the mountains with their arms out, encircling my world, looking over North Haven. They would be there always, and would hold things safe for me. It is such a fundamental emotion, my feeling for them, that I wonder if I were killed whether I would not see them before I lost consciousness, a kind of last homecoming. I thought, "I will lift up mine eyes unto the hills from whence cometh my help" that ends, "He will preserve thy going out and thy coming in from this time forth and even for ever more." I wonder what that means? I used to believe it implicitly.

Fly over Stonington, the quarries, then over Blue Hill. A misty blue day, then over water. "G.E. [Good Evening] Mrs. Lindy" (WCC Chatham, Massachusetts). Try the drift meter. Terrible noise suddenly in receiver—impossible to receive. Work all the time on it, holding lid halfway open, even then impossible. In a rage, to tears.

That first long spit of Nova Scotia—very green, and beaches. Then fly inland—many lakes. Halifax, two arms of bay surround it. Hills very green, pines and birches and that yellow green of [Edward] Hopper's paintings on the banks. A white sail, the city, two green forts, laid out like stars in a formal garden. Big steamships in Northwest Passage, where we land at 21:49 [GMT] time flying 2:34.

Very cold! I wore wool underwear, wool shirt and sweater. Warm with both covers shut, but not when open.

Leaving—"Good luck to ye."

July 12th

Took off Dartmouth, 15:13 GMT. Radio set going perfectly. Beautiful coastline, like Penobscot Bay. Hit Newfoundland about 18:50. Passed Saint Pierre: little harbor, ships on all sides, quite bleak and barren, no trees. Saint Pierre picks up our signals: "What station are you?"—"Lindbergh Plane" "Bon voyage." etc., ending up "Mni tks OM [Many thanks, old man]."

Suddenly, only 25 minutes more to St. John. I send out messages frantically—five minutes more. We fly over it. I am reeling in my 145 turns [of antenna]. A narrow entrance to the harbor between perpendicular cliffs. Lots of green fields, streams, very stony, many lakes, one nice pond surrounded by green and a white fence. We fly over, around the big bluffs, breakers foaming at their feet, along coast looking for a place to land. Finally come back and land in pond. Children, dogs and cattle follow us. Then we are directed to Bay Bulls Big Pond, where we land. Cheers as we come in: "Welcome to NewFound*Land.*" The way they say *New Found Land* makes me think of the Elizabethan explorers. One feels very close to them here.

July 13th, Thursday

Fog rolling by the window—can't see hills—clear at Cartwright. Italian fliers left Cartwright.[1]

July 14th

A beautiful clear bright day, very cold, all the trees blowing. I put on everything I have: two wool blouses, sweater and slicker. We meet a little cart on way to lake, drawn by a dog. I photograph it. The dog is a halfbreed Newfoundland: "There are no Newfoundland dogs in Newfoundland." The lake is deep blue, with whitecaps, and very rough. C. in his slicker suit and sou'wester hat. Spray in our faces. Put on our life preservers. Suppose something cracks taking off! Put my bag over drift meter not to get it wet. Get off 13:08, quickly. Harbour Grace,[2] long arms of sea, long point of bare land, one long runway and a big

[1] Italo Balbo's fleet of flying boats was in Labrador en route from Italy to the United States.

[2] Seaport in Newfoundland, take-off point for several historically important transatlantic flights.

pile of rocks at the end—the last point of land for so many people.

Can't get anyone on radio. Land Botwood 15:13. A rather bare flat promontory sticking out into a protected bay. Two big tramp steamers lying by docks and an engine tooting as we come down. The train and the boats hoot—many put-puts jammed with people come out.

As we take off after refueling (2 hours) 17:54, the official boat waves a telegram for us. C.: "I wouldn't stop for a hundred telegrams!" Pictures. See the first iceberg gleaming white in a distant harbor; it looks very small, like a white sail. 18:46, get a message from the *Jelling* [the Pan American ship] (through Belle Isle) that they are hearing my signals. Follow the coast—more icebergs. After we hit Labrador and go inland, we begin to see snow on the hills—wild country.

20:30, heard the *Jelling,* gave me position of buoy.

Suddenly over the harbor, three big steamers all flying strings of flags. "There they are! One of those is the *Jelling*." A big tramp steamer flying a British flag, the *Blue Peter;* a gleaming white yacht flying an Italian flag, the *Alicia;*[1] and a steamer with a band of blue painted on the smokestack with a white star, flying a flag, white cross on a red ground, the *Jelling*. We circle. Some run out on deck and wave: "There they are!" I get very excited as though we were coming home. That boat down there was for us. Here in this strange land, that was home. They had been watching us, hearing our radio, and now we were here.

The little settlement on the point of land was small, whitewashed houses with red roofs, a pier, a British flag, a white fenced-in graveyard. Across an inlet were several big wooden buildings, yellow, well built, the Grenfell Mission. It seemed deliciously cool as we landed. The gently rolling hills, pine trees, rocky shore, gray water look exactly like all the Grenfell hooked rugs. Rather unspectacular compared to Newfoundland, but pleasant.

[1] Italo Balbo's support ship.

Several boats came up: a white one with *Alicia-Roma* on it in gold letters, and an old one manned by Major Logan,[1] a rosy-faced man in a Daniel Boone cap. Two Scandinavian sailors, flaxen hair and blue eyes, and a dark quick mechanic, Homan. We tie up to the buoy and then decide to move—too strong a tide; have to start engine. Another Italian speedboat with a gray-uniformed, gold-braided officer aboard who salutes, and smiles and bows: "Can we do anything for you?"

We taxi into the cove. The Italians pointing, "Weel you? . . ." offer us the mooring for their plane. We moor and then start for "home." The *Jelling* is quite a big boat but rather old and stodgy. Everyone is hanging overboard to see us. The red-faced short captain wrings our hands and takes us (with much blustering welcome) into his cabin: "Ve do our werry utmost best vor you. Ve do our werry utmost best. I vill leafe you twenty minutes to vash and fix up, vor I know you need to vash up—I tink you need to vash up. Eferting is here—anyting ve can do ve vill do our werry utmost best. It is not werry good, but it ees de best ve haf."

Dinner in the dining cabin—a big table covered with green plush cloth, a swinging gas lamp over the table. An enormous dinner: soup, salmon, meat, vegetables, and two kinds of dessert.

Dr. [Warren] Duffield, the surgeon, a casual, mild, humorous man is very nice, Mr. Jarbo, the radio operator—a pale, rather nervous, quick man in a navy serge suit (like every radio operator). Captain kept me up for about an hour telling me he hoped I would "rest vell in dat bunk—my vife and I, ve haf rested vell in dat bunk, I hope you vind it enchoyable—ve do our werry utmost best."

July 15th

Hearty Danish breakfast! Rice and coffee and eggs and cheese, crackers and hardtack. Over to the Hudson's Bay Post in dory.

[1] Major Robert Logan, in command of the Pan American expedition on the *Jelling*.

A beautiful clear warm day. The dock has boats drawn up and barrels and kegs on it. Walk through a fish-storing sawdust place to boardwalk, past whitewashed, red-roofed houses (hand-hewn planks C. said) to the Judge's house, where we clear for Greenland.

To the Italian boat for lunch. So Italian (and I hadn't powdered my nose), ship gleaming white and yellow stack! All the gray uniforms and gold braid were out on deck as we came alongside. They gave their salute, accompanied with the clicking of heels, a bow and their dark eyes sparkling, followed immediately by a handshake. Then I was bowed into the Colonel's cabin but not left alone to powder my shiny nose. An enormous lunch: hors d'oeuvres and fish and meat, and all kinds of wine. They could not speak English very well, so we struggled along with gestures and various people translating and guessing.

Dr. Duffield said he had just finished explaining where he was born and where he lived only to find that what the Italian really wanted to know was where Colonel Lindbergh was born and where Colonel Lindbergh lived! Then speeches and champagne "toasts." C. made a speech back not as flowery as the one Col. Giuseppe Balba read, but sincere and complimentary.

Every once in a while during dinner I could hear the captain's gruff Danish voice shouting out emphatically: "I saw dem come in von by von—von by von dey come in." [The Italian flying boats.] He shouts at everyone and always repeats as though talking to a foreigner—as we are, of course. The Italians were just amused by him, but he felt ill at ease. He was very red and silent when we left.

I thought them charming and interesting. The radio expert presented me with one of their winged stickpins. Then we were bowed, saluted, and shaken-hands-with off the boat (I with my nose even redder and shinier).

Heavy fog in morning which cleared up in afternoon; watched Homan work on cowl mending cracks, took pictures. It is marvelous to watch a man who knows exactly what he has to do, knows he can do it, has his tools and knows which to use, and sets about his work with speed, confidence, and precision. Added to which this man has a thoroughness and capacity for work, a willingness to do his job perfectly, that is remarkable. He has worked all of two days, and some of the night, not bothering half the time about eating and resting, and he is not (modestly) satisfied with his work. He is impersonal about his work too—doesn't work for praise, but takes pride in its being well done.

The doctor talks to me about photography. He is more scientific than his casual manner would lead one to think. He is a comfortable sort of person—I like mild, balanced people. Jarbo also works hard but is a more introspective type than Homan, probably gets frightfully upset when things don't go right. He has a nice sense of humor, reads poetry, and longs for Miami Beach, or at least pretends to.

Wire from Mother. The baby is so far away that I might not have him and I don't miss him, but I dream violently about him and hold him and feel his weight in my arms.

We leave the boat, as it sails in the morning. It is raining. We wave good-by from our rowboat; they lean over the rail. It is not dark yet, but overcast and rather threatening. We carry our bundles (many mosquitoes on wharf) along a path by the water out to the little white house on the point, "The Hotel." An Eskimo housekeeper came out to welcome us. Our room, small, with an iron bed, old-fashioned pitcher, bowl, and golden oak chiffonnier, no screens, and buzzing flies. I felt depressed. As usual in bad weather, I think we're doomed!

Woke to find wisps of fog forming off water. We are right on the stony beach. The *Jelling* has gone. Back to ship; leave for Northwest River 17:48, over the snow-capped mountains. Ground looks black and bare, hilly and rocky, striped with snow like a zebra. Hit the river inlet, flat and green again—no snow—marshy. Landed Carter Basin. C. is looking for fields. It seems impossible that there may be regular service here, that those marshes could be fields like the Pan American lines south, and yet those places in the jungle were just as wild. In contact with OYKC [the *Jelling*] on way home. "You had me worried when did not hear . . ." Funny how a personality comes over the radio.

Landed 21:15 Cartwright. We walked up to the white-fenced, red-gated graveyard on the hill overlooking the harbor. That lovely springy moss grows everywhere, and flowers. George Cartwright's monument, "who paved the way for the introduction of Christianity to this benighted people." Bad flies. The huskies are everywhere, lying in front yards, under boardwalks, walking on the rocky beach, drinking the sewer-brook water. They have arrogant faces, or perhaps it's their ruffs. The *Jelling* is in dense fog.

Rain and fog. Can't hear the *Jelling,* try all afternoon while C. is refueling. Pick up other stations on short wave. Work very late in afternoon on ship. Pouring rain. We put on our slicker pants and coats and sou'wester hats, but my moccasins got soaking wet.

Still rain—overcast. Out to the ship in our waterproofs. I know the path to the dock well now, first the long boardwalk through the marshy grass, where the dogs are usually lying, then, where it hits the path, lots of blue iris. The path runs along the stony beach of the bay: little white and red-roofed houses on one side and a small sewer-brook, full of flowers, bunchberry, and purple vetch, wild geranium, and mustard. There are always dogs, either among the stones on the beach or on the house paths. We meet little Eskimo girls on the path, brown legs, slant eyes, red cheeks, and smiling, in red and blue cotton dresses, sometimes with the one big Newfoundland dog—an enormous black curly-haired beast, with a magnificent bushy tail. He looks beneficent, kindly and very dignified compared to the Huskies who are snappy and saucy-looking, with their snub noses. I don't feel as though they had much dog *character*. But he comes up to you, rubs his head against your knee as if to say: "You and I, we belong to the same world. We know what companionship means, and affection."

A huge dinner at the [Grenfell] Mission: a long table lined with boys—American, English, Canadian, Newfoundland, and a few women. It reminded me of some school, Groton perhaps. A lovely wood fire, the flower on the table, Labrador tea, big geranium plants in the windows. The boys seem very young, except for one Princeton boy and one English boy.

July 20th

All our good-bys—trudge out to dock. Wind comes up and makes take-off from the mooring difficult. Taxi out past the *Blue Peter,* which toots. All wave from deck. Slowly out into the bigger harbor. Try to take off. Too heavily loaded. Terrible spray in front over wings—not enough wind, just a gentle ripple.

It is a beautiful day; the overcast sky has rolled back and the northeast horizon is all exposed, blue and lovely. The clouds have broken up on top, too, and show blue, so it looks like a Maine day with lots of clouds: two long streaks of cloud, like a single stroke of a brush on the horizon, saffron. But the weather at Julianehaab is rain, visibility six miles only in one direction at Godthaab, and ceiling lowering at the *Jelling.* C. planned to go to Hebron and wait for better weather there even though it's out of the way (a smaller water jump). But we can't get off. He doesn't dare take that triangle trip with less gas, so we come home to await better reports at Greenland, or better wind here.

A long bright evening; home-grown lettuce for supper.

July 21st

Left Cartwright 14:22. Beautiful clear cloudless day. Head over water to Frederikshaab and then change course after hitting fog. Icebergs loom up through a bank of fog. We turn north. Coast terribly cut up, many bare islands and icebergs. Follow on land side of the fog bank, which peters out as we go north. Land at Hopedale on coast—17:00—after looking around for it fifteen minutes. A little settlement at the foot of a stony mountain, snow in the crevasses, a small growth of green pines behind. The harbor, landlocked and perfect, the steep red-roofed houses against the snow on the mountain give it an Alpine look. Two large white buildings, one with a bell tower in the center—the Moravian mission.

The missionary came out in a boat and we went ashore. A crowd of Eskimos, quite dark ones, not like Cartwright, and dogs. I went up into the mission house: a big rectangular building, beautifully built, white inside and out, wide plank floors, big beams. The lower part now used for Hudson's Bay [store], upper for mission family. The missionary (the Rev. Perrett) had been there forty-two years. Mrs. Perrett, white-haired, sharp-faced, kindly, gave me coffee and cake and padded around energetically in her mukluks [sealskin boots] under a black dress. There were two daughters, one fair, with fine features, but very shy, pretty in a pale, quiet way. Mrs. Perrett asked me friendly motherly questions—a birdlike face which flickered. But she asked me about little Charles: "I hope it will not hurt you if I ask . . ." I answered, but it seemed so far away and unreal, and I, another person. I spoke of Jon. The girls took me up into the gardens. The church was white and shining. The girls had been educated in England—they were all born there. The Rev. Perrett's wife, when I marveled at the organ, said, "We must have music here—we couldn't get along without music." C. refueled; took three hours!

Took off Hopedale 20:12; flying up the coast. Struck ice before long, like a white sheet on the surface of the water, not big pieces but a thin film. Coast becomes much more mountainous: great rocky promontories. I have a frightful headache, look up from radio work to see a great giant of a mountain we are flying past. We go up a fjord between great mountains dropping down to sea. The film of white ice stays outside but there are small floating icebergs inside.

Hebron, a small settlement crouched at the foot of a bare mountain, like Hopedale in its Alpine look: white houses, red roofs, perched against a mountain with snow patches. Only there is no green, some moss but no trees. The mountains are very stony and look black and deep-shadowed in the evening light (still bright).

We land in an open fjord and then taxi in between icebergs to the little harbor. The dock is crowded with Eskimos—dark and rather ragged, all hooded, some with fur-lined hoods, the mosquitoes thick around the fur. They smile at us as we climb the dock and the steep hill to the mission. Halfway there a little girl runs out in calico frock and white pinafore, like Alice [in Wonderland], a blue straw hat with mosquito netting around it. She is about four—blue eyes and golden curls. Her father (the missionary) takes her in his arms. We go into the fenced-in yard of the mission (half of it is the Hudson's Bay Co. now) where they are growing vegetables, carrots, turnips, in boxes which can be glassed over.

A well-built Moravian mission: wide planks, big beams, etc. We go down the hall to their sitting room, quite bare except for table, chairs, and the big green-tiled stove. In the window was a small rose plant in a tin can—blooming.

The missionary's wife, in calico dress, apron, and mukluks,

looked thin, white and tired. But she ran about to get us food. "We are almost starving—literally," said the missionary, rubbing his hands together. "Our boat has not come in. Have you any word of it?" We told them it had left Hopedale. They had no flour, no sugar, no vegetables of any kind. He apologized for the meagerness of the food. C. went back to the ship to get our sandwiches and one banana. They gave us tea and canned meat and bread.

I admired the rose, and she said it was the only one of five that had survived the freezing. She takes cuttings every year; all but the mother plant die. They spoke of Hopedale with such homesickness, looking back to it as a land of plenty. "It was different in Hopedale. . . . It was not so cold in Hopedale. . . . Here, in the winter, we leave the room uncomfortably warm at night and the stove going full, but in the morning the room is coated with ice. . . . Oh, it's so cold here."

The missionary talked about the old days. The Moravians went to Greenland with Hans Egede, but were later turned out by the Danes. The Eskimos killed the first Moravian missionary. "Since then we've had no trouble." He said it was no use chiding them at the time they did wrong. You had to try to lead them quietly afterwards to the right point of view. He had converted "twenty-five heathen" that year. I think he had 290 on his rolls. He spoke of the terrible winds there, blowing the graveyard away. He showed us the church, white and clean and with a big stove, only benches (not pews yet, for they were poor and not an old mission). We saw his store houses, his bellows, where they made up parts of engines that broke. Also, he had made three sets of teeth for his wife with no training at all. "In Labrador you must do everything for yourself." "But like everyone with false teeth we do not wear them."

I gave Joan the one banana (the second one she had had); she ate it all and liked it better than the first because it was black! I told her about my little boy, who had curly light hair like hers and blue eyes like her "but no moccasins like that."

Then she wanted to take them off and give them to him. She said she would like to see him and why hadn't I brought him?

When we went to bed it was still light—the mountains purplish and the sky an intense blue behind them.

July 22

Beautiful clear day—no clouds—unlimited. Good contact from water; the weather excellent at Godthaab. We start for Greenland, 16:02. Signals of OYKC [*Jelling*] very weak, get OUGA, Danish boat. "I will listen after you until you are on another side but sri [sorry] Mr. I am not so perfect in English. But I do so good as I can. Here contact OYKC if you have anything for him." Hit fog, low bank 110 miles out. We fly over it, like waves, in lines, try drift indicator.

Finally blue sea ahead, a long line coming in on our left. C. sees the Greenland mountains (about three hours out, 19:35). I try the loop, can't work it. Mountains now a long jagged blue line. We come nearer and can see them white-capped and white-streaked, stretching as far as one can see. Soon they tower up magnificent, high, jagged, a great wall, sky very blue, sea very blue far below us—a few white icebergs, like glistening sails, to the south.

I feel in the presence of a great continent—those giants stretching out before me, calm, still, and white, their peaks towering into the sky. "Greenland's icy mountains." There are many low rocky islands, scattering the coast. I see a small red sail below us, and think of Eric the Red sailing into these giants, and not afraid, not awed, calling it Greenland, so that people would come. It did not look green until quite near; there is green moss on some of the mountains. But mostly they look gray black, volcanic, spectacular. The white sides make them look fairylike—"East of the sun, and west of the moon."

We fly over Godthaab—a big name on the map but a tiny settlement, in a half-moon harbor at the foot of gigantic peaks. They form a background for the town, which is in the scoop between rocky hills. We land outside and taxi around into a steep-sided harbor, narrow, landlocked a hundred times. The statue of Hans Egede overlooks the harbor.

The official boat tows us (our starter won't work) to Godthaab. It is clear and cold, no mosquitoes. The water is smooth and still, the mountains black and purple in the lowering sun. As we come around the point to the town, a cannon goes off three times. The motorboat makes smoke rings. Kayaks are all around us. Like a knife through the water, no splash, no mark, the two-bladed paddle goes deftly into the sea. The town is cupped between the hills, with the jagged tooth of a huge mountain behind it. The houses are beautifully and simply made: square, firmly built, and painted in bright colors, with white trim on doors and windows.

The dock was jammed with people. Coming nearer, I saw the Greenlander women dressed up in high bright embroidered boots, sealskin pants, bright blouses, and tall knitted caps. As we stepped onto the little boat and then onto the dock they all shouted. A little girl in Greenlander costume came down and gave me a bunch of yellow arctic poppies. Then we walked up the street to the local Governor's house, yellow with green shutters, the crowd following.

Mr. Anderson (the Governor) had a son born that morning. I asked about his wife, and I was taken to see her and the baby in spite of my protests that it might do some harm. A ruddy, fine little baby.

Then down to the table, where we were given tea and sandwiches by "the grandmother." The "grandmother," a fine-looking buxom woman, with a ruddy-apple face, held herself beautifully and walked about managing the meal and household affairs, but never joining in. She had the place of dignity in the house, I gathered, but was too busy in her affairs to join in the men's. Delicious toast with egg slices on it, fish and cold meat, all done beautifully, hors-d'oeuvres fashion.

The *Jelling* steamed in, flags flying, and we went out to see her. She looked very big turning around in the little harbor. It was quite cold but clear, the water and sky bright gold near the mountains and green-blue higher up. The Greenlander belles were all walking up and down the street arm in arm in their gay pants.

To the *Jelling:* Major Logan smiling and ruddy, the doctor leaning over the rail, waving. It was nice to get on board again. I looked out of the porthole at night to see the church tower against the distant jagged-tooth mountain, purple in the intense evening light.

July 23rd

The church, set on the side of the hill, is that lovely faded red, but with white trim on the eaves and cornices, a white stoop and green steps. The roof is green, and the steeple is red with little white windows in it on all four sides, and a square white clock. Just at five, the windows flew open and a bell began to chime and all the bright crowd swarmed up the steps. The little Eskimo girls dress like their mothers, but the boys and men both wear European breeches and boots and hooded parkas, often bright blue. The last to go in the door were an old woman, thin and bent but still in her good trousered costume, and a little boy on crutches (infantile paralysis).

"The grandmother" gave us coffee at the Governor's house. C. and Mr. Logan and Mr. Galster,[1] Commander Dam[2] and Mr. Anderson talk shop about Greenland and fjords and Hol-steinsborg, and where we'll go first. Then we tramp back over the hills. The fog hangs out to sea just below the mountains, the peaks showing black on top. Slept on the ship again.

[1] Technical advisor to the Department of Greenland.

[2] Commander Dam was assigned by the Danish Government to act as liaison officer in Greenland for the Lindberghs and for the Pan American Airways expedition.

The next evening we go over in the boat to see an Eskimo dance. A small crowded hall full of Greenlanders, and smelling of mukluks. Two old men with fiddles made their way out of the crowd and sat on the edge of the stage. The dancing began, and couples drew out from the circle, girls in their boots and bright blouses, men in knickers and anoraks, white or blue. The dances were old English and Irish rounds, like "The Hay" and "Gathering Peasecods," and Virginia reels, taught them, I was told, by the early Scotch whalers and traders. A good deal of stamping and clogging; men and girls turning and weaving, interchanging to perfect time.

It is strange but this country dancing gave me the same kind of delight as the harpsichord concert last winter—Bach and Couperin—the pattern continuing, repeating. I am completely caught in it and cannot bear to have it broken—bright boots swinging, arms held out, broad shoulders, straight and still, while feet are going. I watch fascinated, and wonder, caught up in the pattern of it, if there is anything more wonderful than this: pattern and design and rhythm.

I had not expected to find it here, though of course it is everywhere, if one is only tuned to it. Flying has it, and life itself, the beat of the heart and the rhythm of respiration. And the pattern of life has it, if I could only realize it. Birth, and love, and death. I try to realize that it would not be complete without death, that death is part of the pattern, and so I must not be afraid of it.

Then suddenly it stops and they stream out, and we too, out into the cold mist, which blows over us continually. All stroll down the hill arm in arm, and are quiet and shy again.

July 25th

Foggy, though the waves of mist let the sun through at intervals. Commander Dam is now on the *Jelling,* very nice, tall, intelligent, quick to understand. He accompanies us around

Greenland. Lunch on board. Then we watch the ship steam out of the little harbor. We take off 17:28 toward the fog, quickly climb over it, and see it is perfectly clear inland and completely fogged to sea, the demarcation line being the town. We fly over the *Jelling,* which is lying just outside the town. We see her plainly through a layer of light fog, then head inland; many icebergs up-fjord. We can see the inland icecap beyond, a kind of no man's land or edge of the world. C. takes pictures. We fly along icecap edge. It looks dirty, like a week-old snow at home, and streaked as though snowplows had raked over it. C. says those lines are from melted streams running down into the fjords and the horizontal ones, wrinkles, are crevasses. C. is looking for flat places [for possible landing fields]; there are none! Many photos. My hands are cold; send with mittens on. We land at the foot of a high mountain to the north, and taxi up an inlet to a group of houses we thought was Holsteinsborg. Boats come out.

"Holsteinsborg?"—"Holsteinsborg?" They shake their heads and point north. We landed south of town! C. is pulling up anchor when one Greenlander in the nearest boat calmly pulls a pad out of his pocket, writes a note, addresses it, and hands it to C. "Holsteinsborg," he says, smiles and points, quick to avail himself of the advantage of airmail though he has probably never seen a plane before. (The next morning a schooner arrives at Holsteinsborg from this place, with a goose from this same Greenlander and a note on it: "It is too bad I did not think to send the goose by the flier!") Take off again and land a few minutes later in the harbor of Holsteinsborg. A line of mountains shields the town from the north. Houses perch on the hills and the cliffs like mountain goats, with the church and its steeple sitting on top of the hill, guarding the flock like a watchdog.

A snappy motorboat comes out to meet us; three men, Mr. Rasmussen, the departing local Governor, Mr. Nicolaisen, the temporary local Governor, and Mr. Knutsen, his brother-in-law. We go to shore after tying up to a buoy. The stone dock is lined with Greenlanders in bright boots and anoraks, but not as fancy or as prosperous-looking as in Godthaab. Yellow huskies bound around here (none at Godthaab). We climb a steep hill, go under an arch of two whale jawbones, through a red picket fence, past a blue, red, and green church into the Governor's house. They are all very nice and speak excellent English.

C. and Mr. Rasmussen discuss the country and conditions around here. The inland ice: "But you will have to carry all your food on your backs."—"We have a sledge."—"Ah, you have a sledge! You will need a boat also to cross the rivers."—"We have a boat."—"Ah, you have a boat!" We have a nice little room looking out to the harbor. Fog at sea, but not in the harbor, though it comes in by evening.

July 26th

The Greenlander girl "Gunhold" knocks and comes right in, with coffee and toast. A beautiful day. We go over to Mr. Nicolaisen's (we are in a separate house), where they talk plans —maps and weather. We walk out on one of the hills to see if we can see the *Jelling,* then down to an inlet or lake made by the tide, cross a bridge, dogs following us, down to a fish-canning plant, where we try riding in kayaks.

The ship is coming in around seven. The Greenlanders sight it long before anyone else and shout and cry and run to the point, dogs following. After supper we go out in the motorboat; quite cold even in our white Hudson's Bay blanket parkas.

We get on board and thaw out. The town looks enchanting in the evening light. The mountain behind the steeple is red gold, as though lit up from inside.

July 27th

A clear day, but it looks like a fog bank on sea (haze, C. discovers later). So we give up going to Baffin Land and C. takes Major Logan over fjords. I go down to see them off. The deep-throated roar with the engine full open, the foam over the pontoons. Then off on silver skates—the pontoons. The wings look small on top. I have the old thrill—what flying means—a feeling that it does the impossible.

After lunch we hear the Greenlanders cry again and run out —all the children and the dogs. They say *"Tingmissartoq!"* (the one that flies like a big bird). They have seen one other plane. The plane has a whistle or whine above the motor's roar, then disappears. Then another cry from the natives—it has landed, spray trailing behind it in a white path, like a comet.

I have had some kamiks [boots] made for me—dogskin-lined bottom and sealskin-lined top, sealskin outside—very warm—15 kroner.

At night, a party on the ship. Mr. and Mrs. Rasmussen, Mr. and Mrs. Nicolaisen, and our ship family. The captain had strung out the Danish and U. S. flags in the cabin and elongated the table. Homan and Jarbo sat on boxes—a perfectly hilarious meal. The captain shouting Danish jokes the length of the table and talking about his wife: "Tree monts wid de vife on boardt —dat is no vacation. . . . De virst time I came home I had been avay twenty monts and I didn't know her—I had to take out de picture out of *my* pocket. Is dis you, or isn't it? . . . Now I know her vell. I haf been married twenty years." The doctor and I were audience, exchanging smiles. C. was in a blue study, except for occasionally coming up for a teasing remark about kayak riding. I had a nice talk with Commander Dam, who had made an amusing drawing for me. He paints quite well. He is a sensitive, intelligent man.

The lovely warm glow that comes at the end of dinner: laughter and beer and catching one another's glance, and being well fed, all shyness dissipated in the warmth of well-being.

July 28th

Fog, which gets thicker as the day progresses.

Victrola music at night: "The Swan," "Ave Maria," and coffee. The *Jelling* men come over, just like a lot of bad boys getting together in a huddle to tell each other naughty stories. No woman can appreciate the fun of it, just as C. cannot appreciate the jokes, the secret understanding that women have among themselves.

I like Mrs. Nicolaisen. She is having a third baby and working so hard with the other two that she has no time to paint or play the piano or read, yet she is gay and energetic. Many interesting books in the library: philosophy, aesthetics, Clive Bell and Roger Fry on art. Lao-tse.

Mrs. Rasmussen is jolly, loves children and has none, has learned two languages by Victrola method, knits her own skirts and is a wonderful cook. C. adores her vanilla cookies.

July 29th

Fog again. Write and do washing all morning and try to get the stove going. Mrs. Rasmussen takes me for a walk up in the hills. The cotton flower is everywhere and a bank is pink with fireweed. Fog is low on the mountains. A Greenlander woman follows us with a saw, to cut out peat. We see a woman coming back, bent way over with a load of peat on her back twice as big as she. We climb the hill and look down on the town. I see plainly now that there is a center, a green round plot, fenced in, where the flagpole is, surrounded by a dusty path, worn by many feet. Here the dogs lie all day, here the children play in the dust and sand. The store is on one side of this circle and the old blue church-schoolhouse on the other. I bought some paper at the store—a dark shed, a long counter and shelves. The women lean across the counter in their bright blouses and knit caps and the Greenlander storekeepers weigh out things for them, mostly food, which they put, all together, into one paper bag—coffee, rice, sugar, etc.

Hot apricot soup for supper!

July 30th

Mr. Rasmussen raps on our door. "Have you seen, Colonel? It is clear to the west!"

We get up in a hurry. There is still a fog bank out at sea but blue sky above. We start off for the *Jelling,* planning to go across what we think is a thick bank of fog, but when we get up, see it is at least fifty miles broad, as far as we can see, and also inland. We fly along the icecap, very rough at the edge. As we fly lower, I can see rows of miniature jagged mountain peaks, all pushed up into accordion-pleats, and pools on the icecap of intense and poisonous-looking blue. My sending is getting worse and worse. My fingers get stiff [with cold] so I have no control.

Fly over Christianshaab—ceiling lowering—and then up onto icecap where it is clearer toward Holsteinsborg. Pass the mouth of a fjord which is jammed with ice from icebergs breaking off icecap. Take pictures; come in over Holsteinsborg at 6000 ft. We land, tie up, and proceed to the boat (*Jelling*) for supper.

In to shore; it is quite rough. Mrs. Rasmussen welcomes us back. "To Ritenbenk! You have been as far as Ritenbenk!" They can't believe we went so far, but are disappointed we did not get to Godhavn and have stories to tell of the people there welcoming us. Mrs. Rasmussen has a "sweet" saved for us—a kind of Bavarian cream with "Lindy, welcome back," written on it in whipped cream.

July 31st

Get up prepared to fly, but bad weather reports from Angmagssalik and Julianehaab.

Supper. Mr. Rasmussen prophesies bad weather because of the moon change, says wind will be southwest, therefore stormy. The southwest bad weather lasts at least three days and sometimes six weeks. The doctor, Major Logan, Commander Dam arrive for coffee. I have a nice understanding with the doctor—feel very congenial, as though he were my world and we were amused at the same things. C. is telling Mr. Rasmussen his plans: he will cross the icecap from here to Angmagssalik and then back to Julianehaab or further north, so he can see the whole coast.

"You *would*," I say half laughing in an undertone. But the doctor catches it and shakes with laughter. He understands C.'s temperament and the whole situation. Then I have to repeat —and all laugh.

I do not know why I should feel that the doctor "is on my side," so to speak, while Major Logan "is on C.'s side." I feel hopelessly an inexperienced amateur in front of them. And in the last analysis I would be unable to survive in their world. In the doctor's world I think I could survive. (There are other tests, other values.) But in C.'s world I would *not* survive, except for him, and I am afraid of being exposed. I feel insecure. I would like to stand alone once, in that world. I don't know why I want to prove I can. I indulge in dreams of saving the situation, but of course I could not. I would be the first one to have to be pulled out, the weak link. And there must be no weak link in their world. Right now, though, their world, and standing for something in it, seems terribly important. I can't remember that there is any other.

August 1st

Cold and dark. It is *snowing* and sleeting! There is snow on the mountains. We visit the store, a line of Greenlanders bending over the counter. We buy "Bun-nerk" (butter) in a can, cocoa and sugar in bags, chocolate bars, figs and prunes, for food over the icecap. Also a sweater—heavy, blue—for me.

Back for supper. I like these little rooms. First Mrs. Rasmussen's blue kitchen, so light and bright and clean, with two big windows open to the square below, where the children play and the Greenlanders pass to the store. The blue church with the red tower is right opposite. It is always warm, and the two bright-faced Greenlander girls patter in and out, and Mrs. Rasmussen bends over the stove in a blue apron.

The corner window looks out to the harbor and the *Jelling* and the path up the hills from the docks—"The loveliest window in Greenland," with its view of the harbor, the boats and the north mountain beyond.

Grønland,
Holsteinsborg, August 2nd

TO E. L. L. L.
Dear M.

Today—after several days of fog and even snow yesterday!— it is clear to the west, to sea. C. wants to hop to Baffin Land (250 miles) and then back here again before we start out across the icecap to the east coast. We have seen quite a little of this coast.

Godthaab is a tiny place but so pretty—neat square little houses perched around a curved steep-hilled harbor. They are all painted in bright colors and look gay and lovely against a rocky background. The Danes have been good to Greenland, teaching the Greenlanders (they do not like to be called Eskimos here) to build wooden European houses. They are careful to guard Greenland from settlers, traders, intruders of any kind— to keep out white man's evils and diseases. I must say the Greenlanders—at least at Godthaab—looked well and prosperous.

We flew up the coast skirting the icecap, which is terribly unreal—a white dome climbing up gently behind the mountains.

C. has bought a kayak, made of sealskin, and is determined to take it back. They are very light, very narrow, and extremely tippy. You get in a hole just big enough for your body; your legs stick forward into the point of the boat and you sit flat on the bottom; the slightest movement tips you! C. had a hard time getting in but is quite good now. He got everyone on board the *Jelling,* except the Danish captain, to try, hoping that someone would turn over by accident. (The Greenlanders dress themselves in seal-gut waterproofs and turn all the way around—on purpose!) But we were all very careful. However, a young Danish girl up here, not wanting to be bettered, tried it and

WIDE WORLD PHOTOS

Colonel and Mrs. Lindbergh on the West Coast after an inspection trip over the Transcontinental Air Transport passenger route, May, 1933

PHOTO EDO CORPORATION

Charles and Anne Lindbergh with their Lockheed Sirius at College Point, Long Island, early July, 1933. The plane was being prepared for their survey flights over prospective transatlantic air routes

The Lockheed Sirius anchored on The Thoroughfare, North Haven, Maine, July 10, 1933

PHOTO CHARLES AND ANNE LINDBERGH

PHOTO CHARLES LINDBERGH

Anne Lindbergh in the cockpit of the Lockheed Sirius

WIDE WORLD PHOTOS

*The Sirius after landing
at Halifax, Nova Scotia,
July 11, 1933*

*Charles Lindbergh
refueling the Sirius
at Botwood, Newfoundland*
PHOTO ANNE LINDBERGH

Charles and Anne Lindbergh
at Cartwright, Labrador,
July 14-21, 1933

PHOTO CHARLES LINDBERGH

Anne Lindbergh on the Jelling *off Greenland*

PHOTO CHARLES AND ANNE LINDBERGH

The Sirius at anchor in the storm harbor at Godthaab, west coast of Greenland. The Pan American Airways base ship Jelling *in background, July 22-25, 1933*

Field engineer Homan repairing the engine cowling of the Sirius. Captain Hogestadt, Dr. Duffield, and the Jelling's *engineer watching*

PHOTO CHARLES AND ANNE LINDBERGH

PHOTO CHARLES LINDBERGH

Meeting at Godthaab, Greenlanders and members of the Jelling *expedition. Anne Lindbergh in center with Commander Dam.* RIGHT TO LEFT: *Mr. Jarbo, radio operator, Dr. Duffield, Major Logan, head of the expedition*

The Sirius at anchor in the harbor at Holsteinsborg, west coast of Greenland

PHOTO CHARLES AND ANNE LINDBERGH

turned over and had to be rescued. And this cold water is no joke!

We are now in Holsteinsborg, another tiny settlement built on the side of a steep hill.

We have stayed with the local Governor and his wife. They are *so* nice, giving us such good meals, pulling the few radishes out of their garden for us (they grow radishes, spinach, some lettuce, and potatoes, in the short summer months).

Mrs. Nicolaisen has two children, Mona, age three and a half, and Leif (pronounced Life), one and a half. Leif—or Leifling (little Leif), as they call him—is my favorite, though I suppose it is the age. You know it seems unbelievable when I'm off on these trips that I have a child. It seems like a miracle. I try to pinch myself and say, "Did I really hold him in my arms a month ago? Did he really chase me around the sofa on all fours? When I said 'Jon,' did he really look up and smile?"

Charles is now out on the boat, trying to get weather reports either east or west. If it is good east—across the icecap—we will probably set right out and not return this way, and give up on Baffin Land trip. If it is good west we will take a trip over and back again perhaps today. After the trip to Angmagssalik, we double back to Julianehaab, then up the coast again to Angmagssalik, then to Iceland.

DIARY   *August 2nd*

Overcast and bad reports. I dress for flying as usual, and then gradually strip off my warm clothes. It is raining. I start knitting a cap for myself. There is no red yarn left in the village; red is the most popular color. Mrs. Rasmussen is so skillful with her fingers, and with all good "Hausfrau" qualities.

It is fun the way in these small places you can drop right into the heart of their life. From being total strangers you suddenly become friends, allies against the outside world. You are on their side, understand their troubles, take their point of view.

It clears up later in the evening. C. toys with the idea of flying at night (it would be quite light). Mr. Rasmussen shakes
his head. "I think that *maybe* the wind will be north tomorrow
—I feel it in my head—and *if* so then *perhaps* it will be fine."
But it clouds up and we stay and eat chocolate and I knit, very
late, instead. Mr. Nicolaisen ravels the yarn!

August 3rd

It is clear to the west and we start out for Baffin Land. Mrs.
Rasmussen fixes a lunch for us. The radio breaks down in the
air (the dynamotor stops). I try *everything*. No reading on the
dials; I can hear him (OYKC, the *Jelling*), though: reports bad
weather at Resolution. We strike ice halfway across, and fog, and
then high clouds above fog. After flying above clouds for a long
time C. finds a hole, comes down into the dark world underneath. Bare shaley islands break out of the mist—Baffin Land.
Clouds and fog meet. Impossible to get inland. We follow the
coast.

All this time I am changing coils constantly, not knowing
just when OYKC is going to send blind and not wanting to miss
anything. Apparently they [the *Jelling*] are worried and move
out to open sea. We turn around and come back. Mrs. Rasmussen's lunch is very good: sardines on black bread with a little oil
paper laid on top to keep it moist.

Go straight for the *Jelling:* zoom over her and then spiral down
over Holsteinsborg. C. gets the dynamotor going. I feel humili-
ated, it is so simple. The *Jelling* comes back. Jarbo starts to
clean the commutator. If C. had had a regular operator, there
would have been no failure. I feel very much a woman.

I sit in the window and watch the water like changeable silk,
rose and green, and the motorboat rippling it going to the
plane and the *Jelling,* and the Greenlanders padding back and
forth under the window on the dusty paths, or as they lean
against the houses and watch (as I do) the harbor.

August 4th

A pretty good day, high overcast with clear patches of sky. We decide to go across the cap. I get ready and pack, for the hundredth time, while C. goes out to the boat to get weather reports from Angmagssalik and Scoresby Sound. I run over and thank Mrs. Rasmussen, busy in her blue kitchen. She must make us some lunch. Everything is spread out on the long wooden counter under the windows: black bread and white, smoked halibut, sardines, sausage, butter, cheese. Mrs. Rasmussen's hands work fast. "Too fast—eet ees my great fault," she laughs. We say good-by and I really hate to. They have been so good to us and so gay. I love the way Mrs. Rasmussen shakes and the tears come to her eyes when she laughs, and Mrs. Nicolaisen bubbles over with laughter. We write in Mrs. Nicolaisen's book. *"Farvell Leif!"*

We go under the whale-jaw gate with our bundles. All the Greenlanders, even the toothless, bald one with only a topknot left, are standing at the top of the hill, watching us. "Goo'by," some say. "Hul-lo," others. "Farvell," all smiling and waving at us. *"Inudluarna!"* [Good-by].

I sense that the *Jelling* is rather uneasy about this trip. We try the radio out on the water and then take off. *"Inudluarna,"* Holsteinsborg. I hate to leave it, but I always hate to leave, almost everywhere!

We fly north, up as far as Disko Bay, clear and blue, many icebergs. Then approach the icecap, still working hard to climb, up over the rough, jagged, dirty ice. I try the drift meter. It works over ice but not over snow—too much glare. Soon we pass the crevassed area. Radio is good, so little time to look out. Drifting snow beneath and overcast above give a queer sensation. One can't find the horizon; it all looks the same, blinding, like sun on fog, not like sun on snow.

C. opens the window and it gets very cold. My feet burn. I try sitting on them and then wrap a sweater around them; two pairs of mittens on my hands. C. writes on the map: "Every five minutes we save a day's walk!" Communication with Lauge Koch's[1] ship, the *Gustaf Holm,* off Clavering Island, tells us fine weather at Ella Island. We alter course, the mountains rising from the snow all around us.

We are over Ella Island, high cliffs going straight down to the sea. No ice in the fjord, calm, clear, crystallike, and cold. We see the ship *Godthaab* and a plane and one red house and a camp on shore. We land. Dr. Lauge Koch is flying down from his northern base to meet us. They are mapping by air and have two big boats, radios, two planes and a great many men in ground parties.

We had climbed onto the ship, full of ruddy-faced young Danes, when the plane arrived, a low-winged open seaplane with three cockpits. As the men climbed out we could see they had on big sheepskin trousers and coats. Dr. Koch steps on board, a big swarthy man, heavy-browed, shock of hair brushed back from his forehead. He puts out his hand: "Lauge Koch." The crew stand around very excited with cameras—"What a meeting!" Then down into the cabin for a good supper: ham and eggs and all kinds of sardines, cheese, cold fish, meat, etc. Beer and black bread served by a fat chef.

Lauge Koch: "We heard you were in Baffin Land yesterday, so we did not expect you here today!" They go over maps and weather. "Here at Ella Island it used to be (usually is) perfectly calm. Fine weather, always fine weather when there is ice outside. . . . When I was a young man I crossed the icecap. . . . We starved hard on that trip. A man died—starved. I was with him when he died. . . . Here there is a plain [possible landing place], and here, but here it is always foggy."

August 5th

The next morning we start north to Lauge Koch's base at Eskimonaes, Clavering Island. We fly up fjords, over musk ox, run-

[1] Danish geologist, explorer of Greenland.

ning herded together, their great manes shaking. Then a white object—horse? We fly lower. No, a polar bear, white, big, lumbering along near the water's edge. We fly low and he shies off clumsily, sideways. We land at the foot of Clavering Island. It is clear, bright, not a cloud in the blue sky. The cliffs rise up sheer from water, frozen into the sky.

It is cold enough for the white coats and capes. Huskies and puppies are tied up, and a big walrus cut open on the beach. Lauge Koch talking about the north: "We are going up to Peary Land. You are welcome to come. The most wonderful country in the world—always beautiful weather. You will see the midnight sun. . . . The arctic is so easy to destroy. The old explorers wrote about plenty of musk ox, plenty of game—shot twelve musk ox. They did not realize that perhaps there were only twelve musk ox in that valley, and they destroyed them, and it takes generations for game to come back. The Eskimos cannot live without game. And when there is no game and no Eskimos, white man cannot live in this country. It is completely desolate. . . . A little willow, so high, may have taken a hundred years to grow that much." They discuss the various explorers: how Watkins[1] was killed, what happened to Andrée[2] (not prepared for the cold, he thinks).

A good sleep in a nice big cabin, but it is so bright I wrap a towel around my eyes. I wear my blue shirt inside out—it looks a little better!

August 6th

Beautiful clear cloudless day. We start for Scoresby Sound and perhaps Angmagssalik, though rain is reported there. Good radio with the *Gustaf Holm,* so I saw very little. We follow the ice-pack and coast, wild with steep snow-topped mountains. Some of

[1] Henry George Watkins, leader of the British Arctic Air Route Expedition.

[2] Salomon August Andrée, Swedish aeronaut, lost in a balloon, 1897, in north polar region.

the glaciers have stripes down them, like long curving toboggan slides.

C. discovers some mountains and fjords farther inland than the maps show. We go inland, over snow and ice, smooth surfaced, glistening snow, the mountains sticking their heads out of it. We run into storm, lowering ceiling, fog, and very rough air.

I keep on sending to *North Star* and Angmagssalik. Then word from C., "Landing in ten min [minutes] Angmag." I send out excited messages. "OK now, all OK now, will land in ten min Angmag. See you soon." The ceiling is higher, just on mountaintops. A tiny tongue of a harbor runs into a fjord, full of icebergs, white motionless shapes gleaming on the dark water.

Angmagssalik is built up a steep hill from this harbor. There are high snow-streaked mountains on all sides. They look almost black in the overcast light and the snow very white. We finally land between icebergs. There are several little boats in the harbor and Eskimos on the banks in native clothes. All the dogs howl with that peculiarly high lonely sound. On shore we meet Knud Rasmussen,[1] friendly, open and gay. We trudge uphill, a terrific climb, to the Governor's house, where Dr. Rasmussen and the expedition are staying. C. goes over the maps with a young surveyor, Spender, who has painfully, by foot and sledge, gone over so much of the country we flew over.

August 8th

A good day: we dress for flying. Down for radio contact. Hear *Jelling*, fog at Julianehaab. Up the hill again for breakfast. Get very hot, packing. Then we start downhill with our bags. Mrs. Governor runs out and hands me four nasturtiums she has picked from her potted plants. The botanist is picking dandelions and bluebells on the hill as we pass. She hands them to me just as we push off the pier.

---

[1] Danish arctic explorer and ethnologist.

The Greenlanders wave. We start out to the fjord. Will we find a strip free enough of ice to take off? Back and forth past the floating icebergs. Finally: "All set?"—"All right." We get off quickly, head for the inland ice and Godthaab, where it is good weather. Bad radio. I can get Angmagssalik at first but not after an hour or so; no luck with Julianehaab or *Jelling*. Over the inland ice. Smoked glasses let you see the horizon. My feet are warm with four pairs of stockings and kamiks, but I am rather cold without my extra sweater. Have on underwear, one thin wool shirt, one thick wool shirt, and the big white coat. My hands are cold, too, I have to wear two pairs of mittens. We eat the five-day-old sandwich from Holsteinsborg and Mrs. Rasmussen's cookies.

Begin to hit the lakes and crevasses on the icecap edge, then see mountains beyond. Land at ship harbor at Godthaab. A nice Dane helps us refuel. Take off again quickly. We want to get to Julianehaab before dark. Terrible radio communication but a lovely ride down the coast: fog to sea, mountains on our left, the icecap bulging over behind them.

Frederikshaab, Ivigtut—we ride over them imperiously, my head turned to the west to watch the sky. "Will we get there before dark?"—"Long before dark. . . . Landing in ten minutes." We head up a fjord. There it is: the radio towers, the little settlement of bright houses, on a wide curved harbor. The *Disko* [the official Danish supply boat] just coming in, followed by little boats; the *Jelling*'s blue smokestack and a pink sky. We land. It is really dusk.[1] There are no high mountains backing the town; it is low. A line of barrels separate the harbor from the fjord and the ice. There are lights in the town. I see white fences around a little square and a fountain going and a white wooden bridge over a river.

Major Logan, Commander Dam, and Homan tow us to the buoy. We climb out and on board. A nice supper of ham and

---

[1] Julianehaab is the southernmost settlement in Greenland.

eggs, and a light omelet dessert and coffee. Jarbo still buzzing away upstairs. I am very tired; hear OYKC's all night. I wake to find myself repeating the dots and dashes, feel I am fighting something—what? "Darr darr darr—darr dit darr darr—darr dit darr. . . ." Everything turns into dots and dashes in my mind.

August 9th

Over to see the Governor. Up the red sandstone steps of the garden, big rhubarb plants, calendulas, and buttercups; up the stone walk and into a low Danish house (very old—150 years). We climb up two flights of stairs into what is to be our room. "A palace," as Commander Dam says, "hot and cold running water."

Back to the ship, write and have coffee again, and cake. Jarbo and the doctor and I discuss philosophy. The doctor and I, mostly. A gloomy night: wind howling and rain pouring down. We leave the ship in our slickers, carrying bundles, as the *Jelling* wants to sail in morning. I have lost the little comb Charlie played with. We say good-by at the Governor's. Upstairs to bed, feeling gloomy. The wind howls. I can't be comforted.

Julianehaab, August 11th

Another bad day: low fog, a big iceberg comes slowly around the corner of the harbor. I write letters in the dark purple sitting room.

Julianehaab, August 11th

Darling Mother,

I shall never catch up. It is foggy today so we cannot fly back to Angmagssalik (pronounce Am*a*ssalick) en route to Iceland and I have left my log paper on the boat, so I can't work on radio log. My diary is written up so I can indulge in the luxury of writing you. I have just read over again four wonderful letters which you got off on the *Disko*. I can't tell you what a terrific surprise it was—I couldn't believe it.

My first word from home since you sailed! Your cable is about three days late but time means so little here. It doesn't seem to matter. Nothing seems to matter, except this life. It is strange, but Greenland affects people like an enchanted land. I think it is the intensity of the life, the intensity of one's impressions, the sharp outlines of the mountains, jagged, snow-streaked, the bare rocky hills, deeply shadowed in the evening light. The brilliant whites of glaciers and iceberghs (I insist on putting an *h* on iceberg!) against the brilliant blues of sky and water on clear days, and then in this natural beauty, the vivid brave spots of color that the Danes and Greenlanders have imposed on the land. A little colony of red, green, and blue houses climbing up the rocky hills, red and green sails on the fishing ships, and bright boots, blouses, and caps on the people. The grass in the gullies looks *positively* green in this land where there are no trees, and on the grass a wave of blue harebells.

And then because life is slow and rather difficult, it all means so much: a boat coming, like the *Disko* from Denmark, or a party in a low-raftered room, ruddy faces, and Danish beer and "Skoal!" and cigarettes and laughter, and stories of adventures. Or the Greenlanders in bright boots and blouses twirling around in a small dusty square in the evening to the seesaw of an accordion.

Because there is always a tang in the air, good food—fried halibut, Danish coffee, black bread, pancakes—means so much; and comforters and hot water, a pot of nasturtiums in a window, or a warm stove, or the smell of new-baked bread in a blue Danish kitchen.

People's companionship means so much, too. To say *"Ajungilak, tit, ait?"* (Are you fine? How are you today—all right?) to a Greenland child and have her smile back—that is wonderful! The welcoming excited shouts of the Greenlanders when they see a plane and all run out of their houses. The dogs howl and the children shout and point skyward, *"Ting-miss-ar-toq! Ting-miss-ar-toq!"* (The one who flies like a big bird!)—that is thrilling.

And the welcoming handshakes of the ruddy Danes in the colonies, and meeting someone who has any bond at all with you, any connection. I was thrilled to meet a woman who was going back to Holsteinsborg, to take care of Mrs. Nicolaisen (third baby). I said, "Oh, please give them our love—tell them how lovely it was, how good they were to us. I will never forget Holsteinsborg. . . ." Which all sounds quite lunatic. We were at Mrs. Nicolaisen's for less than a week, but you immediately are taken into the heart of the family. You become wrapped up in their problems. You are one of them, and a very strong bond is created.

I suppose it is the isolation of this place. Each colony is completely isolated from the other. The *Disko* is the only boat that goes between them on its three trips a summer from Denmark. Of course it doesn't get to all of them three times. They told us at Holsteinsborg that to get to Angmagssalik (we crossed the icecap to get there) they would have to go to Denmark and then come back the *next* year to Angmagssalik. Each colony is a self-sufficient world: its store, its local Governor (a Dane) and family, its fishing boats, its doctor or nurse and perhaps a Greenlander midwife, its storehouses and dance hall, its accordion player, and—of course—dogs!

The Danes love it here. Many have told me they would rather be here than anywhere else in the world. They came for a year, or a summer, and then came back for life. I can quite understand it. You forget the rest of life, the rest of the world.

We flew from Holsteinsborg north as far as Christianshaab and then cut across the icecap, a big flat dome bulging behind the coastal mountains and spilling down in places into the fjords, where pieces break off and float out to sea as icebergs. The edge of the icecap looks dirty and streaked with little streams running off it. But in the center it is smooth and bright white—unmarked. You can see *nothing* for it is as though you were in a big round bowl with no top or bottom. The east coast of Greenland is very different from the west. The icecap comes closer to the sea, the mountains are higher and more snow-covered. There seem to be no low rocky islands as on the west coast, and the steep cliffs and mountains come right down to the sea. There are few settlements, and it is just now being mapped accurately by two expeditions, Knud Rasmussen's and Lauge Koch's.

Apparently, there is much more field ice (sea ice) on this coast which blocks it for months. The early explorers from Iceland (as the ships now) followed the ice down and around Cape Farvel to Julianehaab, the first place where they could get through. In centuries there has not been found better land in all of Greenland than this first settlement. Now they are growing hay here, and oats and, of course, vegetables, and they raise sheep and a few cows.

We saw a polar bear between Ella Island and Clavering Island on the gray shore of a fjord, loping along; also herds of musk ox. They look like buffaloes but they are an ice-age animal. There are very few left. Isn't that thrilling—to drop into the ice age. I feel it up here, where there are no settlements and the great mountains and fjords are as though just finished by some god. Only a flimsy airplane between us and the ice age!

We flew down the coast to Angmagssalik, passing only one settlement, Scoresby Sound, and a few boats in fjords. The pack ice is just offshore stretching out to sea, and there are icebergs from the glaciers in the fjords.

Angmagssalik is the biggest colony in east Greenland and it looks *tiny*. I could see immediately that this was a much more primitive plane than west Greenland; a good many turf houses and skin tents, and all the women standing on the banks wore native costume with their hair tied into a high topknot, in the old-fashioned way. The faces were dark, and slant-eyed, not intermixed at all, though they soon will be, as there are a good many fair children and several Danish-Eskimo marriages here. The Governor had an Eskimo wife. She could speak no Danish but her lovely dark eyes were very expressive. She had a little nine-month-old baby and showed me how she carried him in a big hooded blouse on her back.

I love to watch the mothers. They go out on a high hill for the sun, or perhaps to watch what is happening down in the harbor —and there they stand with other mothers, pivoting back and forth on the same place, rocking the babies on their backs, saying *"Ajungilak, ajungilak"* (It's all right, it's all right, or, be good, be good).

Knud Rasmussen's expedition is at Angmagssalik, nice young Danes, with two-months-old beards, dressed in hooded parkas and kamiks; surveyors, geologists, botanists, one air pilot and several sea ones. So the settlement is quite crowded now. He is a little man and does not look like a hero, completely natural, without conceit, without pose, but a keen strong face. They all love him and call him with informal adoration just "Knud."

We had a gay party in a tiny room, dandelions and bluebells on the table, black bread, cheese, and beer (a combination I have fallen for), fresh fish, all kinds of hors d'oeuvres, and then speeches and "Skoal!" A great deal of laughter, smoke, candlelight, eager faces, shouts, and general good feeling. "Knud" jumped up again and again and finally presented "Anna and Charles" with an enormous walrus tusk (to be) inscribed from the "7th Thule Expedition."

One of his men made a funny speech about his son at home, playing in a wooden box with a plank stretched across it. When the father asked the boy what it was, his reply was, "Shut up, Father, I'm Lindbergh crossing the Atlantic!" The radio man gave a "Skoal" to me. He spoke English well, hesitating a little, and started by the unfortunate (meaning to be complimentary) remark, "When I first heard her touch I knew—here is no *ordinary* radio operator." Shouts from the room! He ended up, "To the most attractive radio operator I have ever seen." *"Heard!"* corrected someone, then again shouts of laughter.

As we walked downhill to the Governor's house, where we stayed, it was dusk. The white icebergs gleamed in the black fjord below us, and beyond the fjord, the black mountains, with snow white on their sides, and outside the store on the path, you could just see the twirling figures of the Greenlanders dancing to the whine of the accordion. We slept wonderfully in a bearskin sleeping bag.

The Danes usually have only one coverlet, a quilt covered with a case, like a pillowcase. It doesn't tuck in at the bottom or the sides but is laid lightly on top of the bed, so that it is a continual nightmare of "My-feet-are-out-at-the-bottom" or "You-have-all-the-covers-on-your-side." How they exist I don't know! Commander Dam, an extremely nice naval officer who is accompanying us in Greenland, asked us, after our first night at Godthaab, how we slept (with a twinkle). Then he said he was married three years before he could get an extra-long and an extra-wide coverlet made for him which he could tuck in on all sides.

From Angmagssalik we flew back (a beautiful day) across the icecap to Godthaab, refueled there, and went right on down to Julianehaab, where the *Jelling* was waiting for us. (Commander Dam says now he is going to steal the sledge out of the plane so that C. *can't* cross the icecap again!) At Angmagssalik they forgot, in their enthusiasm, to give us any lunch and C. is too polite to let me ask for any. We got flowers instead (which was the most they could give—far more than food). And the Governor gave me a little amulet, an ivory animal, very ugly. "Knud" said it was an evil spirit, "but not if you are strong—if you are strong enough it will help you. Evidently they think you are strong."

I was *very* hungry by the time we got to Godthaab. This was really an awful day. The radio was bad, like a long-distance telephone. You can hear the voice perfectly but just can't make out what they mean. Major Logan was sending frantic messages about what time it got dark at Julianehaab. (We left Godthaab at six in the evening.) He is so careful and conscientious. I am afraid C. has given him a few gray hairs, heading diagonally north across the icecap for no apparent reason, and then crossing right back again a day or two later! I would finally get the message after much double and triple wording and repeating and it would turn out to be something like this: "I said said said your your your dinner dinner getting cold cold cold. Your dinner getting cold," with no way to interrupt him and say: "Oh, all right, I *get* it!"

We arrived at sunset—about 11 P.M. We were welcomed with great relief (I imagine), and we didn't have to be polite and could ask for food!

The next day we went on board [the *Disko*] for "breakfast." A Dutchman introduced himself and said, "I knew your father at the Naval Conference in London." It was so strange; I had a wave of emotion, intense happiness at the same time as intense longing to have Daddy. And yet at his speaking of him, I *did* have him in a way. And I simply glowed at that Dutchman. Everyone else on the boat just disappeared—the captain, the Governor, Major Logan, Commander Dam. They just faded out. They hadn't known Daddy. He said that he was a great man and it was a terrible thing that he died: he was the biggest man of the delegation. I told him that made me happy. "But it is true, it was generally admitted, everyone said so." I said I would write you.

DIARY   *Julianehaab, August 12th*
Weather at Angmagssalik good. I do up the bundles, then run up the hill to radio station.

The whole town sits on a rock under the pier and waves us off. Up through mist, down coast, mist to seaward. Right in among the giant peaks. Can we turn around? Will we ever get out of them? Then looking up to see on the right the end of Greenland, sea beyond. Can that be the end of Greenland? That is the point on the map; the same curve clicks in my mind, Cape Farvel. A geographical thrill. Beautiful clear weather now, "unlimited" north. Pick up the *Jelling*. She is in fog and bad sea up the coast. Snowy mountains down to edge of water, icebergs and glaciers.

Angmagssalik—I shall always think of it like this: the black and white look of the mountain line above the black and white fjord. However, most of the ice is gone. The Governor rows up smiling, and the good-looking Captain Tainer. They anchor us three ways: to each shore (rings on rocks) and then our own anchor.

We climb up the steep hill, very hungry, as we left after "coffee" but before "breakfast." We arrive at 5:30, their time. At last, I think, we arrive at the right time for a meal, a half-hour before their hot supper. But no, we are invited to have coffee, and it *is* coffee and black bread and some sardines, a few slices of sausage on the table. Being very hungry and thinking this was all, I ate a good many sandwiches. Then C. went down to work on ship.

I went up the hill again to the radio station to send a message to the *Jelling,* asking about getting weather from Reykjavik tomorrow. Meet C. in the galley at about 6:30. He has come in thinking it must be time for supper. We walk up to the house but the table is bare. We wait around a little while. No sign of preparation for supper. "How do you make out this supper business?"—"I think they've already had supper, at five. Perhaps we'll have coffee at ten." So he goes back to work. "Let me know if you see any signs of food."

I sit and write until there is a rattle of dishes, so I go for C. Very delicious hot sweet soup—prunes and raisins—then fish. I feel a little too full now.

Rain. Out to ship for contact, but can't get it. Apparently it is Sunday, as all the girls have on their sealskin trousers, red boots and blouses, and "pearl" collars.

C. and I walk over to the Eskimo settlement on the point in the rain: old turf houses, "women boats" turned over, guns lying out wet with other implements, fish and seal meat and birds hung up to dry on a line. An old Eskimo, with pipe, watches us. A woman sticks her head out of a tent (made from flour sacks). He points at her and at himself, also at one of the turf houses. We go into it. Simply filthy inside, a low platform where children were playing among furs and rags; every sort of dirt and filth thrown under the platform, a stove in one corner, a bench, a window. There was an accordion on the bed, a coffee grinder on the floor, and an alarm clock on a box.

C.: "How do these women come out looking so clean—on Sundays!"

Overcast. Climb the hill to radio station for weather. Rain at Iceland.

It clears up in the afternoon. The place suddenly comes to life and color in the sun. At five I stand looking down, past the red church, past the warehouses and men hammering at rocks for a road, to the red plane. I whistle to Charles. It carries and his head comes out of the cockpit: "Twenty minutes more." "OK, twenty minutes." Then we climb the hill for a good supper. Mrs. Berg gives me a Greenlander dress "for maybe a little girl some time."

A beautiful clear day, warm, still, and sunny. C. up early. The *Jelling* is in. I look out the window and see all the Greenlander girls dressed in their Sunday clothes for the benefit of the *Jelling*. Everything shines: the harbor with the red plane sitting in it, the ice in the fjord, the snow on the mountains across the fjord, and the red houses down the hill. I put on my clean blue anorak also for the *Jelling* and to celebrate the morning!

I run down the hill pell-mell over bluebells to C., who is watching the "put-put" from the *Jelling*. We run to the dock—breakfast on the *Jelling*, a good hearty one—then back to pack up. It looks so beautiful; it is hard to go. Good-by to everyone. *"Inudluarna"* to Mrs. Governor, waving, to the Eskimos on the point. Then flying up the coast, over *very* prickly mountains, almost like flames, dancing flames, to Lake Fjord. Then out to sea. Struggling with the radio: "pse [please] try 96 . . . pse try 600 . . . pse try 54. . . ." Iceland thirty miles off. I think I will get Reykjavik to send bearings but it didn't work. It took up time and I lost the *Jelling*. Altogether it spoiled the day—and we were over Iceland.

"Look at the farms." Yes—there was Iceland below us. At first rather disappointing—no mountains. Like Greenland but with the tops of the mountains cut off. Flat-topped bluffs, fjords, valleys. In back of the fjords little green fields marked off in farms. A lot of flat land at the foot of the bluffs with houses sprinkled about much more frequently than in Greenland (where each sprinkling would be a town on a map). There was snow on the high land inland—a volcanic mountain, snowy, spectacular, but not flamelike in shape, like Greenland. I still try OYKC [the *Jelling*]: "Can't copy—pse try 36"—"Q.R.M. [stand by]—pse try 54. . . ." We are following the coast.

Then suddenly C. signing to me "ten min." I rush the message and get a check. The coast is flat below the bluffs and there are several settlements I mistake for Reykjavik. It is much bigger than I thought, rows of modern houses, roads leading out, automobiles, many boats in the harbor. Too rough to land in harbor. C. dives down to the lake and then—in a less windy spot between islands—he lands.

The sun is just going down. Boats come out, a lighter crowded with men and some cameras. The Icelandic flag, a red cross on a white cross on a blue flag. We get on board the lighter and shake hands. "The Mayor of the city." C. tries to explain that we couldn't land in the harbor—too rough—and that he wanted to stay *in* the plane tonight. A bombshell to me, as I had been picturing Reykjavik as the end of all my labors: hot baths, meals, new toothpaste and cold cream, haircut, shoes polished, etc. To sleep on the plane instead, on top of bumpy bundles! No wash, no meal but canned cold beans, hitting your elbows and head as you dressed and undressed, and no tooth-brushing *at all!* I felt crestfallen.

"Oh, yes," said C. brightly, the more they pressed him, "we always sleep on the plane when it's far away. . . . We have everything there—we have often slept in it—we have bedding and food." (Yes, and hot and cold running water, I thought, boiling!)

We got out on the dock. A pressing, interested crowd, but not very gay. They peered at us and rushed after us. We drove off, in a limousine, to make plans. We see for the first time the native costume of the women, big skirts, a shawl, and a black velvet cap with a long tassel, on top of long fair braids. They are all fair and bright-cheeked. The fields look very green; they are haying! Tall blue lupine is growing in the gardens. Ponies and boys on horseback gallop past. The sky is pink-clouded and the bluffs get purple. The lights of Reykjavik on the sky line. We turn back to the hangar and the pier and take the boat to the plane.

C.: "Is that a fishing village? Perhaps we could stay somewhere there?" We can! We walk up the only road. Nets are out to dry, fish in piles covered with tarpaulin. The houses are not bright, like Greenland, but made of painted corrugated iron. The colors are not bright anywhere—not the clothes or the houses or the country or sky—all gentle mild colors, rich but not intense. They look flat after Greenland.

We walk into one of the houses, rather drab but comfortable, a radio and electric lights, photos on walls, plants on a stand. The sixteen-year-old boy can speak a little English. "My Mor"

comes out in a big skirt; long fair braid and round rosy cheeks
and bright eyes—not a wrinkle on her face. There is a daughter
carrying a year-old boy, and two small boys, round, fair, *very*
red cheeks. They bring us supper: meat balls ("Where did this
meat come from?"—"Horse—island horse." C. smiles at me; but
it is good!) and fresh farm milk, and Icelandic bread, like an
unsweetened pancake, and potatoes and cheese and coffee. They
run back and forth, putting clean covers on comforters, water
in a pitcher. Those Danish comforters are here too!

August 16th

Up for "coffee" and a plate of sweet cookies and cake. Then
we start down to the pier. We go into town. Letters from M.
[Mrs. Lindbergh]. Cable from Elisabeth and Mother. A year
ago Jon was born; I am so glad for him. The letters are wonderful. He is there—a hidden treasure.

We are *terribly* hungry by 12:30. A delicious lunch: fresh
spinach soup with an egg, fresh squab and jelly, apples and peas,
and a strange dessert, a kind of cottage cheese with sugar and
milk.

Back to the plane. We walk up the hill to see the sheep, and
the cows, and an old farm; along the fields, up and down hill
where they have smoothed the hummocks and dug out the
lava. The big bluff behind the island is getting purple again
in the evening light. This place has the gentle beauty of places
that have been lived in, and after Greenland fields look like
miracles.

August 17th

We left our little family on Videy island this morning, the
rosy-cheeked mother, the golden-browed children, our friend
the sixteen-year-old boy who stuttered English with difficulty
and determination. We had an amusing dialogue the day before,
starting with his question: "The Greenlanders—are they beautiful?" I said *yes*. He shook his head. Then C.: "I'll give you

something you can take as a fundamental."—"—?"—"A fundamental—something that is true: two plus two equals four—something that is always right."—"Oh, yez—oh, yez—oh, yez." —"There are beautiful girls in every country you go to! That's a fundamental."

Loud laughs from the boy. "Oh, yez—oh, yez—but, no—eet ees not true. There are no such here, on this island. In Reykjavik there is a beautiful girl. I have her picture here (pointing to breast pocket). But my mother and father they must not know I have it!" (He got a great kick out of saying this with them right there smiling, deaf to his English.)

At last down the rocky road with our bundles, the father leading the way, and out in a tippy boat to the plane. We say good-by. Children come down to shore's edge and wave at us. Then off to the Reykjavik harbor. We circle over the village, wave at the little house with its blue monkshood, and then over Reykjavik. We land outside the harbor and taxi in. To the hotel, flags flying. A hot bath. We get out all our laundry in a mad frenzy. It is too good to be true.

We eat with Grierson.[1] He is young and fresh and very nice. The Englishman is the eternal sportsman, never willing to show how dead earnest he is, tossing things off lightly, gaily, "just for fun." It is very gallant, but how dangerous! The American is too earnest, too much a matter of business always, life and death. He shows all he's got, stakes all, and shows it. The Latin overexaggerates the importance. We walk out at night and are stared at but not followed! Except by some children.

[1] John Grierson, an English pilot with a Moth seaplane on a flight from England to Canada.

The *Jelling* arrives. We can see it from the window. It looks enormous. To the Prime Minister at 3:30, to meet the [Danish] Crown Prince. Sherry. "For he's a jolly good fellow."

Sleep late; a terrific gale blowing. Grierson didn't take off—too much wind. Reception for the Crown Prince. Commander Dam calls for us. Lots of cars at the door, women in evening wraps getting out. The panic: "I'm not dressed up at all!"—"That's all right, we're traveling people."

Upstairs all alone to the ladies' coatroom. The same old feeling as at dances, that terrible moment when you are pulled like a limpet from your safe comfortable protecting escort and turned by a stern guardian-angel maid inescapably up those stairs. He can't follow you to give you confidence up there, with the strange coats, the rich fur wraps, the sparkling beauties who dim you. Oh, you think, will I ever find him again when I get down these dreadful stairs, and will I find the person his admiration and kindness makes me, or will it have evaporated in those chilly heights? Oh, those terrible ladies'-dressing-room stairs!

But this time it was not bad. The Prime Minister's wife was at the top of the stairs, and Commander Dam and C. waited for me at the bottom. Then just a big blur of a reception, meeting people and "How do you like Iceland?" and "When do you expect to leave?" and "Are you going to Copenhagen?" and the weather. "It is beautiful," and "No, I enjoy flying."—"No, I am not cold."—"No, I do not get tired."—"Well, it depends on the weather," and tables full of food. Commander Dam's watchful eyes taking care of us. "Your husband does not mind your dancing. It is a harmless pleasure. . . ." Will the Prince never leave? Singing bursts the room. The Prince doing the princely act—going over and talking to singers afterwards. The Prince leaves!

We hop down the stairs, very gay. The air is good, even if rainy. We walk fast and breathe deeply, relieved to be out. Supper. We all go down to the dock to see the Prince off. Singing, high hats, uniforms, salute, cheers and the national anthem, while the Prince stands on the Captain's bridge, with his hair blowing, in salute: A-a-a-a-ah!

Terrible boat whistle. I don't know what there is about a steamer whistle. Wherever I am and whatever the circumstance, when it blows through me, shaking me as it always does, I feel incorrigibly romantic. I am a girl who has just said good-by to her sweetheart, who is sailing to the war. One of these days I shall have to write about falling in love—shy young love, of course, which is built on dreams and an impossible person. Young-girl love, which only goes as far as dreams and catching someone's glance—and boat whistles.

Sunday, August 20th

An English boat has come in and I have mail from Mother. Bad news from Elisabeth and that weight settling back again on the same place in my chest.[1] If the year on her back is only the worst—if there is nothing worse behind that. It takes the joy out of Denmark and Sweden. I am thinking about next winter. I try all day to think of some message I can send her.

Grierson has upset his little Moth in the rough sea outside harbor. Not hurt. I can't help feeling it's lucky. He is such a nice man.

Reykjavik, August 20, 1933

Darling Mother,

I have just got your letter about Elisabeth. How very cruel, when she was just starting out so happily. Your letters about her home and housekeeping were rich and lovely. However, I

---

[1] See note p. 43. Elisabeth Morgan had been told by her doctors that her precarious health necessitated a year of complete rest in California.

think they will like California better than they think. Of course Elisabeth would be just as brave as a flame. It must be worse, really, for Aubrey. California *is* easy and nice to get to, for all of us.

There you are setting out again, for a different place.[1] You are *always* starting out. I hope you don't choose Pasadena (though I will not write this to Elisabeth, as of course it may be best). I think Santa Barbara is much nicer. It is farther from Los Angeles. Santa Barbara may be slightly gayer—younger people—but I should think you could find a quiet spot outside.

I am always looking forward to some mythical time of leisure when we will all be together. It *was* Wales, and now California. We shall certainly be out there sometime during the winter. I shall not yet start dreaming about Christmas—it is too dangerous. But a California winter would be *wonderful* for you, and a lovely place to stay.

People have been nice to us—no fuss, no entertaining. The Crown Prince of Denmark has been here, so there has been some entertaining, but for *him,* not for us. We have met people quietly and they are interesting, sympathetic, cultured people, proud of their long unbroken line of records—history and literature. *Many* of the people can trace their ancestry back to the sagas! And they are so considerate. We walk through the streets —people do not follow us. We waved the Prince off in a great crowd last night on the pier and no one bothered us. If they recognized us they stood back and let us pass. I like these Scandinavians!

Today I went out to Thingvellir, a big canyon or fault in the volcanic rocks that runs through a broad valley. Here in A.D. 930 was held the first parliament [in the world], and for hundreds of years after. Chieftains from different parts of Iceland met once a year. Law was declared by the Law-speaker (who knew all the laws by heart—they were none of them

[1] E. C. M. was going to California to find a house for the Morgans.

written at first) and disputes were discussed, settled, and new laws made. And so the country was governed. I could not help thinking of Daddy as we drove out and could almost hear him say with warmth, "You know, this was a wonderful thing here—this was a wonderful thing, these men . . .," like those rides over Roman roads to Arles and Nîmes.

I have thought so much of Daddy on this trip. Perhaps because I think it would interest him and perhaps because when one is freed of the little everyday preoccupations of home one thinks more of the things that are deepest. The baby, too—Charlie, seems real.

We expect to see Commander Dam again in Copenhagen. He has kept a watchful (guardian-angel) eye on us since Godthaab. Had we enough to eat? Were people nice to us? Were we comfortable? He is quite won over to C. and his theory of never-do-anything-social-you-don't-have-to-do, and he steered us with tact and understanding through the one formal reception here for the Prince. He is bursting with delight at the secret that we are going to Copenhagen and promises a quiet time. I hope so. At least we feel he is an ally.

The last act in Greenland was to have an Eskimo paint "Ting-miss-ar-toq" on the plane. He painted it parallel to the water and not to the lines of the plane.

I long to ask you many questions. (I am thinking of you and Elisabeth and next winter.) What does it mean, flat on her back? Actually in bed, or not walking, using a wheel chair? You know, the rest of the trip does not seem important. I *must* see Elisabeth. I shall write immediately.

To E. L. L. L.   *Reykjavik* [*August 21st?*]
Dear M—
I have a cable here from Mother saying, "Good news from Deacon"[1] so I know all is well. Your wonderful letters about Jon met me here on his birthday and I have since got a letter

---

[1] Deacon Brown's Point, on North Haven, where Jon was with E. L. L. L.

from Mother saying how happy she is at your letters to her, and that you like North Haven.

We plan to go (of course no one knows yet) to the Faeroes, to Copenhagen, then south (see Elisabeth in Wales), and eventually as far as the Azores, but C. will not hop across from there as it is too long. We don't know how or when we'll come home—I guess late fall. The end of the trip will go quickly, perhaps over from Africa to South America, which is a safe, good-weather trip.

We are sending this back by the *Jelling*. They think they may take sixteen days or more. We have had such a good time here. And we can walk out in the streets without being followed. The people are natural and kind, and though they recognize us they respect our desire for privacy. C. enjoys it and I think the Danes and Icelanders respect him for his complete preparedness and care on this trip.

DIARY   *August 21st*

I hate to leave the *Jelling*. It has been half the fun to meet and compare notes. Each time it was like coming home. Jarbo and I shake hands in our dismay at C.'s orders: "No schedules— just pick people up from the air. It isn't necessary. I don't want people to know. . . ." I can see his point: it is a nightmare to step into a newspaper-prepared hell of welcomes at different places. And if you have people expecting you along the line you always disappoint someone, anger others. But Jarbo and I, we understand each other's difficulties. "But suppose I lose you—I'll have all of Pan Am down my neck."—"I know, I know, I told him that. His idea is to contact as *few* stations as possible, mine is to contact as *many* as possible!"—"Exactly. Then if you lose one you have the other." Jarbo looks down at the tablecloth and rumples his hair. These aviators!

Reykjavik, August 21, 1933

Darling Elisabeth,

I feel as if I could not wait to see you, and the rest of the trip does not seem important. Now I have Mother's letter about you, I can't write anything except that you are the bravest person I know, and C. is thinking of Aubrey. Oh, it is so hard to put your roots down and then tear them out again. I know you dread California but I don't think it will be as bad as you think. The sun does really warm you through and through and somehow relaxes you, so you don't care as much and you feel strength coming into you. At least I did, the winter I was carrying little Charles. Health in itself, even in an unsympathetic place, is wonderful, and it does come to people there. Many went out for their health and then stayed. And it is lovely to think our business will take us there periodically! I am now thinking ahead, always one step ahead, to the winter.

But I can't write now. I must pack up to leave. C. wonders if you won't go before October? Please don't dream of waiting for us. Your going is the most important thing. As far as I can tell we might get to Wales the last, or next to last, week in September, if you are still there and should want us.

I *long* to see your house—simply long to. It is real and I want to keep it in my mind, to plant it there and remember it. And C. wants to come, but only if it is right for you. Please write me at Copenhagen (enclosed in an envelope to Commander Dam, the terribly nice officer who represented the Danish Government and went with us over Greenland) what you and Aubrey really feel is best.

Commander Dam promises a quiet time in Copenhagen. I hope so.

DIARY   *Tuesday, August 22nd, cloudy, calm*

Pack. The crowd in the lobby. Down to the *Jelling*. The doctor telling me "What a privilege," and I, embarrassed, couldn't tell him what fun it had been to have his understanding and his humor. Good-by to Jarbo, a hurried "I can't tell you what a help you've been." Thank you to Homan (I wish I'd discovered before he had three children); good-by to the captain (we almost overlooked him—all in uniform, too). Just a "Thank you so *very* much, thank you," to Major Logan, without trying to tell him what a tremendous help the boat had been and how wonderfully he had managed everything. It was all hurried and casual. "Well, we'll see you *somewhere!*"

Over to the plane. The *Jelling* is already pulling up anchor; the terrible grinding noise. It steams out. I stand up and wave both arms; arms and hats waving from the deck. We taxi out of the harbor and out to sea. It is calm but we get off quickly. The *Jelling* off to sea; we can see the blue smokestack. We arch over her and wave good-by.

Then inland, past domes of snow (the mountains are not *peaked* but domed), long fjords, green fields on their sides, farms, streams (very characteristic of Iceland). They glisten down the green slopes.

"Where are you bound?" sends Jarbo, promptly and hopefully. I know he swears when I send back "47° true course."

Cross a stream of lava fanning out below a mountain. Over much steeper peaked mountains, then a long and beautiful fjord, a town on its green slopes: Akureyri. "But don't send as posn [position]." I lose OYKC [the *Jelling*]. TFA [Reykjavik] has difficulty hearing me. "Where bound?"—"South." Start out for the Faeroes; bad storm, terrible communication. A spark station on 600 blots out everything. I get terribly angry. Can't hear OYKC, can't get TFA, can't get anyone else; finally I send CQ [General Call] on 600 and add "Lindbergh plane" after the call letters. Immediately one of the noisy ships I have been hearing "bites." I am thrilled and rush the message through to TFA. "Certainly I will tell TFA."

The day is saved, and my temper. We land down a deep fjord, huge buttes of a mountain on one side, terraced layers of strata pyramiding down. The mountain on the opposite side, green, many streams, waterfalls, and, at the bottom, along the water's edge a town [Eskifjordur, Iceland], one road, telegraph lines, docks and small fishing boats.

We are towed to a buoy and get off at the dock further down. Up the dusty road, past little yards where volcanic stones are laid flat, for drying fish, into the Mayor's house. The table is set by the Mayor's daughter. His fair-haired wife looks almost as young. His mother-in-law is in the old dress, with gold braid and buttons on bodice, a black velvet cap on her white head. A good meal of hot fish and potatoes, then cold sausage, smoked herring, a kind of salad of mashed beets and onions, egg, cheese, and black bread and beer. The Mayor is the only one who speaks English. The trawler who heard me got the message through; telegrams and long distance telephone calls come in.

Wednesday, August 23rd

Good breakfast: eggs! Get the weather at 10:00 on our radio. In front of the house the women, kerchiefs on their heads, are spreading fish out on the stone field. It is going to be a good day, though there is still fog on the mountains. Two sheep start eating the fish and are chased away by the Mayor's little girl.

We pack to take off.

Low clouds over the sea. We hit the Faeroes, wreathed in mist. Fields and hills green and fenced, many sheep, then steep cliffs—some undermined—caves. Tverå is quite a town; a deep fjord, green sloping hills, many ships. Fog is down on top of hills, and it is raining.

The crowd on the pier take off their caps gravely as we approach. Then a set "Hurrah, hurrah, hurrah!" Mr. Mortensen takes us to his house, which was his father's and grandfather's.

I learn a little about the Faeroes. Fishing is the main industry. Whaling is important: a small whale which they drive in herds (by throwing stones in the water) into a fjord and then harpoon.

"And all the sea is blood!" They also catch the sea birds with nets—the young ones on the water before they can fly, the others on the cliffs; a man is let down on a rope. The islands are mostly volcanic and were settled by the Norse, also partly by the Irish. The people on Syderö are supposed to be smaller and darker than those on the Northern islands. The climate is extremely damp—rainy, stormy, and windy!

Telegrams come in from Copenhagen: Where are we going? Will we accept...?

Thursday, August 24th

A reporter from Thorshavn. C. A. L.: "We never speak for publication. We'd be glad to meet you, but we never speak for quotation." (With his brightest, most ingenuous smile!) The reporter is completely crestfallen. He has an invitation from his paper in Copenhagen: "When you come to Co ..."

"We have not yet made any plans. We find we can get around more quietly and do more work if our plans are not made public. On this trip we have had so much time taken up in flying, inspecting routes and working on the plane that we have had to refuse all invitations." Completely discouraged, the man succumbed, and then C. made it up to him by talking to him an hour, answering questions, etc.—"not to be quoted." He left quite pleased.

Our telegram (allowing us to go to the Shetlands) having just arrived, we pack up and walk down to dock; children follow us. I take a picture—a little boy with "Lundborg" and two gilt airplanes on his sailor cap! Boats crowd around us; bunches of flowers. "For your wife, Colonel!" C. swears as a motorboat passes carelessly inches from the plane's wing.

There is still fog around the mountaintops. We start. Out to sea; it is clear and blue. Pass gigantic cliffs, honeycombed, and the surf, boiling white at their feet. Over a rocky island, thousands of birds rise and drift back from us, like sand.

Even the mountains here are green and fenced off with stone walls, for sheep, I suppose. It looks so inhabited after Greenland and Iceland.

Good communication with Thorshavn. The *Jelling* [radio] comes in just as we are about to land. I am terribly excited when I get their "dit-darr-dit" [received], and tell them we're landing Lerwick, refueling, and probably not flying any more today. I got it all through and heard the "dit-darr-dit" in answer! C. let me finish and get Thorshavn and tell *them* we were landing. I felt perfectly satisfied, everything finished and neatly tied in a bow.

Then I looked out at the Shetlands. *So* different. Flat rolling country, much cultivated, not cut up, no fjords; a rather rocky shore line, with a kind of brownish pink growth over the gentle hills—heather. Lots of sheep. The harbor, or passage, *full* of busy trawlers, bustling out like ducks one after another. And the city—for it is a city—all gray, gray roofs, gray steeples, gray stone walls, turrets, and peaks, gray streets, gray chimneys. All uniform, orderly, running down to the water's edge in a fan-like pattern, like a gathering of gray mice.

People begin to swarm on the piers. A big red-brown sailboat swings toward us. The buoy is tied with a flag. Several boats around, but they all back up politely when C. signals. Do they just understand the language better—or machinery? I look to shore. The gray stone buildings come right down to the water—right *into* the water, really—and give the impression of an old walled city, the water of a moat up to its gates. The people peer out of the narrow streets, windows, behind walls. It looks medieval.

"We're verra glad indeed to welcome ye! . . . Ye're now on Shetland grround!" We walk through a big crowd, happy and cheering, up narrow streets with clifflike stone walls on either side to the Grand Hotel.

C. goes back to refuel while I get hot water from a gray tin flower pot and "tea and biscuits" from a fair rosy maid with white cap and blue apron. She wants to know whether we will have "high tea"? "When my husband comes back," I say, pointing to the window, and "Tea for one" pointing to myself (as though she were deaf and dumb—this terrible habit of talking with my hands I have picked up spending a summer with Scandinavians). The landlord brings me a Scotch newspaper. The only American news I can find is "Scot dead in New York." I watch C. refueling from the window, over chimneypots, gulls, roofs, stacks, and masts to the harbor. Now he has shut the cockpit covers and is coming!

Reception at night in hotel parlor—*really* informal. All the women in suits, kind and rosy and unassuming.

August 26th

Leave for Copenhagen. A very warm day; I wear only a shirt and anorak. Good radio contact all the way. We hit land, then mostly in sight of land the whole way. Denmark is perfectly flat, very green, all cultivated, yellow, brown, green, a few patches of trees, groups of neat red-roofed yellow or cream houses. Farms, canals, inlets. Big boats sailing up canals.

Landing in fifteen minutes. Copenhagen, the forts, the harbor, hundreds of white butterfly boats, sails on blue water. The Base—no people. "Good for Commander Dam!"—"No, they're *all* on the water." We land. Boats swarm in like an army after us—brown bodies in kayaks. Terrifying! Take off again, land again. Up to the ramp. Commander Dam and officers. Men wade out to ships. We get out; cameras. Commander Dam taking hold of both hands. The girl pushing me flowers. Into the hangar "for a few minutes."

Their plan is for us to go in a motorboat into the harbor, meet the reception committee, and drive through the street. "One half hour and then you are left alone."—"We just can't do it."— "But, Colonel . . ."—"We just can't."

The dismayed faces, Commander Dam's perplexed brow, the naval officers' wistful expression, and C. looking terribly white and bitter. "Mrs. Lindbergh?" The appeal to me. Agony; try to explain, see an awful situation. Commander Dam hurt, chagrined, upset, and the crestfallen officers. "The people will be disappointed. There may be criticism, I fear. . . ." C. is adamant.

We drive to the mess while they try to arrange a substitution. I am intensely unhappy and wish we had never come. This, the end of our trip, so unpleasant; our nice friendship with Commander Dam spoiled, a frightful entry into Copenhagen.

We drive, mostly in silence, to the Town Hall where the Mayor and committee have been moved to suit our desire for privacy. (We came only on condition there would be no ceremony, of course, and some committee disregarded that agreement and planned a big open-air reception.)

A great crowd already, up through the halls. Trying to smile —photos—faces peering in through doors and reception rooms. The Mayor: "You have disappointed the people, but . . ." Flowers, handshaking. Then we walk into a room with a microphone; my heart turns over. The one thing C. *always* refuses.

But no, the Mayor makes a speech. It is very complimentary —probably meant for the open-air reception but he had no time to change it. I sign the book; flashlights (and I still in my anorak with my hair uncombed), meeting hundreds of people: "Madame Minister." I try to be the gracious lady, *still* in my anorak and dusty shoes! Down to the square. Crowds press against the car—afraid of glass breaking. Finally into the hotel and up to our room.

Whee! I feel quite sick. Commander Dam, C., and I sit down exhausted to supper (of hot milk and toast for me). We are to go to the Legation for a "friendly press meeting" tonight, just to straighten out "this little difficulty." "Now, my dear friend, we must try to smile." Things begin to be better; we meet the press—an interview? "Nothing for quotation." C. stubbornly sticking to his point. Then gradually he talks, sits down among them, they laugh—fencing. The earnest little girl drawing C.'s head. Commander Dam lost in the background. Refreshments in the dining room, "Tea, please." Finally home. I am sick all night, and exhausted in morning.

Sunday, August 27th

Stay in bed all morning. Then out to Commander Dam's sweet little house for "breakfast" at twelve. The green hall with bronze helmets, a sword, a Chinese skirt, and yellow daisies. Black lacquer doors open to the living room. "Oh, what a lovely garden!" with sun and flowers and peace. We walk out onto a green lawn with apple trees. Mrs. Dam, young and sweet and fair. Such an open, lovely face. (I will like her. She is so clear and natural, like Elisabeth.) The boy, fair and shy and smiling like the Commander. Dining room, a *perfect* room, apple green, a fruitwood sideboard and table and chairs, copper on the wall, a big bunch of yellow and burnt-orange daisies.

I feel like a cat rubbed the right way. When Mrs. Dam smiles you *know* she is an angel. It must be nice to be her son. I think they are pleased we like it, and yesterday is slowly warmed out of us. Out for a drive along the water, willows dripping over swans; thatched roofs, rolling fields, rows of trees; the sea and white butterflies; little gardens in front of cottages, sunflowers, calendulas.

Monday, August 28th

We pay calls after lunch on the Prime Minister and the head of the Greenland Department, who says he would rather be in Greenland but he is commanded here!

Tuesday, August 29th

Lunch at British Legation. They were very nice to us—but oh the eternal British superiority. I sensed (though of course nothing was mentioned) their assumption that there is no culture, breeding, taste in the U. S., and though one should (because one is well-born) be polite to these Americans it really isn't necessary to pay attention to them. You can deal with them with half an eye, or no eye at all, just the flicker of an eyelash. All except a nice gay improper Welshman who delighted me.

Wednesday, August 30th

Out to Elsinore with the Vice-Admiral and his wife and daughter. A romantic castle, green moats, swans, great walls, big court and towers, and a lovely view across the water to Sweden.

Thursday, August 31st

We meet the King and Queen of Denmark before leaving Copenhagen. We take the ferry to Sweden, to meet the Crown Prince for "breakfast." Commander Dam goes with us.

Lovely grounds, ugly castle. The Crown Prince is very cordial. She is keen, intelligent and nice (looks like V. Woolf). The Princess, very lovely (Ingrid).

TO E. R. M. M.   *Copenhagen, Friday* [*September 1st*]
Darling,

I have waited to write until we had some plans. Your wire and letter have helped so much. If you will be there that long, C. thinks it better to get the northern places done first before bad weather. He says we can easily go to Stockholm and Moscow (*dead* secret; only a possibility, anyhow—if we can land—) and the northwest coast of Norway, the north coast of Scotland, and direct to Wales and get there by the middle of September. I don't quite see how. But the end of September would be conservative, I think. Is that too late? I am assuming by your wire that it is *not*. It will be better as the pressure of weather will not be pushing us and C. is apt to stay longer. He said "a couple of days" to me, but I think he might be enticed on for a week.

This week in a "gilded slum"[1] is getting on his nerves, and

---

[1] The Morrows' name for luxury hotels.

last night when some perfectly good fish came up all dressed in sauce he nearly threw it out of the window.

I adore Copenhagen but feel slightly imprisoned. The feeling we used to have in the Ritz, with millions of bellboys, carpets, elevators, doormen, and a strange language between you and life.

I love the Danes; they are charmers. Very cordial and gay and natural. I met some English the other day (the kind that you feel may snap the blinds down in your face any moment) and also a gay, charming Mercutio who I discovered soon was Welsh—and a Morgan!

It is strange to be in this atmosphere without Daddy and you and Mother. I have not done one single bit of sightseeing! Do you remember how we used to get up religiously every morning and stamp through palace after palace, looking at old tapestries, dungeons, and armor?

Today I am going but I have told my guide (of the American Legation) that I love beautiful buildings and old china, but I simply hate stalking around looking at old tapestries (though perhaps they would be nice if you didn't have to crane your neck to look up).

Last night we walked through the streets! All right except near the hotel. People stop and look but don't follow. I wanted to go on and on forever, walking in the streets was so exciting, but C. felt we should keep within running distance of the hotel (like Kick-the-Can!).

We will probably leave Monday for Stockholm. Then the coast of Norway, then Scotland, and then Wales.

I am now going out to shop, tra-la. But I wish you were here. I feel very young, frivolous, and daring!

I long to see you, darling, and C. will adore Wales. He is already saying, over the ice-cream castles that the chef sends up, "I wish I were back in Greenland." (Not that Greenland and Wales are alike, but both peaceful and beautiful, I imagine.)

DIARY   *September 1st, out for dinner*

Mirrors and lights and white wine and nicely dressed women and not too obvious music, and strings of lights from the park out of the long windows. I want to dance—how I want to dance! C. and Commander Dam talk about hulls and ships and landing in open water: "Now, I don't say that I know anything about it, but still . . ."—"Well, now, do you consider the flat pontoons . . ." But I did want to dance and it was so strange sitting there, as I used to sit at the table with Daddy at the Ritz watching lovely women dance and thinking that some-day I should be one of them and longing to be a sophisticated woman of thirty, with experience and no longer shy. "And here I am!" So funny, so terribly funny.

Here I am, still sitting, still longing for—what? More glamour at thirty? Will I never settle down and see things in their right proportion and see that C.'s world will still be as thrilling to him long after my froth has disappeared? Things temporal and things spiritual. And yet I did want to dance, out of all proportion. I wanted to taste that world that used to look so tantalizingly sweet to me when I was sixteen.

"Will you try?"—"No, I had better not, there might be a story."—"Well, *would* that matter?"—"Not if it were treated casually, but it would be played up."—"They'd probably say you were drunk?"—"And I want *so* much to dance. Do people dance here when they're old?"—"Oh, you should see them!"—"Then (angrily) perhaps I can dance when I'm an old lady!"

A flashlight reporter in the hall. C. was right.

Monday [September 4th]

Commander Dam arrives before we are up; a rush. Breakfast and packing and addresses. Out to the field, in my anorak and dusty shoes again! Sit in the same room, just where I was when we arrived and I was *so* miserable. Mrs. Dam and I wait for things to be ready. She has great understanding and delicacy of feeling.

Commander Dam comes in and goes over that first day *again*. He wants to justify his position to Charles. I try to explain our position and that C. is satisfied and happy and trusts him. "Then it is all right?"—"Yes, it is all right," and we shake on it.

A man comes in, bows, kisses my hand. "Madame Leendbairgh, I have had no chance to talk to Colonel Leendbairgh, but eef *you* could tell him . . ."

Damn, damn, damn! I am sick of being this "handmaid to the Lord." They think they can wangle *me,* if they can't get at him, make up to *me.* It is not true of Commander Dam. He does not want anything from C. except his respect and trust as man to man, and if he talks to me about C. it is because he thinks I will understand better, which I do. And if he likes me it is not because I am the "worthy helpmeet," a rather pale and good shadow standing in C.'s world, but somebody who stands in a world of her own. I'm afraid it is only the world of "womanly charms." But it is so nice to stand alone *anywhere*— even in a silly little world—for a change, that it is heady wine. Oh vanity, vanity!

Where is my world, and will I ever find it? Yes, but you won't just *happen* on it. You must work for it. That winter at Princeton I tasted it. The Maurois class, the Virginia Woolf world. And there is so little time left. I am almost thirty.

> *"Qu'as-tu fait, Ô toi que voilà*
> *Pleurant sans cesse,*
> *Dis, qu'as-tu fait, toi que voilà,*
> *De ta jeunesse?"*[1]

"And life slips by like a field mouse scarce shaking the grass . . ."

We are all fighting it—fighting the transitory, the evanescence of life, against death and the shortness of life and that futile feeling, the *"Qu'as-tu fait"* feeling. I don't think anything conquers that feeling and that fear. Being young and gay,

[1] What did you do, you who keep weeping, tell me, what did you do with your youth? (Verlaine)

admiration and being loved, and a new hat and pretty clothes all help for a little while; but like any stimulus, they leave you worse than before—afterwards. Children are ramparts against it —for women, anyway. They are eternal life, they are the world growing better and some excuse for living. And the world of art conquers it, catching life in the mold, in the form, arresting life. I'm not sure that work isn't a kind of anodyne too—a healthy one, though—it doesn't help you permanently.

Monday, September 4th

Leave Copenhagen, fly south(!)[1] Then across up over Skåne, flat, fertile, green and golden fields. The sense of a big country still not overpopulated, plenty of room, plenty of woods.

The coast: pine-treed islands, bays, inlets, fjords, all flowing one way, like Maine except for an occasional castle.

Stockholm: spires and ships and towers, bridges, pine trees, sailboats and motorboats. Land quietly at navy port; General Virgin, a few officers, members from American Legation. "We didn't breathe it to a soul, but we had to come ourselves."— "I'm afraid there are people on the road now." We certainly have them scared to death. "To the Automobile Club, which is next to the Grand Hotel but more quiet."

Our new "Commander Dam," Captain Ström, laid himself out for us: anything he can do. He has been in the United States. After we had been driving fifteen minutes he said casually, "You know, I have seen you before, Colonel, at Kelly Field, when you collided with another plane. I was there." We nearly jumped out of the car, and a bond is established. C. is delighted.

---

[1] To avoid press reports preceding the Lindberghs' arrival in Sweden, which they wished to visit quietly.

Darling Elisabeth,

First I shall give you what plans we have. In a day we will probably leave here and go (dead, dark secret) to Leningrad. I don't think we can land at Moscow, so we'll probably go to Leningrad. Anyway, it will be a flying trip, so don't waste a precious letter on it—I'll never get it. Then back across Sweden to the coast of Norway (possible stop in Oslo or Bergen). Don't send any letter there, though, as we will rush through. Then straight to Wales. C. says he should land at the Imperial Airways base (wherever that is—near London. I think it may be at Southampton) and motor up. C. says we can stay a week!

Don't worry about him. He is so sick of besauced food and conversation (though we refused to be entertained) that Wales will be heaven, to be perfectly natural with someone and in the country after rather tense though pleasant city life. It will be just what he wants and needs.

Your letters are such fun. Your "Personal from her sister" causes a rumpus! Commander Dam appeared one morning very proudly bearing your letter—"from her sister"—as though he had laid an egg, and then in true Danish gallantry he said, "Is your sister as sweet as you?" ("Tum tee tum tum tum tum!") I replied, "Much sweeter." "Well then," he said, bowing a little, "I hope you will give her my regards!"

Stockholm is divine, divine! I could live here forever. It is Paris (or no, perhaps Vienna) set down in Penobscot Bay. Venice in glamour, but fresh and clean and sparkling—gulls and gleaming yellow masts and spires and steeples and the sound of water.

I must go out or I shall miss the museums. I will go quite mad, as I adore their glass and their modern fabrics and want to buy for an imaginary home I have not got with money I haven't got!

TO E. L. L. L.   *Stockholm, September 15th*

Dear M.

I meant to write you when we first arrived here. But it is hard to write in a city when it is so exciting and so much to see. We flew up over Skåne, where C. said there was an old family homestead. It is the southern part of Sweden and very rich farmland, green and yellow squares, like a modern blocked cloth (as it looked to Nils).[1] There were little lakes and towns with red roofs. C. wrote back to me, "Very much like some parts of Minnesota!" and later, "I wonder why my folks ever left that place!" When we flew over the coast, islands and fjords and inlets all flowing the same way, I wrote, *"Just* like Maine!"

And driving through the country C. teases me—and I him—whenever I exclaim over some beautiful pine forests or fields and lakes. He says, "Just like Minnesota. You have nothing like this in Maine!"

I have bought Jon a Swedish cap, some Swedish songs, and a gay Swedish toy. However, if I get to Ireland I shall remember that he is part Irish and get him some shamrock!

I got some pictures of Jon the other day which made me homesick. It seems so unreal—a miracle that that beautiful boy should be mine. Is it true? C. remarked as I looked at the pictures, "Very bad for you to look at those!"

Stockholm, September 15, 1933

Darling Mother,

I have had your wonderful letters here about Jon, and pictures! It is heavenly. It was so strange to get your letter about Maine—and a picnic and the water and islands—the same day that I went out here in a motorboat among the islands and archipelago. It was just like Maine. We could have been going to the White Islands, pine-treed islands, hundreds of them, and granite rocks, and a very blue sky, and the pound of a motorboat and sun on

---

[1] The reference is to Selma Lagerlöf's *The Wonderful Adventures of Nils.*

one cheek and wind on the other, and the lovely rhythm of hitting the waves. I sang all the way out. Going out of Stockholm, we went slowly through little inlets and canals, the "suburbs" of Stockholm, lots of bright shining motorboats, red and white summer houses behind the pine trees.

I feel as though I could live here forever, if I could move my family over. You must come, someday, you and Con. You look at old steeples through a forest of masts of fishing boats in a canal, and at night the bridges are arches of diamonds across the water. The street lamps spill across the river from the Grand Palace opposite us. And the Town Hall tower is like one of the slim princesses from "East of the Sun and West of the Moon," with a little crown on her delicate head. I look out every evening and see her against the sky.

In the morning we are waked by chimes playing "Now thank we all our God" in some distant bell tower and the long sighs from the blue trolley cars that climb up and down the grade in front of the Palace.

The people here adore C. A Captain Ström has been "assigned" to us. His wife has helped me shop. In Copenhagen I was rather shy about shopping and went alone, gingerly. I know there must be divine antique shops there, but I couldn't find them.

But here—I have gorged! So much so that my mind is squirrel-caging: "Linen for Aunt Edith, the apple for Elisabeth, but *what* for Mrs. L.? If I give the apple to . . . then I can change and give the glass to . . . No, she must have the glass." Added to which C. is a great help, saying, "No, I think Mother has lots of things like that stuck away in drawers!"

We are waiting for our clearances to Russia. Also we will make another try to see the old homestead of C.'s forefathers in South Sweden without newspapers. There is still Leningrad (perhaps Moscow), Norway, and Scotland between Elisabeth and me, but I am hopeful.

I have eaten too much lunch. It is a bad place for me, as I like different kinds of bread better than anything else, and

every meal here starts with five (or more) different kinds—
with fish, caviar, tomatoes, cheese, etc.—and ends up with a
Danish pastry. I try to limit myself to four pieces of bread and
one cake! It doesn't sound like a limit, does it?

Charles and I have walked through a park here, recognized
but not bothered! It is heady wine. If it were not for the press
we could do it through any street, but photographers popping
out draw a crowd. It was quite good in Copenhagen. The
press was less aggressive. And people by themselves are all
right both in Sweden and Denmark; they respect our wanting
to go about quietly. We can go into any good restaurant with
less trouble than at home (with no trouble at all, in fact).

The winter seems far away and strange. You are already
fixing a house in California for Elisabeth. You are perpetually
doing that. I am glad you had that time in North Haven. It
put the same healthy glow into me just to hear about it.

DIARY   *September 16th*
Now I have caught cold and feel dopey, as though I had been
off on some tremendous emotional spree, the way I used to
feel coming back to college after a thrilling and slightly romantic
weekend where I stayed up too late dancing and then was unable to sleep afterwards for excitement. Rather sad—to feel just
that same heavy "Want-to-go-back-to-bed" feeling—and to have
had no spree!

We must get home and live simply and have a garden and
sun and work and a little girl—to play with Jon. "Down on
your knees and thank Heaven fasting for a good man's love."

Over to the Russian Legation, answering one hundred questions we couldn't read.

Sunday, September 17th
We leave the hotel about ten. Good-by to our lovely view, the
flags flying on the bridges, the sparkling boats under the

arches. Quite cold and blowy but clear and bright—"Perfect Maine day"!

Stiff and fuzzy at radio. It is like going back to school after a weekend and you are tired and have caught cold. Nothing goes right. I know I must get down to work, that I will like it when I get into it, but this terrible stiff period when everything goes wrong and I feel C.'s criticism. He wants loop to work. It doesn't. I have my head down in the cockpit the whole way. I can't get good loop signals or Nauen time signals; very discouraged.

Land at Karlskrona, the island, and pull into the dock—quickly and beautifully managed. Captain Wigert drives us off in a motorboat and then a car down toward Skåne. Lunch in fields, in the sun. I feel happy again.

A bicycle runs into us in a little town; I think the boy is killed, but he isn't hurt at all. My stomach turns over three or four times. C. buys him a new bicycle.

Arrive at Smedstorp near dark. The lake, surrounded by lovely trees; the drive between trees to a big manor house; the old white church with red roof and graveyard. Gårdlösa:[1] white houses, red roofs, red or green doors, hollyhocks and golden glow growing in front. Fields of cabbages and beets, windmills in the distance, gently rolling fields.

No reporters! We drive in the old farm, a white house with a red roof, built in a square, a cobblestoned court. The house is one side; the barns take up the other three. We walk in under the arch, a big pile of hay and a cart in the court. Then across to another old farm where a man lives whose grandfather knew C.'s grandfather.

There are carts in the yard, and geese. "What do you call those—Toulouse?" says C. (his eternal question all through

[1] Village of Gårdlösa, parish of Smedstorp, province of Skåne, in the southern part of Sweden.

Greenland, Iceland, Denmark, Faeroes, Shetlands). The answer hitherto has always been, "Oh, we just call them geese!"

"Yes, Toulouse," answered the farmer. Broad grin from C. at me.

We are welcomed by three daughters and the old mother in a black skirt and apron and a calico kerchief over her head. They ran to get the father. It was a really old-fashioned farm. The dining room had a big table with a stone top, wood base, and wood benches around the walls, all painted blue, with bright flowers on the backs. A painted corner shelf hung up, a big chest, and painted beams on the ceiling. On the walls, a gay piece of weaving. Then a big living room, the walls painted with scenes, rather faded, of old castles of Skåne. The beams in the ceiling were papered. The windows had homespun hangings. There were gay woven rugs on the wall, and the furniture was covered with homespuns. Several big dressers with old copper, kettles, bowls, and one beautiful old blue chest with gay flowers on it, and the date.

The old lady ran around showing me everything. She did not need to talk. I understood what she meant, even to "I knew he would come back, I knew he would come back." And when C. had written in their book she hugged it to her. She opened the chest and pulled out some of the rugs and hangings woven by her three daughters for their "hope chests." She spun the wool for it and they wove it. Then she gave me a runner, pressing it into my arms.

The old man gave C. a pair of glasses his (C.'s) grandfather had sent back from Stockholm as payment on a debt, also some papers. C.'s grandfather had such beautiful writing that they always got him to draft the papers.

The old lady pats my cheek good-by. The people gather around us in the courtyard in the dark and sing the Swedish national anthem and cheer us—a bicycle light thrown on C.

Leave Karlskrona at 10:11; overcast.

Finland—thousands of rocky islands. It is sunny, but low clouds and mists blowing along. Fields between pine trees all striped in lines. Helsingfors; many modern apartments and a few Russian-looking buildings with elaborate domes.

They send up a rocket, and a second one! Then they know we are here. There is a special thrill to that kind of recognition from land to air—the first link after you have been flying for a long time with no communication.

Helsinki, Thursday, September 21st

Darling Elisabeth,

What does Finland mean to you? Quick! Correct—*Emily*.[1] I thought flying in over these modern buildings, "And Emily is my only link!" It looks like Maine, only more so: pine-treed islands, inlets, a little more cultivated than Maine.

I am now safely tucked in bed with a grand Morrow cold which I have dragged from Stockholm to Karlskrona, Karlskrona through Skåne, back to Karlskrona and to Helsingfors. I left it—a horrid remembrance—in Karlskrona, with the nice Admiral who gallantly insisted on kissing my hand three times a day—unsanitary custom!

But now for plans. From here to Leningrad tomorrow; there only a day or two, possibly three. Then straight back to Oslo. We will be there one day after we land (probably) and then take off for quite a long flight—over the coast of Norway and then directly down to the Imperial Airways Base. We don't expect to stop anywhere from Oslo to Imperial Airways, but will probably go way out of our way to see the northwest coast of Norway and arrive too late to motor to Wales that night. We can stay the night, I suppose, in Southampton, and then motor up next day.

[1] The Morrows' Finnish maid in their home in Englewood.

Oh, dear, I can hardly believe it. Will I really see you? It seems so far away from Finland. I will get over my cold, though, before I arrive, and thank God Aubrey doesn't kiss hands!

Don't worry about C.'s enjoying himself or about our meeting any friends or family. (C. likes meeting people, informally—as though you don't know that!) If you don't change your daily life at all we will love it.

It is just this eternal shaking hands with total strangers at airports and saying, "You have a beautiful country." (How do you like Greenland, Iceland, the Faeroes, the Shetlands, Denmark, Sweden, Finland, etc.?) Though I must say people have been perfectly *lovely*. I have a warm feeling for so many with whom I was able to go below the surface.

I met a lovely German woman married to a Swede in Karlskrona. We could talk immediately. She hoped I would see you and talked about her own sister in Germany to whom she was very close. They understood everything—everything—and did not have to talk. "One needs only one person like that in life, but when that person is so far away . . . Still, it does not matter as it used to. When one is older one does not need to see people—one *feels* them."

Now I will get up and dressed and meet the President of Finland (yes—Finland is a republic!). C. says it's a very progressive place too.

> "The men are sailing home from Troy
> And all the lamps are lit!"
> [ELIZABETH MADOX ROBERTS]

DIARY   *Friday, September 22nd, Helsingfors to Leningrad*
Fly along marked route. C. points out seaplane base and destroyers. The mosque on the island of Kronstad. Leningrad; the gold glinting on the dome of St. Isaac's. No crowd at all. On the slip a navy crew, officers and some officials and the press. Drive

into the city. The strange Russian harness—an arch over the horse's back.

An elaborate European hotel. An enormous dinner, starting with caviar, smoked fish, meat, salad and sweet, and all kinds of wine.

After our meal we go out for a tour of the city with a young lady who speaks perfect English, who is assigned as our guide by Intourist. The city is like Paris; wide boulevards, regular squares lined with beautiful buildings, parks, vistas; and the river, crossed and recrossed by lovely low bridges; and the views down the river of towers and bridges and classical buildings—only they are strange colors, a candy pink or yellow. Like Paris except that the sparkle has gone. It all looks slightly shoddy. The paint is coming off the buildings; the stones are crumbling in some places; the shops look like our pawnshops. Crowds on the street.

To the ballet at night. We sit in the royal box of a begilded and ornamented opera house and watch the most conventional and exquisite ballet. All the pomp and gaiety and dazzle of the old regime, and the audience absolutely drab, dressed in dark clothes. No evening clothes at all. It did not seem right. That ballet *demanded* a sparkling audience, jewels, and bare arms gleaming, and shining shirt fronts, and laughter and the hum of a gay and pretty audience. However, it was crowded and there was much applause.

Saturday, September 23

Banquet at night: "about seventy-five people."—"This is the first banquet we've been to in three years!"

Piles of food in front of us: ice airplanes and ducks holding caviar, cake and ice-cream windmills. Toasts, speeches [A. M. L.]: "And I also admire the women of Russia."

Sunday, September 24th

To see Lenin's headquarters in an old convent. Bare rooms. The hall where Revolution was begun, the documents of the Revolution.

Out to see the palaces in Smolny: Elizabeth, Catherine II. Very extravagant: the amber room, the lapis-lazuli room, the room lined with portraits, the Chinese room. The palace of the late Tsar. The Tsarina's rooms: pictures of Germany, her old home, many photos. Icons in the bedroom: pictures of the Annunciation. The baby chair. They do not show the children's rooms. I think it would make martyrs out of them.

Monday, September 25th

Is it good enough weather to leave for Moscow? *"Le brouillard est tout bas."*

To the air base; wait for a long time. Left Leningrad about 2:00; low ceiling. It gets warmer and brighter, sunny. I get GAMS (Moscow) on radio and revive. Moscow—enormous! The winding river—new construction everywhere—the old wall surrounding a lot of towers. The Kremlin. Those big Easter-egg, fairy-tale domes. We land on the river, slipping over bridge. The grandstand, the applause, the handshakes. The Russian aviators, flowers.

A big Russian caviar-to-ice-cream-fruit-and-coffee meal.

The opera. People are better dressed here.

Moscow, Tuesday, September 26th

The Kremlin wall—crenellated red brick with towers regularly piercing above it and then, beyond, an unbelievable brilliant and fantastic group of gold bubbles—domes of the churches in the Kremlin Red Square. The fantastic Arabian Nights Church of St. Basil, its jeweled bubbles looking as if they had just risen from the ground or from the wand of a magician. The white wall, the gold domes behind, the row of trees. Two red towers at each end of wall—Lenin's Egyptian-like pyramid, low in front.

Wednesday, September 27th

Nursery home.

Institute for the Protection of Motherhood and Childhood.

Lunch at aviation factory.

To Kremlin museum and palace.

Drive through the Park of Culture.

Big banquet at 9:00 to 12:30, given by Civil Aviation people, [including] women in Civil Aviation. The girl who carried the mail had flown eight hours that day.

The Grandfather of Aviation: "For we are a people who appreciate daring and technique and science."

Friday, September 29th

Beautiful day. Up, pack, and breakfast. C. to river to refuel.

Last view of Kremlin across river. All our friends on the dock. Good-bys.

The other plane following us. C. points out a field full of planes, also towns of poor houses with a big stone church (like Mexico). C. says the farms are good.

I try to write in my diary and sum up impressions of Russia —in five days! One's conflicting feelings on first sight—rather disturbing. The bad roads, the houses gone to pieces, the ugly outskirts, rubbish heaps and debris. The guards in their long blanket coats, thin horses being whipped.

But no, that isn't fair. The first impressions before and during the landing were of surprise and admiration. The number of planes—modern planes—well flown. They had prepared well for our arrival, everything went perfectly, no press and no crowd, and then we drove into the city.

The people, compared to America, shockingly dressed, old black shoddy short skirts, shawls, bandanas on heads, poor shoes.

The wide streets, cobblestoned and not well kept, not clean; some being repaired as if there had been a great flood and a lot of debris left.

The magnificent buildings, slightly shabby too, crumbling in places, marked with shots, and the paint coming off. The crowded streetcars; dull, drab, poor-looking people, but all busy. The feeling of a glittering city gone to decay.

The grand old-style hotel. All employees well dressed, lipsticked women on each floor, smart maids. Our rococo apartment with a tin [inventory] mark on every object. Looking out beyond the lace curtains to the crowds of black somberly dressed people in the street, honest peasant faces, old men with great beards. The sense of all the work that is going on: building, repairing roads, people with the same intent expression on their faces, all poor, all workers, all going the same direction.

One's depressed feeling: "And this is *improvement!*"

The old palaces and museums surprisingly well preserved (inside). They are proud of them.

The marvelous and healthy enthusiasm and interest of the technical people (especially aviation). The enormous generous splurges of meals for us, the songs and parades of boys in the streets. Children are better dressed than older people. Lines in front of stores. The modern buildings, food kitchens, and Halls of Culture. Lenin's picture *everywhere,* even ash trays made in his image. The outskirts of Leningrad: big factories going up, big apartments, feverish activity. Few cars, many trucks, and *many* heavy carts.

Arrive Tallinn [Estonia] about 4:20. A fairly flat, wide-mouthed harbor. Red roofs, with white chimneys. The houses are all close together, narrow streets, as though they had been playing follow-the-leader and got wound up in circles. We land and are towed up into the hangar. Very few people there, no cameramen. And *no hurry,* no pressure, no intensity. I feel as though a fever had dropped from me.

Our hotel is right in the old wall. You climb up stone steps through the thick wall and ring at an old door, then walk through empty old rooms of a private house.

I sit in the wide window seat and look out at the wall and a cherry tree with red fruit and listen to the quiet: nothing is stirring. And I feel so relieved.

Saturday, September 30th

Pack up. Breakfast at a round table in the dark dining room. It is very damp. I am terribly cold. The coffee isn't *really* hot. I shall never get warm and get over my cold! Weather too bad to go. We unpack, do some writing.

Sunday, October 1st

Clearing. Pack up and out to slip. Bad weather between Finland and Sweden and over coast of Sweden, which I recognize by its red houses and pine-treed islands. Clear sky as we come over Oslo, about 4:30: a town thinly scattered over islands in a big harbor (the end of the fjord, really). The plane pushed up in the hangar hardly fits in. We go off in a boat. The old wall and castle guard the water front.

We drive through the streets of Oslo. People are well dressed, children rosy. The lovely Legation, piles of golden leaves being raked up. Delicious tea upstairs, hot bath, with a washcloth! Every comfort.

Monday, October 2nd

An absolutely perfect breakfast: croissants and marmalade and really hot good coffee! It is a golden day. I walk through a children's park. It is all countrylike and provincial.

C. goes to the Foreign Office and we go to meet the King, then to see the Viking ship. Beautiful and proud lines—that high curved stoop, the carved keel, the breadth of it.

Dinner at the Legation; the Norwegian Crown Prince and Princess. She is Swedish and very keen, appreciative, and charming. We talk about children and traveling.

Oslo, Monday, October 2nd

Darling Mother,

I am writing in pencil because I do not want to leave the sun— a delicious open French window and warm Indian summer sun, the sound of leaves blowing gently, and a golden glint to the trees. We are on our way to Elisabeth's, back from Russia through Norway. Tomorrow we hit the coast of Norway and the day after Southampton.

Until we left Stockholm I was perfectly content with this life, but ever since I have been homesick. It doesn't matter how beautiful or interesting anything is—I want to go home. I can't absorb any more or ask any more intelligent questions or admire any longer. As I looked ahead to Russia I thought, Well, I'll just get through it, that's all, shut my eyes and mind and not make any effort.

Of course it was impossible, and you can't visit Russia even superficially without being terribly upset one way or another. It is tremendously absorbing and challenging: you simply *have* to meet their unspoken "Well, now, what do you think of us?" Those crowds of shabby, somber, intent-on-their-work people trudging the streets, the tremendous amount of work everywhere, the enthusiasm and unity of purpose, the ceaseless energy and determination. You want to say, "Where does it come from, this push?" Their tremendously daring jumps ahead in certain lines—aviation—and in maternity and child care, their single-track minds that drive you almost crazy.

You can't look at a palace, museum, new or old art, or architecture from an aesthetic point of view. It is always, always the social point of view. After I had been through several galleries with every object pointed out as showing "the oppressed state of the worker before the Revolution, now we . . ." I wanted to shout with annoyance, "I get it—*see*? I *get* the point, now for heaven's sake stop talking about it."

It was on the whole much more impressive than we expected

and gave us a great deal to think about. But oh, it was a relief to land in the quiet, peaceful, slow, little town of Tallinn.

DIARY   *Tuesday, October 3rd*
Up and pack. Long wait out at the island before taking off. Fly across mountains to Bergen—snow on the bare round tops. Beautiful fjords along the coast like Greenland, but here, green sides and cut-up fields and little red-roofed farms. Bergen, in an arm of a fjord.

Stavanger: little boats and cameras and a crowd on the pier. A man hits C. so hard on the back I think C. is going to start a fight.

Wednesday, October 4th
"Weather dark and gloomy," mist which blows thick one moment and clears the next.
Direct course to England. Can't get any of the English weather stations; very discouraged. Can't tune loop. Fly very high. Southampton: houses all in gray rows, like caterpillars. The big calm river, with a procession of steamers coming up from the sea. Where are we supposed to land? Other planes chasing us. Finally an amphibian shows us a little canal, right in Southampton. Aubrey is in the motorboat leading us. Planes dive over us. Aubrey motors me to a private hotel outside Southampton.

Thursday, October 5th
An early start. Foggy. The steam buses on the road. Hedges and bicycles, English inns with their signs, "The Golden Stag," "Ales and Stout." Every house with a neat fenced-in garden. The long old walls around estates. Beautiful trees. No road signs or ugly things along road. Aubrey talking about all the land being *owned* and every man having a pride in keeping it beautiful.

Cardiff: a modern commercial city, low buildings, rows of stone houses, fields and forest in the middle of the city.

The Renwicks' house[1]: the white gate and fence, the blaze of dahlias along the drive, ivy on the house, a prim lawn and rose garden and Elisabeth waiting for us. Their lovely house, Elisabeth's portrait downstairs, all those no-colors that are soft and unobtrusive but *not* pastels, not pink and blue—parchment colors, colors of birds' eggs, greens and blues. Elisabeth (in the portrait) very pale and long and ascetic and her eyes (painted larger than they should be) startling out of her pallor, giving exactly the right impression. Like a good portrait, it doesn't look so much like her as suggest her emotionally.

Downstairs to lunch. Sherry, sausages, and scrambled eggs. Salad in a Waterford glass bowl. Afterwards, sitting by the coal fire upstairs, on the old wood foot stools, Elisabeth and I talk until tea.

Elisabeth ordering Michael[2] around, talking about "Cook" and "Mr. Aubrey." Tea and Welsh scones. Aubrey's brother and wife for "sherry." A quiet supper. "What is the savory?" "Herring roe and anchovy," answers Elisabeth docilely, like one of Chaucer's model housewives.

Aubrey talks history at night—pre-war and after-war alignments.

Michael upset by our bundles all over the floor. "What can I do, Madam? The things are *all* over the floor."—"What kind of things, Michael?"—"Why, Colonel Lindbergh's suit that he's just taken off!"

Friday, October 6th

Rather foggy. Clear out our bundles. Perfect breakfast in the upstairs sitting room: a fire; blue and white china, red and blue hand-blocked tablecloth. C. and I walk through the fields along

---

[1] The house the Morgans had rented in Wales, called Tynewydd.

[2] The Morgans' Welsh maid.

blackberry hedges, like Peter Rabbit, with always a distant view of green fields and beautiful rounded trees on the opposite hills. The local people's pride in protecting us against the press; the constable coming round.

Tynewydd, St. Brides-super-Ely, Glamorgan, Sunday, October 8th
Mother darling,
It is really too good to believe that we are here. Aubrey met us at Southampton. Elisabeth had packed the car full of maps, guidebooks, a sweater for me, a note. She had planned everything, even our route: Winchester, Bath, Bristol, with the places underlined in the guidebooks. She thought we might see Stonehenge or Mells Park on the way down, but we were too anxious to get to her for lunch, the day after we arrived in Southampton.

(In the train to London—Wednesday)
Darling: We have had such a wonderful time. It has gone so quickly. We are going up to London for a few days, back for the weekend with Elisabeth, and then on to Paris.

I think Elisabeth is remarkable. She did not look as bad as I imagined, only thin, and stands much more than I thought. She does not seem to tire easily and is not discouraged. She was sitting on the white bench outside the door when we arrived, peering out for us in that shy half-mischievous way (like a child who must wait for the plum pudding to be passed to all the grown-ups before he can take any)—sitting perfectly still, but everything sparkling in her eyes. She peered out at us for just a minute before scampering around in her red shoes to hug us (*me,* that is!).

The house was a little like a dream come true because you have told me about it. There is so much of Elisabeth in it and such lovely things of Aubrey's: the china blooming on the dark wood dressers. Great splashes of dahlias everywhere against the cream walls.

In our room Elisabeth had arranged everything: digestives in a jar beside the bed, Virginia Woolf's *Flush* on the table, special books, Corliss[1] on Russia, Lisbeth Longfrock (Norway), on the desk, all toilet articles in the drawers.

The great thrill was this strange and yet completely familiar Elisabeth playing house—"Winston,[2] tell Collins that Mr. Aubrey will be back at 1:30 and to have the gate open."— "Michael, will you tell Cook I want to see her about the dinner." C. was in great spirits and expended it teasing Elisabeth, Aubrey, and Peter [Elisabeth's dog]. He sat on a bathroom chair for lunch as he disapproves of the lovely old "Post chairs," which he says he slides off of.

Elisabeth has had quite a bit of family entertaining, and yesterday Lady Astor[3] for the night, whirling through on the way to open a nursery school.

Elisabeth will have to rest while we're gone and then a quiet weekend, now all the family have been entertained. The soufflé didn't *set* for Bernard[4]—terrible tragedy. "Winston, can you run out and find Mr. Aubrey. The soufflé hasn't set and what *can* I give?"—"How about a compote of fruit?"—"We've only got peaches and we're having those for supper."—"Well, how about some canned fruit?"—"We *have* no canned fruit, and anyhow I couldn't give *that* to him even if I *did* have it."— "Well, how about that nice chocolate cake you had for tea?" —"Oh, *Anne,* you *never* serve cake in England at any meal except tea!"

How strange to be going to London without you or Daddy or Elisabeth.

[1] Corliss Lamont, teacher of philosophy and author, a long-time friend of A. M. L.

[2] E. R. M. M.'s Welsh parlormaid.

[3] Nancy Witcher (Langhorne) Astor, wife of Waldorf Astor, 2nd Viscount. The first woman to sit in Parliament. The Astors were old Morrow family friends.

[4] Bernard Morgan, Aubrey Morgan's older brother.

DIARY   *Saturday, October 14th*

Home to Elisabeth—very discouraged at the doctor's saying she can't get up *at all*, must be flat on her back as long as possible. "And I may not be any better." *It* comes back and sits on my chest in the same spot.

Tuesday, October 17th

C. and I talk about next winter. He tries to tell me it makes it easier if you are prepared beforehand for someone's death.

Elisabeth standing at the door, saying good-by, looking just as she did when we arrived.

All this visit I felt as though something were hanging over us. I couldn't let go. Not only our trip back, which I have been dreading, but Elisabeth's. If she can get to California—if she can just get there all right. We are *always* saying that. If she can get to England—if she can get married—if she can get away . . .

Saturday, October 21st

Drive down to Bottleigh Grange, outside Southampton.

Letters from Elisabeth, Mother, and Betty.

The baby—I just can't bear it. He is mine and I'm not having him. Will I ever get home? It is like looking down a tremendous ski jump. The bottom is not so far away in time, but in effort and all one has to give to it, such a mighty jump.

Sunday, October 22nd

Elisabeth telephones me from the hotel in Southampton! Very satisfying to hear her. It must be such an awful day for her.[1]

It is raining and cold. I sit at the desk and look out at the dark cedars; my feet get cold in spite of the gas fire, but I finish my log. Great relief—now it is all behind me mentally and emotionally and I can and must start over again.

It feels like college. C. is away and I alone. The little room,

[1] The Aubrey Morgans were sailing to the United States from Southampton.

the rain, the Sunday feeling, the cramp at the desk, the work
hanging over you and Yorkshire pudding for lunch.

Galway, Ireland, Tuesday, October 24th

Mother darling,

I spent all that day in Southampton, the horrid dark rainy Sunday that Elisabeth sailed, working on my radio log, which was
back to Iceland! It was better to get it done, especially as if I
had really let myself go writing you I should have been so frightfully homesick. I can hardly bear to think of Jon running about.
He is mine, and I am missing it, and no hope of immediate return. Ireland—Scotland—Paris—Spain—Portugal—Azores—Madeira—South Africa—South America. Will I *ever* get home—ever
ever *ever!*

After we leave Paris we'll go quite fast, so I'll have more idea
when we'll get home. C. and I plan (it is nice to talk of next
winter; it makes me feel more that we really *will* get home) to be
in Englewood for two or three weeks, meantime looking for an
apartment, and to stay quietly in New York all winter except for
a trip (probably) to California.

Elisabeth will have told you about Wales. We had such a heavenly North Haveny visit: a good deal of fog and sitting by the
fire, and long arguments between Charles and Aubrey about the
state of Europe and Germany before and after the war, and *Are
Disarmament and World Peace possible?* Peter and Bogey coming in all wet from the fields and delicious sherry and cheese wa-
fers at 12:30, and Mrs. Morgan dropping in to arrange the dahlias.
"You have no idea, my dear Anne, how much it helps to cut off
the stems." And Elisabeth sending Michael out to find "Mr.
Aubrey." "His cousin is coming for dinner, and how *shall* I use
those gold salvers he gave us?" I thought Elisabeth quite wonderful about her winter and their leaving. And C. was impressed
with Aubrey's courage at facing things. I am so anxious to hear
that they get there safely. Do let me know.

We had a good time in London, though I felt quite shy and scared when we arrived, as though I ought to know these people very well and I didn't know them at all! The first visit, we went out to supper with "Charlie Whigham."[1] I felt extremely shy and C. felt shy, and C. W. doesn't exactly throw his arms around you. I couldn't help thinking of being there in that dining room with you and Daddy and Michael Herbert. It must have been after we left Elisabeth in Grenoble and Con was too young to come out. I felt exactly the same age, but rather cold without that nice sheltering wing, that protective coloring of "And you know Anne, of course."—"Oh, of course." It always threw an invisible cloak over me. One sank into the blissful background the rest of the evening, feeling warm and comfortable and happy in the glow of older people's conversation and silver and candles and food. One didn't have to come up at all until the end of the evening and "Good night, Anne." But last week I had to barge right in alone, really carrying Charles too, strangely enough, because, of course, I knew that they were taking us in because of you and Daddy.

I have not been shy all summer. I am always meeting strange people, different kinds, and as C. never will stoop to small talk, I have to, and feel I can manage pretty well now. But with your friends I felt exactly the same age I was when I was there before—the same age and none of the advantages!—saying to myself all the time, "You must do it—you must do it—you must be your father's daughter."

Aubrey gave me the most marvelous party at the Berkeley [planned by Elisabeth]. A delicious dinner, perfectly ordered by Aubrey; an old-fashioned bouquet for Elisabeth's long velvet coat, and orchids for my dress. We went to *Richard of Bordeaux*. Aubrey and I and his party danced at the Berkeley till the music

[1] Charles Whigham, Michael Herbert, friends of D. W. M. and partners of Morgan, Grenfell & Co., London.

stopped! I came home absolutely satisfied with my gay evening to "poor Charles," who I found had been to see Josephine Baker with Mrs. Grenfell!

Mr. and Mrs. Grenfell[1] were lovely to us, took us at our word, let no one know we were there, let C. come and go as he wanted, did not entertain us or bother with us—were, in fact, wonderfully understanding.

I am simply enchanted by her. In the first place enchanting-looking; I love to watch her. And then it was such fun—I felt young and gay. I loved going to Fortnum and Mason's with her, or walking down Bond Street, very busy and bright and glistening with lovely shop windows. I think she is a perfect Mrs. Dallo-way,[2] always calling up "an old singing teacher" and taking her to the movies, or "a cousin of mine from the country," or "poor dear Mrs. —— has been so frightfully ill," or "I promised to run in to see ——, she has a new baby." "Monday—all day Monday I am down at the Settlement."

In the meantime she was arranging some kind of benefit performance for the Russian Ballet. At tea or lunch people would drop in and go over lists. "Now if we could only get Noël Coward, he would be perfect. How about Osbert? You know Osbert—could you reach him?"—"How about young debutantes —do you care about them?"—"Well, no, I don't think they have much influence." In the meantime running into stores with samples and stopping to ask, "*Could* you get that new tea gown ready by Monday night instead of Tuesday?"—"A day *early,* Madam?" Don't you think she is like Mrs. Dalloway? Mrs. *Dalloway,* remember, *not* Mrs. Ramsay!

I must finish London. We went to see the American Ambassador for tea. The Ambassador is a quiet intelligent man. He made a great hit with me because instead of saying in a big

---

[1] Edward Charles Grenfell, head of Morgan, Grenfell & Co., London, and his wife, friends of the Morrows.

[2] *Mrs. Dalloway,* novel by Virginia Woolf.

blah way, "I was a great admirer of your father," he said, "I admired the work your father did in the war, and of course in Mexico." Only the people who really know about it speak that way—the work during the war.

And then Charles came back one day and said we were having dinner with Sir Ramsay MacDonald.[1] He had been taken there after some lunch. There was no one there except "Ishbel"[2] in Scotch kilts and some friends of hers and a Mr. Thomas and his wife. I must say it was interesting—the house itself, 10 Downing —and then he is very charming.

He showed us all his paintings, some old, some new, with real feeling and no affectation, reminding me a little of Daddy. And one lovely small bronze head of a child called "Joy." "The privilege," he said, "the privilege of living with that every day of your life." He showed me his study. "Your father sat right there, on that verra couch." And he asked about you, as of course everyone does in London. I liked her too—"Ishbel"—such a clear, shining face. We talked about (1) Elisabeth; (2) bathing babies; (3) housebreaking dogs!

People over here seem quite worried about us (the U. S. at home). C. talked to Mr. Grenfell. They seem to mistrust Roosevelt's experiments. Mr. G.'s attitude seems summed up in "Well, you can't tell, America is a strange country. It might work there."

DIARY   *Monday, October 23rd*

Left Southampton 11:25. Hazy and fog. Down through a hole to the industrial valleys of Wales. Fairly clear over the coast and channel. A mountain rising and the coast of Ireland—very green —rolling country, thatched roofs, haystacks, stone walls. Valencia —the coast where C. touched[3]—clouds and mists and sunshine.

[1] British statesman; Prime Minister at the time.

[2] Daughter of Sir Ramsay MacDonald.

[3] On his flight in the *Spirit of St. Louis* from New York to Paris, in 1927, Captain Lindbergh made his landfall near Valencia.

Circle Galway. The long stone breakwater and children running down, waving hockey sticks. The brown-sailed fishing boats coming in swiftly, noiselessly. The small boy with his father in an old rowboat pulling us around. The Irish brogue, the shouting: "Welcome, Colonel, and God bless you!"

Tuesday, October 24th

A low, thick day. C. up early to get ship out of dock and to refuel. I go down to breakfast alone at eight. It is gray and dark. They have the lights on. Not a sign of life on the streets. I write all morning in my room. It is very damp and quite cold.

I had a talk with Mr. Q. this morning. The Irish mourn for those provinces in the North: "Those are the six provinces that aren't with us."—"But the North Irish—they're a different sort of people altogether. We're much more akin to the Scotch now than we are to the North Irish." At lunch, he discovered that *Morrow* was a North Irish name! (C.'s ancestors come from Killarney, "Kissane—a fine old Irish name!")—"The North Irish are black. It might be MacMorough, though."

After lunch we drove out toward Connemara. Whitewashed cottages, with the smoke curling out of the chimneys; two-wheeled carts, and donkeys, two gray donkeys tied under a big oak tree by a gray wall; barefoot boys, women with big red skirts and huge black shawls (blankets) around their heads and shoulders, falling down the whole length of their backs.

Galway to Inverness, October 25th

Good-by to the green fields of Ireland.

The rocky coast of Scotland, great bluffs and bare heathery hills. Up the Caledonian Canal, mountains coming down steeply to the lakes. Very rough—a high wind. Inverness, a gray mouse town on a river. We anchor in mid-tide and then C. spends six hours fixing a broken cable, changing the ship to better anchorage, and refueling. It is bitterly cold—a north wind—and it rains before the evening is up. I wait at the hotel where a nice man (in Aviation) and his wife give me tea and then, when C. doesn't turn up, supper, and then wait up with me until C. comes in cold, tired, soaking wet. "I don't mind—I enjoy an evening like this. I like working hard. I'd a hundred times rather spend an evening like this than one in New York."

Great excitement in Inverness about some "big beastie" in the Loch. "Don't shoot the monster of Loch Ness."

October 26th

Still very cold. More snow on mountains. We leave Inverness [for Paris] at 1:13 with a roaring north wind at our backs, straight across the mountains, over snow and under heavy white clouds. Terribly bumpy and cold; we slow down at the big bumps and then lose altitude. I am relieved when we are across. Hit the Firth of Forth in three quarters of an hour! On down the route across England; the Channel—lowering clouds and a rough black sea. We find where we are and start across. It gets blacker and blacker. That was a brave man who first flew the Channel! Is it really this dark or is it just the clouds? How long it takes to get across. Bad luck we haven't a clear day, it would stay light so much longer.

The beacon ahead—the coast—the harbor with two breakwater arms stretched out to the sea—terribly rough sea, even in the harbor. We head straight inland. It is getting dark. I keep my eye on the bright bits in the sky, on the reflection on the wings, but they go out one by one, quite suddenly like electric lights. It is black to the east and dusk to the west. If we don't find it [Les Mureaux naval base], where *can* we go? We have never landed on pontoons at night. The feeling that there is no port we can reach. You can't steer back into day. We could go back to the coast and land by flares, but in that *awful* sea? At five, C. says fifteen minutes more. He must know then where we are. Can it last fifteen minutes more? I start to count the seconds by my breathing. In, out, one, two. . . . We hit the Seine. The lights going on. Circling different points. Finally, the lights, the hangars, the little group of men. Perfect landing on river—practically dark.

Darling Elisabeth,
That awful Sunday you left Southampton I was dying to see you or call you but C. and I talked it over and thought it would be hard enough for you anyhow—and not to add another good-by. I feel as though I should never never feel sorry for myself when I look at the way you go on. You were so wonderful in Wales about leaving. That place was really you and Aubrey. I shall never stop being grateful that I saw it just for that reason. And perhaps it will help make it more permanently yours because we have all seen it and keep it in our minds. It was such a warm and glowing thing. But I know you can do that with any place you are—like Mother.

And then you saw the little farm in Princeton. I have really no feeling, or such mixed feelings, about Hopewell that I want to wash it off the slate. But the little farm I can't bear ever to see again in someone else's hands. Because we were so happy there, and did not realize it. I remember everything in that house and always shall, though it was not as pretty as yours and I took no pictures of it.

I think there must be shut cupboards in one's mind; you think you have forgotten things and yet they are all there, safe and perfect. Sometimes, of course, you lose the key! But still, everything is there.

Paris! We arrived from Inverness in the evening on the Seine, an hour or so out of Paris. A very small group of Navy officials on the banks waving excitedly. A man in uniform in a motorboat dashing up: "Good-by! Good-by!" he said excitedly, shaking our hands! Then the thrill of hearing French again: *"Doucement, doucement!"* to the motorboat. We got out on the mudbank and had flowers handed us, hands kissed, and I was taken off to have tea (still in my white wool Eskimo cape and sealskin mukluks—

PHOTO CHARLES AND ANNE LINDBERGH

View from Governor Rasmussen's house: the harbor at Holsteinsborg. S. S. Jelling *at anchor, July 25-August 4, 1933*

Anne Lindbergh in a kayak, Holsteinsborg

PHOTO CHARLES LINDBERGH

Greenlander mother
and child

PHOTO CHARLES AND ANNE LINDBERGH

*Taken from the Sirius: approaching the Greenland icecap before
crossing to Scoresby Sound on the east coast, August 4, 1933*

PHOTO CHARLES AND ANNE LINDBERGH

PHOTO CHARLES AND ANNE LINDBERGH

The Lauge Koch camp at Ella Island
on the east coast of Greenland, August 4-5, 1933

LEFT TO RIGHT: *Charles Lindbergh, Lauge Koch, and member of*
the expedition at Eskimonaes, Clavering Island, August 5-6, 1933

PHOTO ANNE LINDBERGH

PHOTO CHARLES AND ANNE LINDBERGH

The Greenland mountain range discovered by the Lindberghs on their flight from Clavering Island to Angmagssalik. (The altimeter indicated the peak to be over 12,000 feet high)

Glacier flowing into the Greenland sea, east coast

PHOTO CHARLES AND ANNE LINDBERGH

PHOTO CHARLES AND ANNE LINDBERGH

*After landing among icebergs at Angmagssalik,
east coast of Greenland, August 6, 1933*

PHOTO CHARLES AND ANNE LINDBERGH

*Eskimo women at Angmagssalik;
Jelling in harbor in background*

PHOTO CHARLES AND ANNE LINDBERGH

Julianehaab bridge

Iceland's plateaus

PHOTO CHARLES AND ANNE LINDBERGH

PHOTO CHARLES AND ANNE LINDBERGH

Approaching the Faeroe Islands, August 23, 1933

Boats surrounding plane after landing at the Faeroes

PHOTO CHARLES AND ANNE LINDBERGH

WIDE WORLD PHOTOS

The Lindberghs leaving the Shetland Islands,
August 26, 1933

it was quite cold) and to attempt to speak French. It was great fun. The officer in charge was overflowing with sentiment. It was so beautiful, so romantic, our coming down out of the sky *"comme une Princesse Lointaine,"* with that beautiful white coat! "How about the boots?" I interrupted. We were now in the warm teahouse and those sealskin boots smell to heaven!

It was very quiet—no reporters. We drove into town, through Saint-Germain-en-Laye (do you remember sitting on the terrace, having tea, and the brown chestnut leaves over the ground?), and then after an hour driving looked down a long avenue to the lighted Arch. The Champs Élysées look entirely different with those big show windows but the other streets exactly the same, the same advertisements—"Dubonnet"—that funny waiter with a long apron holding up a bottle. I think the Place de la Concorde is quite thrilling lit up, theatrical but extremely French. But to light up the Madeleine down the end of that dark street is too much. It makes it look like papier-mâché—no depth or solidity.

We went to the Crillon (the Air Ministry arranged it) and out for supper, to a little restaurant, Au Grand Veneur. It was heavenly, as no one had yet discovered us. C. was touched by the enthusiasm of the officers. They called up Coste[1] and said he must come, not telling why, and he arrived to find C. *"Ah, mon brave!"* And two of the officers' wives—very French, simply but perfectly dressed, in black, of course. (And I also feeling smart in your black dress. The flaring ruffle is quite the newest thing!)

But what is there about a Frenchwoman? She is always smartly dressed and yet never conspicuously so. You never think, as you do with an American or an Englishwoman, "How perfectly dressed she is!" (with a sense of the effort it has taken). If you think at all about it you only think *"Of course* she is well dressed." Everything is in that "of course."

Well, we really had a heavenly evening, before we were dis-

[1] Dieudonné Coste, French pioneer aviator. Piloted first nonstop flight from Paris to New York.

covered, though in Paris everyone on the street stops when they see Charles. *"Tiens! C'est Lindbergh!"* Even though there had been no publicity and they hadn't expected him. So we quickly had reporters gather and the papers came out the next morning with the indecent headline "Lindbergh reported found in Paris hotel."

The next morning things started. Ted Marriner[1] came over with Mr. Tuck of Press Relations and tried to arrange how to deal with the crowd of reporters below. Our quiet time in Paris was over. From then on it was one hectic rush. We refused all big dinners, clubs, etc., and yet from morning to night there was a stream of people in and out of our rooms, telephone calls, messages, letters, and everywhere we went we were followed by reporters and cameramen. I didn't go into a single shop or museum while I was there. If I went out to walk I was followed, so I just turned around and came back.

The second morning I got out while they were following C. and once free, walked to Place Vendôme, then down the Rue Saint-Honoré. Everything looked so heavenly. You know that "first morning" feeling when you just taste everything; my great mistake was not to buy that morning for it was the only chance I had to get the bed jacket, and that was what you wanted most. Paris was *the* place to get it, and there is no other place as good. It wasn't the bed jacket you wanted so much but something enchanting to wear in bed *from Paris*.

Looking back it seems hard to realize that it was so hectic. Why couldn't I have got things arranged somehow? But everything was done under the watchful eye and eavesdropping ear of the press, and I had that same hunted feeling I had at the time we were engaged. If you jumped into a taxi they jumped into one behind you.

It's impossible for C. ever to be in Paris inconspicuously. They still regard him as a romantic young boy—the Fairy Prince.

---

[1] Theodore Marriner, Chargé d'Affaires at United States Embassy, Paris.

Women bang at the door of his car, crowds collect as he leaves the hotel.

Except for the American reporters, I could get around quite easily, more easily than in many other cities. I am not connected with C. in the French person's mind. They simply can't think of him as married. It is like a famous movie actor. He is Romance. You can imagine how he took to that! And of course the French show it. No one has any reticence about joining a street crowd or shouting.

And to Charles it was just bitter medicine. It was very sad. He talked about giving up Aviation, never going to any cities. It was pretty awful—and yet he likes the French, he felt moved, I think, that first evening coming back. But then the Air Ministry people were the finest type, and their enthusiasm was very nice and there was no press that first night.

The last day we saw Mme. Carrel. She is a marvelous woman—a scientist, and yet a marvelously womanly woman. She talked to me about C. and the work with Dr. Carrel. It was thrilling, and she told me I must tell Charles to encourage him. She is very wise. I hope all that she said about C. and the work is true, for it made him happy, especially at that moment when life seemed unreal.

I got quite a lot of fun just from the social side. The game of it is fun, though you crack after a while. For instance, at a dinner party I am talking to Mr. Stone on my left, Ted [Marriner] on my right. C. is across the table between two pretty girls, to whom he is not talking at all. Mr. Stone and I have talked long enough on eugenics (one can, you know!), as he remarked in the middle of a sentence, "How *did* you get onto this subject anyway!" We switch to Russia. Problem: how to get C. into the conversation, which Mr. Stone will like more than talking to me, and which will pull the end of the table together? Answer: The Gold Ruble story. So I begin and then drop my hook over in Charles's lap: "Charles, have you a gold ruble in your pocket?" The pretty girls lean forward. Mr. Stone and C. meet across the table. Ted looks up from his preoccupied stare down the length of the table (where he has been looking nervously to see how people have been enjoying the party), turns to Charles, who, smiling, picks up the ball and starts to talk. Ah! I sit back with great relief.

I had a nice time with the charming wife of Captain de Villatte, the Air Ministry officer. She wanted to take me around to some shops where she had seen things *"tout à votre style."* In an American you did not know well you might resent that, but she simply took it for granted that, though one should not spend much money on clothes, one *must,* of course, be interested in that, *naturally.* I could not explain to C. but there was something charming in that attitude of hers, like the care one might spend on a perfect soufflé or a perfect dinner. And her interest in clothes did not annoy me, as it would in a vain person. She had absolutely no vanity and I knew had little to spend on her clothes. But her attitude was that it was the right and proper duty of a decent woman to dress well, as it might be to cook well. She described a dress to me that she had just bought and never once said, "I can't wear ruffles," or "Gray is becoming to me." Perhaps it is a kind of objective sense of the artistic. A lovely dress is a lovely dress— one does not wear it just to show off one's figure. One must dress well, but never to make an impression, a furor.

We are going to Geneva and then to the north coast of Spain, then Lisbon—Azores—Madeira. I have figured out that we should be home by the 15th of December. It makes it easier, to put a date on it.

DIARY   *Monday*

Out to Le Bourget. Lunch at field with pilots. Family dinner at M. Blériot's—films of M. Blériot's first flights.[1] She was a courageous woman.

[1] Louis Blériot, French engineer and aviation pioneer, who built France's first airplane factory and was the first to fly across the English Channel, in July, 1909.

Paris to Amsterdam [and The] Hague, Thursday, November 2nd
The war country completely grown over, plowed over, except for
a few big holes. The trenches show jagged lines, a lighter brown,
zigzagging across the dark brown fields. There are trees and
farms and cattle. It seems impossible and horrible that so many
men died fighting over that little stretch of ground.

Stormy weather.

Everything is square in Holland. Straight lines of water
(canals) and fields.

The Hague to Amsterdam, Saturday, November 4th
Sunday, November 5th

Motor with Mr. Plesman[1] to Utrecht.

Rows of willow trees, small stumps, along the canals through
the fog. Beech and oak forests brown and gold.

That stormy look of a Dutch landscape: the skies high and
cloudy and, way off in the distance across flat fields and canals,
the silhouette of trees and a windmill and a church spire.

November 7th

Amsterdam—toward Geneva and back to Rotterdam. Left Amsterdam in fairly good weather, local storms. Flew into fog and
storms after leaving Holland. C. tries to go around. We plow
around for about two hours, sometimes wheeling close to the
ground under low fog, sometimes flying between two layers, the
dark ground slipping under us beneath wisps of fog. Find a fairly
clear spot, with a circle of high clouds and fog on all sides; no
light spot anywhere. He goes right back into it again. Lighter
ahead? No, just a bank of white fog. Is that black ahead of us
more storm or is it the solid earth showing through?

I was in sheer physical terror the whole time. One of those times
when life is not worth it. "If I get out of this alive, I will never

[1] Albert Plesman, founder and head of K. L. M. Dutch Airlines.

fly again." Speculating on whether we could land on that canal—or a lake. He looks back at it. Why doesn't he land? I keep looking out on the good side, hanging on to a road, to a line of trees. We're awfully near those coal-pit hills. There is clear weather ahead—there *must* be clear weather ahead, they said so. We must come out sometime. He said we could land on the ground, wipe the floats off—that would be a relief! We might get banged up a little. I didn't mind the thought of that so much, but the hell of fear I would go through before we landed. It would have to be absolutely impossible before he would do that. And I couldn't stand it—the pit of fear to go through before we landed. How illogical.

I poke C. for a smile—something. He only looks annoyed. I can't have him feel that way. No, he smiles now—that is better. I feel better. I will shut my eyes and have faith in him. When I open my eyes it is always worse—much worse—as though fate took advantage of my napping. I try to say poems to keep my mind off things, for I am shaking. That is silly. If I were in a transport plane I would have to control myself. All kinds of poetry come to my mind: "Fear no more the heat o' the sun . . . as chimney-sweepers, come to dust." "I will be sorry for their childishness. . . ."

Where are we? The compass keeps swinging. Now it is north. We are going back. Thank God.

Better and worse, better and worse, till I get sick of following it. He says we are landing. He circles a lake . . . we will land—good! He circles and circles and circles—and goes on. We hit the sea and a town with a harbor and lake. Here we can land. How wise of him. It is a big town, too. I look at the map—Ostend—a nice reservoir to land in. We circle, weather is worse, we can *just* get in. He circles—and goes on, up the coast. He wants to stop at a smaller town. How wise of him. Here is one—a big canal. He looks at it—and goes on. We must be going back to Holland, to land on Dutch soil. Here is that first hook of sea. He is following it up . . . Oh, Antwerp, of course. He will land there (how wise of him), a good big Belgian town. Then we will stop in Antwerp, up the river. He circles and circles and circles—and goes on.

I am simply disgusted by this time. Are we going to try to go back to Geneva? Why doesn't he tell me something? I wouldn't *mind* going on if I knew how long it would be. I would settle down to it. I am cold, but as he said we were "landing" an hour ago I did not put on the flying suit. Now I will put it on, stop looking out, and simply try to go to sleep. I sit scrunched up. C. wiggles the ship and points at something—fortifications. Damn! I go back to sleep, wake up—still over Antwerp. Damn! I think wildly about going home, the train to Paris. I have a five-pound note. I could get more at Paris. But the newspapers: "Are you getting a divorce, Mrs. Lindbergh?" Damn the newspapers.

C. pokes the stick. "Back to Amsterdam." All right, good. The weather is better now, and no customs trouble. Very wise of him. We land at Rotterdam harbor, next to airfield Walhaven. It is 4:30 and darkening.

Up to clubhouse. I am cold and tired but happy. Hot soup. Other pilots caught in fog behind us. Ostend: "Fog right down to the ground." Ostend! I think, that was one of our *brighter* spots.

Rotterdam to Geneva, November 8th

Get off, after waiting for better weather, about 11:30.

Coming into Geneva. That high glistening crown of snow-capped mountains, floating on a blue haze above the lake. We dive down into it, leave the mountains behind. Geneva.

November 9th

Reception by the Mayor in the old Town Hall.

November 11th

It has snowed during the night. Cars are covered, and roofs, and the plane—a snow sky. Wake to very bad weather, but struggle to get *"météo"* from the airfield on telephone. Don't know technical terms. *"Les prévisions ne sont pas bonnes. S'il n'y a aucun changement . . ."—"Les nuages sont très bas."* Out to Yacht Club, row to the plane. Good-bys in the boat, trying to keep steady, handing up the baggage. The step onto the pontoons, three jumps up to my seat and slip down into it, take off my tam and put it under seat, on the life preserver. Put on my white coat, cotton for the ears, red mittens, take the helmet off the drift meter where it has protected it from rain, etc. The sky is lightening a little. Can we get over the mountains? I will be good. I will "have faith in the pilot and always look out on the best side of the plane." But it is better than we thought—get through the pass by the river— scattered clouds. Keep sight of ground below—sometimes over, sometimes under light snow.

Arrived at Santoña [Spain] at four—just in time. It had been getting worse and worse. But I was not afraid, as one could follow the coast line fairly easily, even in the poor visibility and rain, until the mountain behind Santoña loomed up ahead on our sea-side. Rowboats come up, full of fishermen in slickers. It is raining and windy. *"No hablo Español."* C. says to me (as though I knew *anything!*) "Tell him I'll come in just a moment." *"Momentito!"* They understand "Estados Unidos" and "Lindbergh." Big crowd on dock. We go around to the other side of the pier and anchor. It is dark when we go in.

Supper at ten. After supper the Mayor and "corporation" come and want C. to write a "reference" for the town harbor. Before they leave, the wind gets louder and C. says he is going to look at the ship. He gets word that it is drifting. He runs down to the dock and finds a terrific wind. The plane has dragged both anchors and is drifting down the length of the pier. They work three hours and come back at two. They get the ship tied to a hydrant at the end of pier and two bigger anchors behind. C. goes down again after two, to see if still OK. Wind howls all night; we sleep badly. C. uneasy about ship, and the wind bringing back that night to me.

Santoña, Sunday, November 12th

After breakfast we go down to see the plane. It is still raining, and a rough gray sea. All the fishing boats are in the harbor. The town reminds me of Mexico: the square with the bandstand and plane trees, the signs, "Pulqueria." The dark-eyed women, sometimes with a black shawl, in the doors on the narrow streets. The donkeys carrying panniers. But the men look Basque, in blue jean fishing clothes and black tams pulled over one eye. Men and women both wear big wooden clogs with toes pointing skyward. The little boys all crowd around C. on the dock.

Santoña, November 13th

The weather is better. We feel rested. C. writes the letter [of recommendation] for the Mayor. Good-bys on the dock—"And give a kiss to your baby." When we are taxiing, a boat, trying to stop us, comes up. "Storm at Vigo. You must not go."—"Oh, we'll go see what it looks like."

Leave about eleven. Same kind of day as when we came in: local storms, lowering sky. A line of dark mountains and, behind, a line of snow-capped mountains. Surf pounding up by the cliffs, rising through holes in the cliffs, like geysers. Try to cut across the mountains, clouds down on them. Try a second time, follow the river in. After we get over one range we hit a big plateau. Weather gets worse, but no hills, a few lakes. If only we would strike one of the rivers. Worse and worse—we start turning and trying again. C. asks if I can get weather. I try 600—no answer. When I don't look for a while, it gets worse.

We strike a river! And mountains. The river is running down west. We must be on the west coast. Deep gorges—we are down in the canyon. Could we land? Shallow rapids. C. keeps hugging the sides of the gorge so he has room to turn around. Fog hanging on the sides. I have never kept "ground contact" *sideways* before. I keep trying the radio and think we have never been in a position like this. We turn with river. It is good to have it to hold on to. It gets broader—the valleys are broader—must be nearing coast. Fog gets lower. After a half hour C. turns and gets ready to land: 150 feet of antenna out! I pull for my life—only get 110 in before I feel it strike the water and jerk away. But thank God we are down safely. "I've lost the antenna, Charles!"

We plow up river against a strong current. C. finds a quiet place behind a sandbar. We anchor, safe and still. People begin to crowd both banks and shout at us. After a long time a boat makes its way across. We can say "Lindbergh." *"Mal tiempo, Santoña—Lisbon, mal tiempo . . . no puede . . . Lisbon . . . aquí."* Also, *"Persona Inglesia?"*

They row back for someone who speaks English and they show us a map. We are on river [Minho] dividing Spain and Portugal. Lots of boats come up now—Spanish soldiers and Portuguese. Both banks are lined. We decide to anchor in a small inlet, quiet water off the main stream. We pull up to the bank, and C. ties down to willows and anchors to the hill. A group of people watching: "international" police and a lot of poor peasants, bare feet, and in rags. The women look quite lovely with a strange color yellow bandana on their dark hair.

Someone who speaks English persuades us to go to the nearest Portuguese town—Valencia—where the Mayor invites us. Soldiers will guard the plane. We row across the little inlet, up the crowded bank and are driven on a bad road into the city.

Finally, very tired, we drive back with several bouquets of flowers to the river and row across to our plane. C. makes a marvelous bed: take the stick out, fill up the holes, all the hard things first, make everything flush with the rudder bars so C.'s feet can go under the seat, use our coats for pillows and on top of slickers, flying suit, and rubber seats, in our sleeping bag, we go to sleep.

We are waked in the night by an argument across the stream. C. throws on the flashlight: "Hello." "Hello, Mister Lindbergh— there is a telegram for you."—"Who from?"—"From Lisbon."— "Who from?" "From Lisbon—a telegram for you."—"Oh, never mind it." "Mister Lindbergh—a telegram for you—from Lisbon."

"Yes—never mind—in the morning."—"A telegram from Lisbon," etc., till finally we shout out, "Mañana!" and they leave us.[1]

November 14th

It is quite cold. We wake to hear voices and a boat and then more voices. People are gathering on the banks. Dressing inside the baggage compartment; my sore finger hits everything; I have lost my handkerchief; I have spilled oil on my trousers. Always in a time like this little things that wouldn't matter at other times matter terribly. The cold-cream tube has burst in my purse—I probably sat on it. Impossible to pull trousers on in a sitting position. My comb breaks. I can hear voices get louder and louder and can see through cracks.

There is a large crowd on the bank in front of us—several cameras—and the banks on the other side of the river are lined. Two or three rowboats are ferrying people back and forth. There is a continuous chatter, like a theater before the curtain goes up. And all eyes on the plane.

That strange feeling of dressing, doing one's complete toilette in the middle of a crowd of watching eyes, covered only by the thin body of the plane. Also knowing that the minute one sticks one's head out one will be shot at by photographers. "The Lindberghs after their night in the plane."

We get out, C. first, and shake hands. The Mayor of Valencia, the Captain of the River Patrol boat, the head customs officer, the boy who speaks English ("New Yorkese"). C. pumps out the pontoons. It is a very bad day. The man comes with gasoline and C. fills with a ten-liter can while the Captain of the patrol boat explains the weather (in French) to me. Fog is low on the coast.

Finally we go off with the Mayor to an inn in Valencia. We have lunch, a long, long lunch, with three or four different kinds of meat, five or six courses, wine. The hall is crowded. We wait for hours—from 1:15 to 3:30. We have champagne.

[1] The telegram turned out to be: "Welcome by Portuguese Baptist Convention."

My French is long ago exhausted. Then a walk up the hill, around narrow cobbled streets, past women carrying big pots on their heads, to the cathedral. All the town follows us, the children screaming and running ahead. Then back down the hill and drive "home." The muddy boat across the stream. It is about five. The officer says that we must be tired . . . so many people. He will put a guard there so that we are not disturbed. All the people are driven off peaceably, like sheep. We are alone and fix up the bed, take our shoes off. The plane is covered with mud from C.'s boots and the muddy bank. The mud dries on the floor and the dust gets over everything. We sleep quite well and hear rain rattling on the wings.

November 15th

The clouds are off the hills. The same crowd of people and more photographers. The cabin is in the most awful mess. Will it ever be clean again? The Mayor announces that he is naming a street after us. Charles takes some pictures of the cameramen, causing great amusement. C. repacks. Good-bys, we warm up the engine, and shove out from the willows into the river, across the current, and upstream. We scrape on the bottom several times! Crowds of people run along both banks, pell-mell, children, men and women, dogs, all falling over each other, all watching the plane and running to keep up with it, like the Pied Piper. Most of them in bare feet. I notice a mother carrying a child, followed by a lamb. When we get quite a way up we turn and start to take off downstream, all the people running frantically the other way.

We circle Valencia and Tuy and cut across to Lisbon. Suddenly in sunshine—a great bay full of boats, warships, tugs, sailboats, passenger liners—and a big city, distinctly Latin, white stone, or pink, gleaming in the sun. Rather a choppy sea. We taxi into an inner breakwater full of fishing boats. The boats all toot as we enter. The usual crowd and barricade of cameras as we step on the pier, flowers, introductions. Up into the office of the Commandant, the welcoming drink of port wine. The nice fat officer, very serious, exploding with an "Ip—ip—urrah!" Mrs. Caldwell[1] takes me to the Legation, where a hot bath, decent clothes, and a delicious lunch make me feel in bliss.

The little Portuguese maid unpacks *all* our carefully packed bags and spreads the things around the room in four bureaus, throwing C. into a fit. We spend the afternoon trying to locate them.

To bed very sleepy.

Lisbon, November 16, 1933

Darling Mother,

This place—at least the Embassy and garden—reminds me of Mexico. I awoke this morning in the high-ceilinged old-fashioned bedroom to all kinds of sounds and impressions that made me think of it. That kind of fresh chill to the air that you know will disappear in the sun, for I felt that we were again in a warm country. And on top of an underlying impression of peace and quiet, the superimposed sounds, very clear and vibrant, of morning in Mexico: street cries in the distance, monotonous and carrying, but not shrill at all, just continuous and almost musical, like some kind of bird. Then the shrill cries of children and the clatter of turkeys, over the next wall. And then, nearer, under one's window in the garden—oh, delicious!—all gentle lovely sounds, sweepings and rakings and scratchings of some-one working in the Legation garden. The thud of straw baskets put down to collect the weeds. And feet clapping clearly down stone steps and the occasional twitter of birds and the unmistakable smell, vaguely pleasant, of something burning. We had it in Mexico and never knew where it came from. It wasn't a cooking smell and yet not distinctly a burning-leaves smell—what is it they are burning? Anyway, I couldn't resist walking out before breakfast.

[1] Mr. and Mrs. Robert G. Caldwell, American Minister to Portugal.

This grand old house is built on the side of a hill. You look out down hill, over red roofs and occasional palms, to the big harbor full of boats from all over the world. And on the near hillside is their closed garden, which has three terraces up from the street so that you walk across a bridge from the second floor into the garden. It is completely walled, mostly grass and trees and garden beds around the outside next to the walls. In the garden, palms and pepper trees, and bamboo, and up the sides of the palms and the walls, climbing pink geranium, poinsettia and dripping fuchsia.

It seems heavenly to us—sun and flowers—as we have been in bad weather all through Europe, cold and wet and damp. And along the coast of Spain and across to Portugal simply *terrible* fog and storm.

I am really frightful about fog. I hate it beyond words and am in a panic the whole time, and every time we go through a day like that I think I cannot go on with that kind of life. Of course, when we get down C. says we never were in a bad position. I do trust him perfectly and know that he is very careful and does not take chances, but it is a kind of uncontrollable physical terror, exaggerated by imagination.

I had a funny experience in Rotterdam. I often think that you can't help another person, except accidentally, and one never knows when one does. But in Rotterdam someone helped me quite accidentally. We had tried to go to Geneva and after two hours fighting through fog, turned around and came back. When we finally got down again, in the warm clubhouse near the field there were several other marooned pilots talking. I felt terribly shaken and aggrieved. Someone sat down next to me, a rather nice gentleman-pilot, and started talking to me about how lovely it was for us to be able to fly together.

It wasn't exactly the time to talk to me that way. I felt he didn't know anything about it and felt rather bitter about this ideal picture he was painting of us. Then I began to realize that he wasn't painting us but his own experience. He apparently is a very sensitive man who has a business of his own but often goes off on long flights with his wife. They just go together, doing everything themselves, completely dependent on each other.

I don't remember exactly what he said, but he was talking about his wife. (She had just been terribly ill, which I suppose had heightened his feeling about it.) He appreciated my courage (!) because he knew what the hardships were, but how wonderful it was to have it together. *Especially* flying. There is something binding about flying together, because it is such a lonely thing. One is so dependent on the other person, the experiences are so *peculiarly* one's own. "You go through good weather and bad weather together." It is all quite true, too—only I had forgotten it.

I realized then, in one of those strange lightning-storm moments when you see yourself, that C. feels that way about me, although he couldn't express it that way or wouldn't think of expressing it, and that I took it for granted and almost threw it away. And that the picture he was painting was us, or *could* be us, if I would just put out my hand to take it, if I would stop fighting it and accept it and realize that it was probably the happiest time of my life, that we were young and happily married and having everything together.

I *do* realize it and *have,* of course. In Greenland we had it. But somehow fear and homesickness and a weariness from the pressure of too many and too unreal people and the tension that the watchful press put one under have all combined to create in me the desire to get home, to get *through* with this as quickly and painlessly as possible—a feeling of impatience for a *real* life, not realizing that this is real life. Do you remember Proust's wonderful saying about the future's not being a cake that was handed to you in one piece but something that you were nibbling into all the time? It's that, of course. And it is dreadful to waste it.

I don't know why I write you this, except that you will understand better than anyone and it makes it realer to write it to you. Of course you yourself are the most wonderful example of that. You and Daddy had so much together. It must be a satisfaction to realize that you never backed down on anything—Mexico and the campaign and so much before I even realized it. You always went the whole way and got the most out of it. Mexico seemed a kind of culmination, perhaps because I was there part of the time and saw, or rather felt, the results of what you did together.

But it is hard to take examples from one's own family: the situations do not seem the same, even when they are. And I have felt rather better, after my time in Rotterdam, about the rest of this trip which up to now I have only been dreading. There will be something for me to do, as there was in Greenland. That makes it more fun, and more mine. There will only be the work of flying and radio, nothing outside to detract from that. The flights—from here to the Azores, from the Azores to the Madeiras, and from Africa to South America —will be long and tiring but a definite job. Not just sitting in the back cockpit trying to be calm, when you think you may run into a mountain.

We will wait for the best possible weather on these trips and hope to have good communication. Also, as C. says, we're on the way home! I have been saying we'll be home in a month —that sounds near. So much ground to cover that the *time* seems almost meaningless. I can only think of it in terms of space, distance, and amount of work.

DIARY   [*Lisbon*], *Sunday, November 19th*
Drive into the country; valleys and hills, rather bare, covered with vineyards and plowed fields. Here, rows of eucalyptus, gray olive trees, bent and wind-blown, brilliant little towns in the sunshine.

The Minister telling us about a certain ridge of mountains, "The lines of Torres Vedras," which cut across the country north of Lisbon from the sea to the Tagus River. This sharp line was always the last stronghold of the defense—Portuguese against the Moors, Crusaders against the Moors, and Wellington against the French in the Napoleonic Wars. There is one gap in the line, a long valley at right angles to it. In this valley, on a high stony ridge, is Obidos, an old fortified town guarding the approach to the lines of Torres Vedras.

Our first view of Obidos:—a Crusaders' town on a rocky island in the big plain, completely walled and a castle at each end, an aqueduct leading out of it. We climbed the old wall and looked down on russet roofs at all angles, higgledy-piggledy, dovetailing one another, narrow twisting cobbled streets, here and there an orange tree or a cypress or a small grape arbor, green against the white stone houses. Way down below us, bright roosters in a little court and a gray donkey nodding up the street.

We ate our picnic in peace in the south tower. Our eyes followed the irregular jagged line of the wall and beyond, the plowed fields of the townspeople, who from medieval days could work in their fields outside and hurry back at night to the safety of the walls.

Monday, November 20th

C. not home for lunch: too busy with engine. He is doing hard mechanics' works—doesn't trust leaving it to other people.

[Lisbon to Azores] Tuesday, November 21st

Called at four. Pitch dark and rather cold. Everything is packed, so there is no rush. The Minister and Mrs. Caldwell get up and have breakfast with us. The whole household rises. Terribly nice of them. A good breakfast before we start down to the dock. C. got the plane into the water and refueled yesterday. It is raining by the time we go out to the boat by lantern and car lights. But it is light to the east.

We take off, spanking the swell, at 7:08. In bad storms and low clouds the first part of trip, strong winds and static, but later almost clear skies. Then again, after we hit the islands, rain squalls. The only excitement of the trip: when I was flying while C. took sights, was seeing the volcanic slope of Terceira going up into clouds.

After Terceira we are in sight of islands all the time. Local storms, clouds boiling over the hills, very rough winds. Land in the little harbor at Horta: a steep hill at one end of harbor and a steep cliff at the other. Come down in a curve and then straighten out.

Ville d'Ys, French warship, in harbor. We last saw her in Greenland at Godthaab. Thrilled to see her again and wave frantically.

We climb out, shake hands in the bobbing boat. The French boat comes up. A bunch of camellias tied with a blue ribbon with *Ville d'Ys* on it. We row to the dock, cameras and clapping and a crowd and lots of girls with flowers. I take the first two bunches but can't carry more. C. has a hard bunch of camellias thrown at him! They scatter them at our feet. People want us to stay at their homes. "Are you tired? Do sit down. . . . Did you have a pleasant trip?"

C. insists on going to the hotel to think things over. We take bumpy road down the one street and stop in front of a yellow plaster house with stained-glass windows—*Hotel.* Up two flights of stairs to our room. It looks clean, painted white with faded blue curtains, a big dark wood heavy bed, tin washstand and pail in corner. I sit on the bed. It does not give at all and rustles slightly—a straw mattress and bolster. A girl brings in a pitcher of cold water for washing.

The English family who have urged us to come to them stand in the door and say, "This really is rather uncomfortable. Why don't you come home with us and have a hot bath and a cup of tea?"—"Oh no," says C. brightly, "this looks *very* comfortable to me—it looks, uh . . . clean" (which is all one can say for it). I lie down very tired—too tired to take my things off and wash in cold water. "What would you like?" says C. "I would like a hot bath and a cup of tea."

He comes back an hour later and we go over to the English family and have tea and Madeira and a hot bath and supper.

To bed on our corncobs; that awful hole in the middle of your back.

Wake at four and can't get to sleep.

I don't feel homesick when we are flying, but when we stop for a day, in the early morning and before we go to bed, I am wildly impatient and count the probable time it will take. I can't think about the next day or I don't go to sleep. I don't let myself think about getting home and the baby. It is too precious. It might undermine the chance of getting home.

Wednesday, November 22nd

A dark sky and torrents of rain. We call on the local Governor, then on the head of the Port, then on the military head, then to the Vacuum [Oil] office. I am very sleepy, climbing up steps past men saluting into an inner office. We are bowed to the seat of honor, the sofa, we present our compliments. It is translated. He says, If there is anything we can do, we are at your disposal. It is translated. We smile. He asks us when we leave, or if we are going to America. It is translated. We answer. It is translated. "Thank you very much . . . good-by."

C. thinks the harbor is too small to take off with a full load and the sea outside has too big a swell. We may go to Ponta Delgada. Ponta Delgada is bigger than Horta—a bigger harbor, longer breakwater.[1]

Thursday, November 23rd

A lovely day. We take off easily [with a light load] from inside of the harbor; in the air by the end of the breakwater, about noon.

[1] Colonel Lindbergh was considering a flight back to the United States by way of Newfoundland.

In one hour and a half we arrive at Ponta Delgada. Have a terrible time anchoring. The official motorboat comes too near, almost banging into a wing, then tows us too fast. C. is afraid of banging into a boat. He cuts their rope to free us! Great excitement among the Portuguese.

It is fairly hot. I have been flying with a wool shirt, sweater, and wool blouse on top. I take off the wool blouse. We push up to the dock in a small boat. A picturesque old landing: two open arched stairways leading down to the water, almost Venetian. A great crowd on dock, shouting, waving, crowding, pushing babies at us. We finally get to an open car and drive through crowds who throw confetti and roses at us from the balconies of the narrow streets. Very Latin, like South and Central America. Into the Consulate. Have a hot bath and tea; then we go out to pay calls—on the Naval head and on the Governor, who is also a U.P. reporter and runs the local newspaper!

Friday, November 24th

Called at 4:30. C. has an awful time trying to get a buoy on the anchor rope, shouting and pointing. They do not understand and don't want to say they don't (my policy always in arithmetic). It takes a long time. In the meantime the wind has risen and it is day. However, we get off all right. A beautiful day, good communication to Madeira, which C. hit right on the head. I took a sight when almost there, which put him very near. We looked up to find it dead ahead. Madeira, a pretty, steeply terraced green island. Quite a sea and a very small breakwater. C. circles and circles and finally goes on toward the Canaries. Through some rain and then out into clear weather.

Land at Las Palmas. A long breakwater, an outer harbor, a big port at the foot of two bare black mountains. The town at the foot looks very Moorish; flat-topped white buildings. We taxi into the big port. Many ships—British, French, Portuguese, Spanish, Swedish—and lots of fishing tugs. Two Englishmen take us into port, where by this time a crowd has gathered. Push through the crowd to the Captain of the Port's office, then to call on the Governor of the Canary Islands. We go to bed early and sleep under mosquito nets.

Sunday, November 26th

Up at 4:30. Out to the dock. We take a *long* time to get ready. Finally we leave. A beautiful day—clouds on horizon.

Africa is just as I thought it would be—dry, brown yellow sand as far as one can see, falling down abruptly in steep cliffs to the sea. Villa Cisneros, on a spit of land between the bay and the sea—nothing but sand. A big, white, flat-topped fort, a hangar, a square of flat-topped houses, and a settlement of dark brown tents. We landed in the bay in the middle of the morning. The light was brilliant. Bright blue bay, bright shadowless desert, a sharp line where the cliff made a shadow.

A boat came out to meet us, a Moor standing on top in ragged European clothes with a dark blue turban wound around his head. They had a buoy ready for us. C. had caught it and I was down on the wing about to fasten the rope to the pontoon. Suddenly—splash, and out of the water right at my feet came a curly black head. One of the Moors had jumped off the boat and swum to the plane to help us. Finally moored, we stepped into the boat. The Governor, a large man in white, was Spanish, cordial, and spoke bad French. We struggled along: *"Pas d'essence."—"Nous partirons demain matin."*

We get onto the dock. Lots of Moors squatting about. How do they sit that way, all hunched up and motionless with their dark flowing clothes wrapped around them and dark eyes peering out? The mouth and rest of the face are covered by the hand. They do not move or seem to notice you. They walk with a certain rhythm. The women are slim, swift, and noiseless, like wild animals. You don't realize they are following you.

As we approach the square fort, some lanky yellow dogs run

out barking. Here are two sentinels—Spanish, somewhat de-jected-looking. Inside, a few scraggly trees, white sand, white walls. We walk up stairs into the Governor's apartment.

The Governor has a car and we go out *"faire une petite promenade."* His wife and small son come with us. We stop at one of the white houses and meet some of the Air France people. Apparently this is a regular stop and they have three or four men here: a mechanic, weatherman, and pilot. We drive over the field to a line of forts with a thick wall of eight or ten rows of barbed wire joining them together. There is a gate which swings open. Here the desert really begins. Looking down that stretch was like looking out to sea. Trails ran off, and in the distance we could see a group of small figures, a camel or two and men, on the way out.

Conversation goes slowly. The Governor talks to the officer in Spanish. He repeats it to me in French. I repeat to C. in English. He replies in English. I translate . . .! After lunch, C. and I are dropped at the plane, where we do odds and ends. I paint the ship—think it more restful than talking French. At twilight the colors are heavenly—the sand, a dull gold, not brilliant but a soft glow and the water and sky, a dark green blue. It is very clear. Something about the clarity and sharp colors reminds me of Greenland evenings.

Tea with the Moors. They invited us in the morning. I had been trying all day to ask in French whether or not it was safe to drink the tea—*not* that I was afraid of the Moors, but the tea. *"C'est bon. C'est très bon. C'est sucré."* Finally I ask: *"Il ne donne pas la maladie?"*—*"Non. C'est bouilli."*

It was quite dark. The Moors rose from nowhere as we approached. We went inside a small lighted room, hung with cloth, rugs on the ground. A circle of people. We sat on cushions. There was only candlelight. Two Moors in the center had trays, pitchers, glasses, and big cones of compressed sugar. They hammered the sugar up and put huge chunks of it into the teapots, measured the tea in their brown hands, turned the teapots and poured a little in each glass, then filled up with boiling water (a great noise) as they poured from high up. They were little glasses and you were supposed to drink three!

The turbaned heads were all in one corner. The Governor began to talk to them in Spanish about C. "The first man . . ." They listened with attention and perfect dignity. Then one who could speak French (very good-looking) got up and spoke to me: the heads of all the tribes wanted to say welcome to us, and bon voyage. C. said I was to say thank you very much and how happy we were to be here and how much he liked the tea—at which some more was poured out which I couldn't drink.

Villa Cisneros to Porto Praia, Cape Verdes,
Monday, November 27th

Wake early. Breakfast and off across the sands to the wharf. It is fairly cool and there is dew on the sand and stones. Mrs. Governor carries some ostrich feathers for me. I carry the camera and radio bag, C. the sextant. The bags go in the car. When we get to the dock the boat is not there. *"Le matelot dort encore."* There is a group of Moors in dark clothing huddled on the dock, veiled up to their eyes, motionless, not watching, yet aware of us.

Take off easily. Good communication from Las Palmas. Pass Cape Blanco. Try to call PAA [Pan American] stations on 24 [short wave]. I hear WSL [Sayville, Long Island]. I call WSL—he answers! I am hot and cold inside from excitement —don't dare touch the set. KHCAL comes back clearly, QRK [I receive you well] and QRU [Have you anything for me?], casually like that. I say, "Lindbergh plane, en route Cape Verde Islands, min pse [please wait a minute]. Then I poke C. vigorously and he gives me a position for PAA. I get it through OK and plan another contact at 13:00 GMT, but can't get him again.[1]

Find Porto Praia in early afternoon—a small port, not sheltered, and a big swell outside. We circle. Below Porto Praia is a tiny opening at the end of which is a hangar and crane and pier—the Air France base. Rocky coast and breakers. We circle and circle and circle, come down once or twice about to land, and then go off again. I begin to get nervous. It looks worse than Madeira. Finally land—spank terribly and, when we stop, bounce on the waves. A very strong wind; we can't get into the tiny opening to the harbor. A boat comes out rowed by Negroes and a white man with a helmet.

Well, I think, there seem to be only one or two houses and a few huts, but where there is Aviation there is usually a certain amount of efficiency and comfort. We drift back and finally get in harbor, riding on the swell. We drop our anchor and the boat comes up. The man is French—Air France. He looks rather bad and is sloppily dressed. He tells me he has a high fever and came up out of bed. I feel worried and don't dare ask what kind. We finally get tied to some big rocks on shore and anchored twice, and go ashore. Another man, tall, thin, part Negro, fairly well dressed, steps up. He speaks some English. He is in charge of the Air France station. He introduces us to his pretty little wife, only a girl with a sweet sad face. She also wears a helmet. The heat on one's face and head is terrific.

We talk about lifting the plane out of the water into the hangar, but there are no shackles the right size. A car comes down over the hill with uniformed officers in it, from the Governor. There is a strong wind blowing—the trade wind. It is hot and dusty and dries one's face. *"On n'attend pas de tempête de cette direction-là?"* (from the sea).—*"Jamais."*

---

[1] This contact established a record (over 3,000 miles) for radio communication between an airplane and a ground station.

We decide to go into town to get the shackles—also to call on the Governor. Up the steep stony hill by a few huts. A rough ride, bare hilly country, volcanic rock, loose stones over hillsides. Everything is dry and a browny red color, a few grayish scraggly trees, all bent in the same direction from the trade wind. Men and women barefoot, in ragged clothes, carrying loads on their heads. We learn a few things from the Air France man. The Company has stopped operating; the chief has left. He was the radioman and is now in charge. Will we go to Praia or stay near the plane? Then we will stay in his house. The first aviators he has had as guests since he was made chief. We ask about the mechanic and the fever. "Oh yes, he has fever, but it is just the fever we all have here."

After a long ride we come down a hill into Praia, past more huts sprawling with poor-looking women and naked children with great swollen bellies. The town itself looks fairly clean. We stop in a square full of trees; the Governor's house. Upstairs into a big ballroom where we sit down (C. and I always on the inevitable sofa!). The Portuguese Governor speaks excellent French and is intelligent, with a pretty wife and daughter. We promise to come for a meal the next day.

Then off, to a kind of hardware store, to look for shackles. "No, there are none. He is sending a man for some."—"Well, can't we go there ourselves?" We start up the narrow street to the Harbormaster: "No, he isn't there." We walk further up the street. "No, he is back here." "Ah, he is here." "No, he has none." But the mechanic says he can *make* some in an hour. "It will be too late," C. says. "Haven't you any cable?" *"Un câble d'acier?"* Yes, perhaps. We will go to the mechanic's shop. Uphill again. C. looks around—no cable. "No, but he has sent the boy for some." "Can't we go ourselves?" "No, he is coming now." Finally he comes. Yes, he has some cable. It is too big, but it can be unwound and will do. We start out of the garage. A large crowd has gathered. The sun still beats down. We push through the sticky crowd to the car.

We take the long drive back and arrive about twilight. After looking at the plane and its anchorage (the wind always blowing from the northeast), C. decides it is all right there and to move it in the morning. We take our bags out. The Negro boys carry them uphill to the chief's old bungalow. C. goes out in a rowboat to look at the sea. (Will we *ever* get off this sea? Especially with a full load?[1] Is it ever smoother?)

The girl decides it is too dusty in the bungalow and we had better sleep in hers, so we trudge down the hill and up the opposite one to their bungalow next to the radio towers. Off a small porch there is a tiny room where two Negro women are cooking, and two other small rooms; one, filled up with a big bed, the other with a table and cupboard for food. They apologize for the house. "We are in the country." Both speak good French.

When C. came back he asked me to go out for a walk before supper. The Frenchman had told him that someone in that house was very ill with consumption or something. He, C., could not understand, so I must speak to him. We met him and he told us it was tuberculosis and the house *"est tout contaminée."* We must leave at once, use his house or the old chief's house on the hill. We thanked him. The tall operator was horribly thin and had a blue tinge to his face. We had been planning to sleep in his bed, but now felt we couldn't, but we didn't want to hurt his feelings.

After supper we broached it to him (and I felt very un-comfortable through supper, afraid to use the napkins, the towels, the glasses, noticing his cough, etc.) that we couldn't use his room and would use the old chief's house.

What an uproar. The company had sent him wires to do everything for us and we would not use his room. Over there it was dirty, it had not been cleaned: *"Il y a des bêtes qui*

[1] To make the transatlantic flight to South America, the *Tingmissartoq* would have had to take off with a heavy overload of fuel.

piquent" (bedbugs?). Well, we said, we'd get our own bedding. *"Jamais!"* With all the beds not being used in his house, he *couldn't* have us use our own bedding! We walked down the length of the bungalow and saw there were unused rooms and decided on one of those. They shook out the mattress (it was falling to pieces) and brought clean sheets and covers (all stained, for the former occupant had used them for tablecloths).

The little girl looked at me sadly and said that I had never slept in such a terrible bed. I said she didn't know where I had slept. Then again she spoke of *"les petites bêtes qui piquent."*

They left us and we started to unpack. There was no chair in the room and lots of bugs on the floors and the cracked walls. I sat down on the bed and looked at it. "Is that a bed-bug?"—"No, just a roach." I started to get undressed: a little black tick on the coverlet. "Ah-ha!" said C. "A bedbug?"—"Looks like it." He tried it with his finger (horrible thought) but it would not bite. However, I soon found another—several. C. killed a few, one on the table. "They're probably in the walls too." He thought they might not be bedbugs and we might try it. I was for going down to the plane immediately, but he said we'd better wait.

He took one of the bugs in to the radio operator to ask him if they bit. "Yes," was the verdict, "they bite, but not badly." That was enough for me. However, C. wanted to pour citronella all over us and try to stick it out. I absolutely refused. I said I would walk all night, or sit on the table. ("You won't be safe from them there. You're all in, and it'll be too uncomfortable on the plane and we won't get any rest.") I refused. There were other things, too—small pale nameless insects crawling about.

C. finally conceded and we decided on the plane. He took one load down, I shook and brushed all the baggage off, the boots, the camera, and waited on the porch in the dark, the wind still blowing from the northeast. Then we walked out quietly and down the hill again. I didn't even feel tired; I was anxious to get away and so glad to be spared the night in that bed. The two Negro boys, startled from their sleep by the dock's edge, rowed us out. It was cool on the plane, the wind blowing hard, and it felt clean. C. made up the bed and we slept in peace, though I had nightmares. We were waked early by the sun in the window. And the family down to meet us, quite chagrined at our action of the night before!

Tuesday, November 28th

A hot day, and still that wind, roaring, from the same direction. I get up and try to do all the regular things inside the plane: wash out of a canteen with a handkerchief, cold cream and powder on the face, comb the hair. The clothes are messy, as we used them for pillows.

Up the hill for breakfast. Good coffee and bananas and eggs. After breakfast we see the oil and gasoline people, who have come over. We have all our gas here and it looks as though we couldn't get off. They say the wind blows hard for six months of the year and it is never calm.

We try to wash up for lunch at the Governor's. C. cables Dakar for permission to go there and get reorganized. Evidently we can't take off here with a full load [of gasoline].

Drive into Praia. I felt well dressed when I left, but very shabby as I arrive at Government House in my piqué hat that has been folded for five months and my mussed cotton dress. A long and delicious meal and I feel civilized. The Governor talks good French and I have no difficulty in making him understand.

Back to our harbor. Refueling. By this time I am dead tired and have an awful headache. That hot wind blowing all day long makes you feel as though the place had a fever. It makes me feel, too—when we are sitting on their little porch—that we are at sea. I feel the house tip like a boat.

Telegram back from Dakar: "Eminent danger from yellow

fever . . . quarantine . . . etc." The couple explain to me that yellow fever attacks whites more than blacks. *"On vomit du sang et c'est fini."*

Again supper. I am so tired I can hardly keep awake. Back to the plane. C. remakes the bed. Same kind of night—too hot *in* the sleeping bag and outside the coat does not cover me.

Wednesday, November 29th

Second morning's wash in the plane. Breakfast and back to the plane where I lie down again. Tired and headachy. C. sends a telegram to Bathurst requesting permission to land there. He works on the ship, painting. Up to the house for tea. They think there will be fever all along the coast soon; very discouraging.

Just before supper we get the cable from Bathurst: "Pleased to grant authorization"! We are cheered up. C. says we *can* get off here with a light load.

Back to the plane and to be waked at 4:30 because it is calmer in the morning.

Thursday, November 30th, Thanksgiving Day

Wake early. Feel very dirty. Good-by to our strange group. We are towed out to the lighthouse and taxi for a long time before taking off. There is quite a swell. We start. I hold my breath. Frightful whacks—something *must* break; it is worse than landing. I think we are off several times after a big bounce and we come down again even harder. C. stalls off—whee! relief.

Good communication en route to Bathurst with our [Porto Praia] friends.

Bathurst: flat and green, palms, a harbor full of fishing boats. A muddy river, small ripples. Land easily. A motor launch with white-uniformed officers in sun helmets. It is frightfully hot. Climb up the pier and into a car, to Government House. Nice streets, fences, freshly painted houses, a cricket ground, the English flag—Order! C. says, "It always feels good to get onto English territory."

The Governor's wife, young and pretty and dainty in lavender voile, runs out to meet us.

At Government House, lovely high ceilings, a bathtub and hot water and nice soap, a delicious meal. (She apologizes for the fish —a little too much cooked! As though we would notice it.) Everything clean, cool, and glistening. Silent, efficient Negro servants in long white coats, red sashes and white fezzes. I wash my hair and rest. Tea at four and out to see the English planes here on a trip—three bombers. A good night's rest under mosquito nets in cool white sheets.

I wish on a first star. I find I am saying simply "Charles!"— an old old wish. I don't remember now, exactly, what it meant originally. But it was enough just to say "Charles."

Bathurst, Friday, December 1st

We bought sun helmets in the English store. Moslem dress prevails in the street. Many women wear what looks like a child's dress (as blouse) on top of a skirt, but some have a big flowing robe and sweep along, glorious-looking, gold in the ears. Children are strapped low on the back. Colors: many blues, sea green. A strange headdress, little braids sticking out in front from bandana, or a knot on top. Some primitive half-naked women with shaved heads.

C. refueling. No wind in the evening, he thinks we must go in the morning.

Saturday, December 2nd

Write up diary, pack up to go, C. refueling. Where will we be tomorrow night?

1933

Sunday, December 3rd

Called at 3:30. Up and dress, coffee from thermos bottles, hard-boiled eggs and bread and butter. Mr. and Mrs. Parish[1] get up to see us off. Good-bys. She is very sweet and is, I think, really concerned about us. We are rowed out to the plane. A bright moon. We are all packed up and it is still dark, pink streaks in the sky.

We start off about six and taxi miles out in the bay. Very little wind. More wind farther out. The ship is terribly heavy—the floats way down in the water. It heaves from side to side as we taxi, looking to me as though the wing were touching the water. I start having indigestion from excitement.

"All set?"—"All right." Terrific roar, terrific spray, all over the wings, streaming down for hours it seems, but not bumpy. Then C. pulls back the throttle. Can't do it. I look at my watch: two minutes only. I start breathing again. We go back and try it again. Same thing.

Finally we go back to the dock to take out gas. The pump won't fit into the gas tank; we have to siphon it with a small tube. We try pumping to start suction, then one of the boys sucks and spits and gets it started slowly. Then C. sucks and spits to try to get it faster. Finally we use our bilge pump. It takes a long time. C. looks over the pontoons. The anchor box is full of water. He can't get at the back compartments (under water), so he gets a boy to lift up on the tail (from the rowboat).

We start out again, but the wind has dropped to nothing; it is better and we get up on the step—but we can't get off. Finally we go back to the wharf. It is 9:30 and the sun is hot now. We decide to wait for a wind. We go back to the house where the Parishes wait for us, and have a good breakfast.

I lie down until twelve. Lunch. After lunch I sleep a little. At four we go out to the "Cape," a lovely house on a cliff,

[1] Acting Governor of the Crown Colony of Gambia, West Africa.

165

overlooking the sea. It is delicious and cool. We sit on the terrace and watch the stars come out. The skies are calm and clear; quite a wind blowing here. C. thinks we might take off at midnight by moonlight. We walk out to the point after we get back; a wind on the pier. At 9:30, get ready to go down again. Work on the plane pumping out pontoons, etc. Taxi out into the bay. Mr. and Mrs. Parish are on the wharf.

"All set?"—"All right." Terrific noise, spray. I hold my breath; think we're going to get off, absolutely tense and terrified. Can he see well enough? Can he control it—so heavy? Couldn't a wing hook into the sea? Would we be thrown? Drowned? (Balbo's accident taking off.) Watch the end of wing—fire? No, the red wing-tip light. He pulls back the throttle. We can't do it. What is wrong? I wish he would tell me—something, *anything*. But he only turns the ship, heavily bouncing in the waves, and goes back. He will try again.

I feel rather sick. I don't want to be sick. Why is it we always start under the worst possible conditions? I look up at the stars and wish they could give me the calm that they did this evening on the point. The feeling that human misery is small, human life unimportant. I will try to name them. That big circle—the navigating stars. Castor and Pollux? There is the Southern Cross—points to what? The ship bobs up and down. I get out the watch and try to see by moonlight. I can quite well.

"All set?"—"All right." He tries again—same thing—and yet there must be a wind, a good wind. He turns—why doesn't he tell me *something?* He cuts the switch. "What are you going to do?"—"Don't know—thought we'd think about it. It *almost* gets off—almost."

I don't dare say anything, don't know which way to swing things. Shall I say, as I long to, "Let's not take any more chances . . . go back to bed," or shall I force myself to say, "Let's try again." I say nothing. Finally C. says we'd better go back and get a good night's rest and think things over. I feel relieved and tired. "We'll try again on the way home." We do, trying to rock it off. No use.

We taxi back to the lights of the town. I try to think what it means. He said he would not take out any more gas—that would be taking too many chances. We had a good wind and hadn't got off, with a load we'd taken off with before. Would we wait and wait for wind? The moon was waning now. Would we tear every unnecessary thing out, floor boards, etc., and try again? Would we move to another place—Portuguese Guinea? Could we get off at all with enough load to make it? Go home by boat? After this preparation and fuss, how would C. feel?

It would take time, anyway—weeks perhaps. Christmas, and getting home, and the baby vanished, and I felt very tired— infinitely weary of the whole thing. And yet I mustn't give in to it, at least not ostensibly. C. felt worse. His ship had failed him. He couldn't understand it. We seemed to be at the wall, at the last margin, and what was he to do? What was there left to do?

We hardly spoke, put things away. C. got the buoy fixed. The little boat with the boys was there. I got out the bags. There was still someone on the dock—I hoped not the Parishes. I couldn't bear to see them, or anyone. It was about one o'clock. We were rowed back to the dock. A nice Englishman who had stayed helped us up, without saying much. "What was the matter now, Colonel?"—"Don't know. Overload, that's all. Don't understand it—it's taken off with that much before. It must be different down here in the tropics."—"It's been very damp today," he said comfortingly. The Governor's car was waiting for us. "Well, we thought we'd sleep on it."—"Oh, yes . . . always wise."

We drove home in silence. No one on the streets, a few huddled forms asleep on stone benches. We stole quietly into Government House. C. said, "It's better not to get too tired, then you begin taking chances. A great many accidents have happened that way." His mouth was rather set. "We've still got a few tricks we can pull." Then to bed, without talking about it at all.

Monday, December 4th

Woke very tired. After breakfast, went back for a rest. C. is taking out one of the empty tanks. He is going to patch up things and try to stop up the leakage in the anchor box. We are dumping all our clothes and are going to try again. He says, his optimism restored, "It's very interesting, this experience!" It is hard work, as he has to snip inside the fuselage. The fumes are terrible and it is very hot.

I sleep, and instead of thinking (there seems to be nothing helpful to think about) I learn poetry:

"Brave flowers that I could gallant it like you!"

C. comes back tired and hot just in time for supper. After supper we look at the sea—calm, very little wind. C. decides to get a good night's sleep and try tomorrow. Except that we will have less moon, I feel relieved. C. needs the rest.

Bathurst, Tuesday, December 5th

After a good night's sleep, C. decides we are going to try again at five (if there is any wind) or at midnight. "Could we take off tomorrow night, Charles?" "Yes" (very cheerily), "but that's the last."—"Can you get off now with *no* wind?" *"Almost!"* I began to realize that tonight at midnight (or tomorrow) is our last chance, because the moon is getting less and less and there is practically no chance of taking off at five, when it is always dead calm. I take an hour's nap before motoring out to the cape, where we were the other evening. I can only think about the wind. There is not a breath, even there. Coming home, I watch the palms, the sailboat in the river, the flagpole outside Government House. Not a stir.

It is the quietest evening yet—this of all nights! Mrs. Parish and I walk out to the end of the pier. Not enough wind to lift a handkerchief. We'll never get off. I feel quite desperate. Before supper I walk out again. There is a change—enough to blow out a hanky. I tell C. and we walk out together. "That helps!" We think it will come up with the moon and the tide. C. admits to the Parishes that if we don't get off tonight we'll "have to change plans."

We walk out again. The wind is a little stronger and the moon is up, reddish and terribly squashed-in since last night. I look at it with a sinking heart. "Well, this certainly is the last night we can use *that*." We say good night soon after supper and, in bravado, that we'll see them at breakfast. Mrs. Parish squeezes both my hands again. The Governor wants us to wire if we get there. I say over and over in my mind, "Listen—the wind is rising and the air is wild with leaves."

C. has gotten a great deal out of the ship: the chocolate we got in Greenland, the anchor and rope, the tin bucket, lots of tools, the flying suit, the sleeping bag, etc. I have a sick headache but otherwise am fairly fresh. We leave the house about 10:30. Bump through the streets in the dark. Someone leans out of an open lighted window to see what it is (if only it were that casual to us!). Our luggage looks very light. C. takes only the suit he wears, his helmet, one rain suit (not even a razor). I take one silk dress with slip and stockings and small hat. In through the gate by the dock, not a breath of wind on shore. There is more wind out at the ship. The Captain of the port comes out in a boat, to stand by. I tell C. it is as much wind as the morning we tried before. "But not as much as the night?"—"No. I had my sweater on that night."

The moon still gives a fair amount of light. C. starts to pump out the pontoons, the back hoisted up by the rowboat. Then he seals up the anchor box with putty to keep the water out. I hold the flashlight or sit on the front of the pontoons, to keep the weight forward. "There's about a five-mile wind right now," he says to the Captain, who holds up his hand. "You air folks must look at it differently."—"Why? What would you call it?"

—"Almost a dead calm!" However, a little breeze did come up before we started—enough for me to put on my sweater.

C. takes off the lantern and gives it to the Captain, also the bridle: "If we come back we'll want these—otherwise . . ." Then finally his cheery "We'll have another try," and we start off. I look in the back for obstructions, put the radio bag in the seat beside me, and fasten the belt. The lights of the town are on our left, the palms outlined plainly in the moonlight, the bright path of the moon on the water. We turn and slow up, throttle down, pause a second for breath. "All set?"—"All right." The roar, the spray. I watch it over the wing and then look at my watch. "Well, it won't be more than two minutes, and then we'll know. You can stand two minutes. Look at the watch, that's your job."

Now the spray has stopped. We are spanking along, up on the step, a good deal faster than before. Sparks from the exhaust. My God, we're going to get off. But how long it takes! We're off? No—spank, spank—but almost. Sputter, choke, sputter—the engine! My insides turn over. It's coming then— Death. He's going on just the same. We're off—no more spanks —sputter, sputter—he is turning? Are we going to land again? He is pumping the wobble pump. The watch: just 2:00 GMT. Yes, we're off! We're rising! But why start off with an engine like that?

But it smoothes out like a long sigh, like a person breathing easily, freely, almost like someone singing, ecstatically climbing. We turn over the lights of the city. The plane seems exultant now. We did it! We are up—we are off. We can toss you aside, you there, way below us—a few lights in the great dark silent world that is ours—for we are above it.

C. switches on the lights in the cabin to look at the compass. We turn over the land, quite low. I write by moonlight, "Left Bathurst 02:00 GMT," thinking, Well, I needn't be so excited —we've got the whole trip ahead of us.

I can almost work by moonlight. The dials of the receiver are lighted. I decide not to turn on the light until we get over water, as it may make it hard for C. to see. I start to send to CRKK [Porto Praia], trembly with excitement still. At 03:00 I hear a reply. Through terrible static, I can just hear our name, or it sounds like that, out of the welter of sounds—KHCAL. From then on through four hours of darkness I stay bent over in front of the dials, straining to hear (it is so terrible almost to hear, and then the crashes of static).

After four hours it gets a little better. I realize for the first time that we really got off and are on our way to South America. (The whole thing seemed unreal till then.) And I realize that I am terribly tired. I am sending with my eyes closed. It is a kind of rest to send. Sleepy already? And I have the whole day yet. But still that would be *day*. Night is the worst. It would be all right after it was day (just as I had said, "It will be all right after we get off!").

Then we begin to hit clouds, lose the moon for periods, for longer periods. We are flying under clouds and can still see a kind of horizon, where the water meets the clouds—a difference in darknesses, that is all. But it seems to get darker. Are those dark clouds or is it the sky? We lose the water. (I turn the light off quickly so he can see.) We fly blind. Now out again. There are holes. One can see the dark water and holes through which one can see the dark sky.

More blind flying. I am afraid. This is it—this is what people forget. This is what all the ocean fliers go through . . . absolutely blind . . . and dark. But day *is* coming. It ought to be day before long. I try to figure out: in an hour? Can we go through it safely for an hour? We climb up. "QRX—QRX [stand by], going through clouds—min [minute] pse [please]." We come out into stars, my hand steady again. Clouds ahead, again blind flying. It is colder. I put my mackinaw on and try to work. But I cannot receive in pitch blackness and don't dare turn on the light, making it harder for C., so I send "QRX" and "all OK."

Finally get a message from him (to send) "eight tenths over-cast scattered squalls viz [visibility] three miles. Daybreak." Daybreak! What a joy! I can't see any sign, and yet more and more clouds distinguish themselves from water and sea. The next blind flying is not so bad. We are still flying through clouds when sunrise comes. I take something to eat, start writing notes to C., feel relieved. I can now see the dark thunder-clouds that we graze under, bumping heavily. The weather looks better ahead, also I get a good report from PVJ (Rio) about Natal.

I am still sending on 57 when WCC barges in calling "KHCAL ans [answer] 57 or 36." I am quite surprised, but the whole night is unreal. I answer casually on 57, not bothering to change, and he comes right back! He is so loud, I can hardly believe it is Chatham, Mass. I take down his message. "Would you answer . . . few questions for the Boston *Herald*. . . ." Newspapers here too! It was so disillusioning. I reply that I am too busy to send a long message and must ask for weather from PVJ.

The sun is up and the day fairly good. I am so tired that it is hard to keep going. I am not at all quick getting the messages and turning the dials. I am tired of that bent-over position. My ears hurt from the clamp of the phones and my fingers are sore from pressing the key. The thought of the whole day ahead is terrific.

For a while I did not seem to have enough strength of will (it is your will that goes when you are tired; you know what you *should* do, but it doesn't seem worthwhile doing), then slowly "came to": "Now you *must* do something about this! First get the canteen. A drink of water and a little on the handkerchief to wipe off your face, then a sandwich." It did help very much. I revived and did not feel that way again until the sun was well up in the middle of the sky and it was hot.

But I begin to lose PVJ [Rio] and C. wants me to fly while

he takes sights. The flying is refreshing, sitting up straight and looking out at the clouds and sea. I try to read C.'s face as he takes the sights. He doesn't seem satisfied. For two hours I lose PVJ, and everyone. I try all their wave lengths and listen on all; can't hear anyone on anything. C. is taking the sextant to pieces; then something is wrong. The sights no good. Here we are about halfway and it is very important to get radio. Finally I get CRKK [Porto Praia]—a godsend. Very pleased, plan next schedule, but don't get him again; discouraged. Start C.Q.ing [general call], signing "Lindbergh"—my best fly. Immediately get a bite! "Lindbergh—Lindbergh—Lindbergh." A boat, *Caparcona*, gives me its weather and position, and says it will notify all stations. I also hear DDWE, the *Westfalen*, a German Lufthansa aircraft carrier. I feel relieved with two stations.

After that we started passing boats. The first one—a white speck to our right—was quite a thrill. Then we went right over it—*Aldebaran*. For two hours I had the *Westfalen*. They took our bearings and gave us a bearing relative to them. We thought we would try to fly over them. I now felt quite refreshed. It was cooler and bright and clear when we found them and dove down. They gave us a course to Fernando de Noronha.

I felt all was easy after that. Only the radio in my ears was a constant annoyance. It got to be something really hateful. I have never felt that way before, my ears physically tired so that noise pained them. Soon we hit Fernando de Noronha, a bare little island with a huge, round rocky volcano, like one of those long French rolls, sticking straight up in the air. C. went on the inside of it too—just to give me some bumps! Then I tried again to get PAA [Pan American Airways] and did, and, satisfied, kept them till we were five minutes off Natal.

C. pointed out South America, low and green in the slight haze ahead. We came on it quickly, following the coast until C. put his hand back and opened his fist—five minutes more. I tried to clean up a little, comb my hair, cold cream, etc. It looked flat and green and muggy compared to Africa. It was nice to see the Pan American barge in the river, flying its flag. We circled and landed down river.

Suddenly it was terribly hot and close and I was very sleepy. We were pulled up to the barge, where there were a few cameras and officials. No sun helmets, I noticed. We were in America and the hard flat straw hat began to appear. We stepped off onto the float. I felt rather shaky, a little drunk really, and I couldn't talk. But we went quickly in a launch to the dock, up the street and uphill to a lovely cool house looking down on the town, the palm trees, the river, and the white caps of the sea we had just crossed.

I let myself think about getting home and Christmas and seeing Jon.

December 8th
Leave Natal for Pará

Storms the last part of the trip. Thrilling to come into Pará. Big PAA hangar gleaming white, the red sign, the ramp, the people, the little boat, and officers waving.

The ladder on wheels rolls out to take us on shore. Walk in the boiling heat into the hangar. The big PAA Sikorsky. One of the office girls fanning me. The radiomen can't speak English—all Brazilian.

We are going to Mrs. Gordon Pickerell's—a nice big cool rambling house, verandas and high ceilings. I am terribly sleepy; to bed early.

Saturday, December 9th

C. goes to make calls; I go with him to call on the Governor. It is getting terribly hot again and I feel as if I could go right back to bed.

C. comes back to say that we will go to Manáos, a thousand miles up the Amazon, "on our way home"! I feel the way I did that time out west when we had a landing on the edge of a canyon[1] and walked down into the canyon that night (the blisters swelling on my feet) and up again the next morning and miles down the side—walking back again in the afternoon. By the end of that afternoon we were all dragging (two archaeologists and C. and I). We were so tired, yet I didn't realize it while walking on the path. I walked a regular fairly fast pace, rhythmically, never stopping. I felt as though I could go on automatically forever, but then suddenly we stumbled off the path and I could hardly stagger.

Well, as he says, I shouldn't fuss, really, as Mr. Trippe[2] wanted him to go to Montevideo, Rio, Buenos Aires . . . and he himself wanted to go to Bermuda "on the way home" but has now given that up.

I had a nice time at dinner, talking to Mr. Kuzmik,[3] very amusing and intelligent. I was so delighted to hear that language spoken again that I suddenly realized how long I'd been without it. What language? The language of a person who reads a good deal and observes keenly and can express himself. So when Mr. Kuzmik talked about the "trimotored mosquitos" at Paramaribo and his hating to kill a mosquito who had worked so hard all night to find that hole in the net, and James Truslow Adams' books on American history, and the plane being like a race horse, finally back in its own stable, I felt refreshed and stimulated, as though I'd had a cocktail.

Wonderful story of Mr. Kuzmik's about the radio operator's not believing the operator KHCAL was a woman [after] the 150-word message: "My God—she got it!"

Sunday, December 10th

Get up early. Drive down to the PAA hangar. The ship looks like new, the pontoons all painted and greased, the engine gone

[1] De Chelly Canyon, Arizona. See *Hour of Gold, Hour of Lead,* p. 101, and photograph between pp. 52–53.

[2] Juan Trippe, President of Pan American Airways.

[3] Pan American Airways manager at Pará.

over, the cowl mended, the floors varnished—very good mechanic. Finally off. It is overcast, low rain clouds. We follow the river. It gets lower and lower, going through rain. I can't hear anything because of static; sick with apprehension. "I didn't want to go—I didn't want to go, Charles" (to myself). We are skidding over the tops of tropical forest, flowering trees, a great deal of swamp, lakes, streams. We think we are following a river and we come to a round end—a lake! C. looks back at me and throws up his hands as if to say, "God knows where we are!"

Then we cut right over the forests, covered with wisps of fog, like thousands of feathers, flying quite low, "to get out of the Delta," C. writes; "will then pick up Amazon." I hope so! Just as it is getting very bad I see a break in the fog belt ahead—a river. I feel relieved. C. passes back a message: It is the Xingu river!

We have been three hours getting here. Three hours should have taken us halfway, and this is only a fourth. There are little huts on the side of banks, boats, clearings in the jungle. After we hit the Amazon it is better weather—low clouds, but clearer ahead. Communication pretty good. Lots of green swamp and a good deal of cleared land. The river is very muddy. I get Georgetown on the radio! Maybe the next flight won't be so terrible if I can hear Georgetown all the way.

Manáos, the place where two rivers meet; one can see sharply where blue meets brown, curls of blue in the muddy water. White stucco houses and towers, a few smokestacks, a big pier jammed with people. There are lots of boats out in the water, little racing shells, rowboats, motorboats, flags waving.

I suddenly have a loathing for this all over again for the millionth time and even for seeing a new place. That was why I didn't want to come. If we had gone on up the coast we wouldn't have struck a single new place (how blissful to come *back* to a place!) then the impressions wouldn't hurt as much. They wouldn't bang on one; they would just fit into their old places quietly with no commotion.

We land and the boats come round, as usual. C. in a fury waves them off. We circle [taxiing] for hours, with everyone waving us in, thinking we don't know where the buoy is. We don't dare go back into that mess of boats, have them crowd up, not be able to stop, and someone be hurt. Finally they push back and we come in. Then they crowd in again. One American, a nice intelligent-looking man, is shouting frantically to the boats to keep off. He is insistent about one which seems very much in the way. The man shouts back at him, "Captain of the Port." This is taken as a great joke by everyone. The Brazilians think it is a joke that the American is making such a fool of himself shouting at the Captain of the Port to keep away. And we Americans think it is terribly funny that the Captain of the Port should be as bad as any of the other boats crowding around. We catch his eye (the American's) and laugh, all three of us.

We get into an overcrowded boat, meet officials, are taken up the pier through a shouting crowd and up the streets to a nice house which is given to us while we are here. Everything is ready and clean and pretty, and two Brazilian servants bowing and smiling as though we were coming home. It is a delicious luxury to be left alone to wash and eat. We felt as though we were playing house!

A call on the Mayor, the Governor, the police head, etc., and wives. The inevitable sofa and "What are your impressions of Manáos?"

Back for supper at "our" house. We are tired; to bed soon. C. has a bad cold and a fever. If we can only get out of the interior, I feel we'll be all right. C. tells me to ask for a blanket. The couple speak only Portuguese. I get out my Spanish dictionary: "manta." She understands and gives me linen spreads. Also C. draws a picture of a clock pointed to 8:15 to show when we want to be called!

December 11th

I stay all day in the house, write up the diary. It is a dead morning, hardly a breath of air. Across the street someone is pounding exercises on a piano: "*tum* tum tee *tum*—tum tee *tum*." In the afternoon after a long hot rest C. and I go to the rubber factory. A stupid American blundered out excitedly, "You know, we were the first to hear of the kidnapping here!" C. and I were so stunned that we both smiled and murmured something. I: "Oh, really, were you?" and then we were silent with the shock. It suddenly turned everything quite black. That thing—it happened, it happened here too. I had thought in this faraway place it had not happened.

C. went out and started feeding the monkeys.

A bad night: hot and mosquitoes.

Manáos to Trinidad, December 12th

Called at 3:30. Said good-by to our house and the nice couple standing staunchly in the door till we were out of sight. Down to the water by the first streaks of day. The plane is still hanging with lanterns, like a Christmas tree, one on the tail and one on each wing. The PAA man has a huge lunch for us. Calm water, but we get up all right. The sky seems overcast until the day gets brighter, then the light seems to push the clouds back to the west. I keep thinking, "And not by eastern windows only, when daylight comes, comes in the light."[1] I have said the words over so many times trying to be hopeful about something that now with the first line, "Say not the struggle naught availeth," hope surges back like the blood pounding in my veins.

We followed the river in pretty good weather till it divides, then the Rio Branco, quite rough. I could see mountains, rising on the skyline out of the flat jungle and pampas. The jungle is only a narrow strip along the banks of the rivers. Round pools in the middle of the pampas, as though it had rained a lot.

[1] From a poem by Arthur Clough.

We leave the river and head toward the mountains. I begin writing indignant notes to C. I have good radio contact with Trinidad, and good weather. Many clouds but visibility unlimited. The clouds increase as we go over the mountains, which I don't like. We are flying through them, diving through big piled-up white castle-y clouds. No rivers below, or valleys. We can see jungled mountains in between the clouds. I write notes to C. "Are you sure you're flying high enough to miss the mountains? There might be some unmarked!" Silly notes—for I knew the answer, but I wanted to get one of C.'s encouraging mocking smiles. I notice a river below us. C. points at it and pats himself on the back—as though we could land on it! But it is flowing the wrong way, still flowing south into the Amazon and not to the northeast.

Finally we see a waterfall and a river [the Cuyuni] flowing northeast. We are across the divide. Then we start going down, diving through clouds and rainstorms (I wish I could get out of the habit of holding my breath through them) to flat country— the valley of the Orinoco. Storms over the Orinoco mouth, getting increasingly worse.

Across from the mainland to Trinidad we fly close to the water; violent rain—visibility practically nil. We are going frightfully fast—now wheeling—and black on all sides. I pull the antenna up in terror and wait for God knows what. Finally C. looks back and nods. All right now. He sees land—Trinidad.

I make a face at the bad weather behind, and he agrees, for once! "Bad stuff." Then we follow the coast of Trinidad, covered with low clouds and rain, to Port of Spain. It is raining slightly as we land. I see the PAA ramp and pier. Very relieved to get through that trip. To Government House, which I remember —a great big sprawling house, like a palace, in the middle of laid-out gardens. We have the same room, the big bed in the center draped in mosquito netting.

December 13th

Quiet day. I go down to the radio room of PAA. Early lunch and a rest.

December 14th

Left for San Juan [Puerto Rico]. Cloudy and heavy at Trinidad but beautiful weather all the way. Just as I remembered it—that harebell-blue water, a little hazy, soft, and then the green mountain islands set in it. That was the first long trip I took.[1] I thought it was the loveliest flying I had ever seen and the loveliest islands—and still do. C. took me over the Virgin Islands where he landed *The Spirit of St. Louis* on a golf course, up the side of a hill with a mountain topping it!

Hit San Juan quickly, dazzling white buildings, big boats flying the American flag, the old field and the hangar where we landed the first time. Land against a stiff wind. The old walls of a fortified embankment on the bay look familiar. Lots of Americans and newspapermen. Acting Governor Horton and his wife take us to *Fortaleza,* the old Spanish fort that is now the Embassy. American signs in the streets.

December 15th (the day C. said we would be home!)

San Juan to San Domingo—short flight. Arrived about noon, circled the small harbor many times—big swell—landed OK, spanking a good deal. As we came up to the dock, I could see Mr. and Mrs. Schoenfeld.[2] We talked Mexico all through lunch. I feel at home.

December 16th, Macorís to Miami

Up early. We fly over Santo Domingo, the river, the old *Memphis,* the ruined castle of Columbus's son. Over the airfield we landed

[1] Pan American Airways mail inauguration flight to Paramaribo. See *Hour of Gold, Hour of Lead,* pp. 79 ff.

[2] Arthur Schoenfeld, in the Embassy at Mexico City under D. W. M. See *Bring Me a Unicorn.*

on the first time, then across the mountains—north. C. keeps me busy with long messages about the latitude and longitude of Miami, the viscosity of Wolf's Head oil, etc. Finally we hit the water and follow coast, flying over Christophe's Castle, on top of a jungled mountain, big battlements, a thick wall, and a sheer drop into the jungle below. We cut across the water, over Tortuga Island, past Inagua Island; then we hit the Bahama bank. I recognize it by the color—glorious clear greens and blues, dazzling and jewellike. Get Miami here—messages which suggest pressure.

C. says fifteen minutes more. I see the coast and the white skyscrapers of Miami. We are over the bay and the white corner in the bay that is the new airport. Several planes come out to meet us. We land and are quickly moored by PAA mechanics. Then past the doctor and customs, on the PAA barge, and talk to the radiomen. Then a drive to the hotel. *NRA*[1] signs in all the shops, attractive clothes in the windows, girls walking around in pajamas, and a poster advertising beer. A wire from Mother. They are in New York and waiting for us! And a fat letter from Elisabeth.

Sunday, December 17th

A lazy morning. Go to bed with a frightful headache I've had all day—think it's a fever and malaria!

December 18th

Wake at daybreak as usual, my headache gone. Guess not malaria! Down to the PAA barge and leave. I feel sorry to see the last of PAA. I can't resist listening on the radio. I heard KHCAL once, and I answered, then went off watch and wrote in my diary. We see the flats of Charleston in about four and one half hours—a paltry trip! I feel as if we had just got started.

[1] National Recovery Administration, established under the New Deal (June, 1933) to control major industries of the United States.

Landed in the river by the Navy Yard; a swift current and the wind against it. Finally get anchored. Admiral Raby, who knew C. when he was twenty-one and came to Pensacola, takes us to his big verandaed house in the middle of the live oaks. We go up to bed, very sleepy, at 8:30.

[*Charleston to Flushing Bay, Long Island*], *December 19th*
Get off easily—no reporters. I am trying to prepare myself for the impact with New York. The kind of pressure I haven't had on this trip, except in Paris. In the first place, family, which is heavenly, but that is why it is an interruption, usually pulling, unconsciously, in the opposite direction. There will be hundreds of people wanting to see us. We will be in everyone's mind for invitations, also requests to be on committees, etc. There will be real friends whom I'll try to fit in and others I'll have to decide not to. There will be letters of congratulations and other-wise from people on the trip. Letters of thanks to write, pictures to send out, presents to the family and relatives for Christmas. And this trip—finishing up odds and ends, making a radio report to Leuteritz.[1]

There is the apartment to get and the book to start and pres-sure on all sides for all of these. I must try to keep well. C. will be restless and impatient with the complications and details piled up.

This life is hard in one way and I want to get home, but at least it is simplified: just one job to do, one objective. You only have to look to the day you're in. Your work is finished at the end of that, results are quick, and when the job is done well, C. is pleased. Except for physical fear, physical strain, and tired-ness, it is easy. Your life is in your control. I must try to control my life this winter—have courage to say *no,* to do the things I want to and to keep a peaceful home for C.

[1] Hugo Leuteritz, chief communications engineer for Pan American Air-ways.

Darling Elisabeth,

At this point things are still so frightfully mussy and mixed up that I feel I should not sit down and write a letter. But I imagine they will be mixed up for a long time so I might as well forget it. I have had three satisfactory days out at Falaise[1] with Jon all by myself. Then about three here with Jon and Betty and Elsie and Mrs. L. He is pretty spoiled. It seems impossible to get the idea across about letting the baby do things for himself. Everyone seems to think they know better than I how to treat him, so it is hard to start reforms immediately. He is irresistible when he is in a spirit of fun. Perhaps he will have that quality which C. and I lack, and you and Dwight have to perfection, of somehow making a party wherever you are. Of course Daddy had it superbly; Mother has it too, but hers is more acquired—not quite the same hilarious letting go.

I have taken a horrible dislike to Christmas this year, perhaps because away from all of you: the disgusting advertisements, enticing you to buy, the horrible stores' claws out to nab you. It seems very far from anything real.

The baby has many too many toys. At the G.s' Christmas tree there were presents for all: gay balls, decorations, lights, stuffed bears and horses for Jon, and a stocking. I had to laugh at Jon who got down under the tree, picked up two small red berries, and brought them back to me ecstatically!

A long lovely letter from Mother brings such good news from the doctors [about E. R. M. M.'s health]. I am going into town to look for apartments. Though I want to get our own home, I dread living in New York and we will certainly miss Englewood. It has been beautiful lately in *real* snow.

I think, though, if we have our own home we will enjoy and appreciate Englewood more. It *has* been a haven to us.

[1] Long Island home of Harry and Carol Guggenheim, close friends of the Lindberghs.

1934

TO E. L. L. L.   *Washington, D.C.* [*January 24th*]
We have rented an apartment—not very large—a penthouse. It
is supposed to be a good building with nice people in it. There
is a terrace for Jon with sun and another big one with a view for
C. and me. Jon will sleep next to us with a bath between—open at
night. We will probably have Skean and Wahgoosh[1] in with us,
and occasionally Thor! There is no guest room but an extra bed
in Jon's room, when you come—I hope soon—or else we can get
a studio couch for the living room.

C. likes it very much—our having our own place again, even
if it is temporary and in the city. I did not realize that there was
so much work—painting, papering, and linoleum. I suppose it
will be another week or two before we get in. I am trying to spend
a great deal of time with Jon and also to finish what I was writing
last winter about the Orient trip before I start on Greenland.

Jon is in splendid shape. I bought him a slide, mainly for the
apartment terrace. It arrived before I did one afternoon and Jon
and C. explored it together. C. showed him how to use it and
Jon had no fear at all. He went round and round shouting,
absolutely absorbed in it.

He is beginning to eat fairly well with a spoon now—he takes
three or four mouthfuls very nicely and then he gets tired of always shoveling that stuff *into his mouth!* Why not spread it
around the table and the floor!

"Admiral" Jerry Land[2] came here for supper and asked about
you.

Now waiting for C. to come back. The plane looks beautiful in
the museum[3] against a painting of a tropical sky, but it seems so

[1] The Lindbergh terriers.

[2] Rear Admiral Emory Scott Land, cousin of C. A. L.

[3] On returning from their Atlantic survey flight, the Lindberghs gave the
Tingmissartoq to the American Museum of Natural History in New

dreadful never to be able to fly in it again. We rented one to come down here.

[Englewood, February 11th]

Darling Elisabeth,

With one ear on the Philharmonic and the other for Jon upstairs I am going to try to scribble you. Charles is in town, as he was last Sunday, on the air mail. When I clear away all the minor worries from my mind I find that is there in the bottom. I suppose you have followed it. On the presumption of collusion, all the airmail contracts were canceled, some of the companies not hearing it definitely until it came out in the newspapers.[1] Last Sunday C. sent a wire to President Roosevelt appealing for only one point: *fair trial before conviction.* You have probably seen the flurry that followed. The White House move in return; one of the President's secretaries saying that (1) it was bad form to send a message to the President and make it public before giving him a chance to reply; (2) it was evidently for publicity purpose (which naturally it *was*—a public appeal for justice); (3) the President hadn't done it anyhow but [Postmaster General] Farley; (4) the White House is not opposed to commercial aviation—look at Mrs. Roosevelt, she uses commercial planes when she could use Army ones.

Then a storm of editorials and letters, etc., mostly (both in the *Times* [Democratic] and the *Tribune* [Republican]), supporting C.'s plea; some of them were *very* funny. Did you see "The Shrinking Violets of the White House" in the *Tribune?*

However, no move from the White House, except a wire to C. saying that if he knew what they knew he would not object. C. feels if they have such additional evidence they should show it.

York. It was later transferred to the Smithsonian Institution in Washington, D.C.

[1] On February 9, 1934, the cancellation of domestic airmail contracts was announced by presidential decree.

Tomorrow the Army starts flying the mails. It is hard on them, as they haven't the equipment or training for that kind of work. Three pilots have been killed already just *practicing* on cross-country routes. C. is afraid more will be, as the Army spirit is to push on in spite of everything and that is just what kills pilots in bad weather. And as they are spunky men who have been told they *can't* do it, naturally that is a challenge, and they are going at it in that courageous and fatal spirit.

The result on the commercial lines, C. feels, is a terrible setback. Some of the companies will go right out. Some will continue with passengers for a time but they cannot keep up the same service. Pilots and others will be put out of employment and our commercial aviation, which is now the best in the world (the English and the Dutch have just decided to copy us), will rapidly drop down.

C. felt it was unjust, whether or not the companies are innocent (he believes some are), to condemn all without trial. He felt he must protest for that principle anyway.

Of course, C., being a technical man, was never in on the subsidy conferences.

Also when the Black committee talks about the fourteen million that is squandered in subsidizing mail-carrying lines they do not mention that the lines are handing *back* about ten million of that in postage! TWA in fact has not only paid back all the Government gave them in subsidy but has made money for them!

We have had a good many telegrams. The ones pro are from rather intelligent people (this sounds too naive to put down!) and the ones against—about one to ten—fanatical: "You'd better be careful and learn that anyone who criticizes Franklin D. Roosevelt isn't going to last long." That kind of thing, which perhaps isn't so fanatical after all!

Jon has refused to eat the last two nights. He simply wants to play and throws spinach all over the room and is so happy about it! I have put him to bed hungry both nights but I wonder if I am on the right track. I cannot manage him at all this week. I keep thinking he is possessed of a devil, but perhaps it is because I am very tired from moving and my fingers are rough and catchy. Everything goes wrong when one's fingers are catchy.

I bought a pair of red shoes the day the airmail business blew up. They help a lot.

[*New York, February 15th*]

Darling Elisabeth,

I wonder now why I ever left that beautiful clean home in Englewood. I weakened at the last moment and brought Thor in, besides letting Elsie bring Wahgoosh and Jon bring Skean. The roof is *frightfully* dirty—and blowy. A cold wave when we moved in made it icy and Jon was blown right over and got things in his eye. The dogs use the roof all right but they are demoralized by it being so like indoors and consequently treat the screen and piano as pipes and fire escapes! They track the house up with soot. Jon cries whenever he is left alone (just like the dogs, he feels "it is different here" and the same rules don't apply)! Betty says the dogs *must* go. Elsie says Wahgoosh *must* stay! Charles thinks everything is perfect and that I am wonderful and that everything is going smoothly. Ha! Well, that is something.

But *quick*—your advice about nursery schools. I have fought them off, feeling a dread of sending Jon out into that strange world C. and I are in, where we are "different." And yet I realize that the sooner he goes out into it, and with the youngest possible children, the easier it will be for him. Also, I *hate* the attitude that I know will be applied to him: slightly "hush-hush," and looking for traits in him, and expecting him to be different—"over-cherished at home," therefore . . . And yet he does need it *terribly*. He is frightfully active and hasn't enough to do and doesn't know how to do it. I don't want him made self-conscious. Is there one like yours[1] with horse sense?

[1] The Little School started by Elisabeth Morrow and Constance Chilton in Englewood.

Mother darling,

Yesterday I had lunch with B. at her enchanting house. It is all *perfect*—clear and cool and clean, all in key, nothing out of place or wrong; white walls, white and yellow curtains, fruitwood light golden furniture, sofas covered in nice materials. There was nothing left to do. Everything was right, even to the pictures and glass and china. It seems a blissful state to me. I can't sit down in my living room but must jump up every moment and change everything. Even if I force myself to sit still, I keep on thinking, "I must get slipcovers, I must get curtains . . ."

I know it's supposed to be more fun to do it slowly. But I somehow feel it would be wonderful to get it done all at once and have it perfect to sit in and take for granted.

I came back and realized that I had five little tables in my living room, all different styles and all dinky!

Your letter about Elisabeth sounds wonderful and I'm so glad. I hope you just sit and sit in the garden.

I sent Elisabeth *another* nightgown! I was looking for a different bed jacket—something fresh and flowerlike but not bedroomy, like a first spring hat. But they were all pink and lacy and frowzy like old powder puffs. The only springlike thing was this nightgown. Do explain it to her.

TO E. L. L. L.   *New York [March 26th]*
Dear M.

I have started several letters to you. What happens to them? They never get finished. I have thought about you all through the airmail thing.

Oh, I was so proud of C. for his testimony—so perfectly clear and straight. Of course he believed it all firmly, knew he was right, knew his ground. Everyone has told me that he was a *wonderful* witness, that among the confusion down there C.'s testimony stands out as the only clear thing.

TO E. L. L. L.   [*New York, April 26th*]
Dear M.
I don't know why I have dropped into this life where I never
read, or never sit down to write letters. I think it is because I try
to write on the "book" about the Orient trip. When I sit at a
desk I am doing that.

I feel as if it had been a terribly long time since we'd seen you.
When are you coming on? When is school over? I wonder what
you would think of Jon—and Charles. It has been a hard winter
for C. But he seems happy in what he is doing and though he
hates the city he likes the independence of it and comes in for
lunch and sometimes the afternoon. I really see much more of
him and he sees more of Jon.

Jon seems so wonderful to me that I can hardly believe it. I am
more thankful every day to have him.

                                        Englewood, June 7, 1934

Darling Elisabeth,
I have just read your three articles.[1] They are so good that I will
have to write and say that tonight, even if there isn't time for
more.

How could you remember it all? They glow with reality. You
have re-created something, *selected,* which is the hardest thing on
earth, and *shaped,* joining and piecing bits that belonged in
character if not in time, following the same color thread through
many patterns.

Oh, Elisabeth, I am glad you have done it. I feel, too, that you
have saved something from the scrap basket—no, from the old
scrap sewing bag, bits of old material that mean so much.

I am working on an article for the *Geographic,* to cover the
whole trip in ten thousand words, in two weeks. We've already
had two or three that I diddled, writing six thousand words and
only getting to Cartwright. I have spent a week cutting that part

[1] E. R. M. M. was writing a "Family Album" of childhood reminiscence.

in half. The Orient book—first writing—is finished. I have not gone over it, because of the *Geographic* pressure.

I think we will go to Maine for July, *in our plane!* C. has bought, or will buy, a small closed two-seated plane—quite fast. He now has one borrowed from the same company. But in the end of July, or first of August, *our plane*[1] will be ready, and we will—so C. says (I don't dare trust to it, as anything may happen) —go out to Saint Louis (where it is being made), pick it up, and continue on west to the coast, arriving I imagine just when everyone else does. Never mind, you never can tell, we might move out to California for good, probably just as you leave. C. is ramping and raging about "New York life," which is pretty hectic and we neither of us like it, and saying we must live somewhere else.

Jon is such fun. He is in the "Go wup in a gahden an see the tuwips!" stage now talking. Miss Watson[2] says he is like you. I gather that is the height of compliments.

North Haven, July 11th

Darling Elisabeth,

I have not yet got down to reading or writing and am wallowing in a heyday of sunshine, sleeping, and eating, and hours doing nothing with Jon, which is bliss. There is still that divine feeling here that summer is eternal and that there is really nothing to do except ride around the island and wait for teatime. The place is full of old summers: old books—*The A.B.C. of Aviation,* dieting books, outgrown poetry. And also records—*Who* and *Allá el Rancho Grande,* and old sweaters, a blue one of yours with turquoise squares on it, and Mexican hats . . .

I keep thinking of you in the downstairs room telling me about Aubrey, and thinking it must have been last year. It is very strange

---

[1] Single-engine, high-wing monoplane, built by the Monocoupe Corp., Lambert Field, Saint Louis, Missouri.

[2] Of the Child Education Foundation School in New York City.

not to have you, and to have Jon. I have never been here for any time with a child. It is wonderful to have a child here. You begin to like the things they do, and it is so restful: flat stones on the beach and dark places under the pine trees, and finding mushrooms, and sticking pine cones up on end, and sitting on a branch of the apple tree ("Jon go way up high") and just rushing outside in the morning because it is heavenly.

TO E. L. L. L.   *North Haven, July 27th*
Dear M.

I have not been busy, just soaked in a wonderful life of swimming, sailing, picnics on the *Mouette,* and having Jon whenever I want! I wish you could see him. He looks so brown, legs and arms and back, and his face like a ripe apple, a few freckles on his nose, and his hair in tight curls. He goes in swimming every day in the pool. We have a "never-sink" jacket for him in which he really *swims.* He spends most of the day on the beach, collecting stones and snails and wading. Charles plays with him a great deal, carrying him high on his shoulders, Jon clutching at C.'s curly hair.

The day we arrived C. took Jon and me for a flight, putting cotton in his ears and trying Jon in the cockpit on the ground to see if the noise frightened him. He did not mind anything except the wind taking off (through the window) and Charles banked and turned quite steeply. Jon wanted to look out, but not seeing very much wanted to get down—until he discovered the window shade!

He was interested afterwards in watching the plane take passengers up. The other day I was carrying him so that his head turned up to the sky and I said, "Jon, look at the lovely sky." Jon said merely, "No planes in that sky."

Betty has gone and Shirley Grant is helping me with Jon. I wake every morning thrilled to think I can go down the hall and see him and have him all day. We have a little more time here as the ship is not yet ready in Saint Louis.

The last *Geographic* proofs are off—after a struggle over the picture titles.

North Haven [*July 29th*]

Darling Elisabeth,

There is a delay on the plane, per usual (I once waited three months in California for one to be finished). It is to be finished "about August 15." I think that means at least the twentieth, perhaps later. There is always more delay in Aviation than anything else. I feel a little uneasy about this. I hope it won't just peter out. However, I think we will get to California. The business trip ought to come off sometime this summer. The days are full of Jon and C. and feeling wonderfully well, and sunshine and the smell of hay and pines, and salt and wood fires.

Saint Louis, Thursday, August 23rd

Darling Elisabeth,

We are waiting here. I knew it would be this way. I have absolutely no faith in airplane manufacturers as to time. When we arrived on the 20th and went to the factory, they were surprised and slightly crestfallen. "You didn't get our telegram, then?" (Apparently to delay us.) I looked grimly at them. "Well, the ship's coming along fine, hope to fly it tomorrow." (Liars, I thought.) We went over to look at it, a nice-looking plane, about six people working on it at the same time. I observed: no instrument board hooked up yet, no cowl on the engine, no glass in the windows, no seats, no pants on the wheels. The most serious thing, I guess, being the cowl and the pants, as they are new types and probably won't be right and will have to be changed.

The thing that worried me the most was the experimental tone they took about it and their other planes—a good trait in getting the best plane, not a trait that leads to speed in getting work finished. "We're interested to see how this cowl works. If it adds speed, we intend to change our others; if it doesn't, we can always try . . ." etc. That kind of remark, and "If the pants aren't just right, we find it decreases the speed instead of increasing it." Charles was as bad as any of them: "We had to change the cowling on the Sirius several times."

I felt very discouraged and thought the only hope was to go out to the coast in our old ship and pick this one up on the way back—which Charles had suggested once, when you said you hoped to have us out there by the end of August. I asked C. about how long he thought it would be before it was ready. He said four days! (I know you are saying, "It took her six pages to say that one bit of news I wanted.") I don't really believe him but that means he doesn't expect it to be a long job. I guess a week, as they did *not* fly it the next day *or* the day after, and *hope* to fly it today. That will tell everything. I will write you as soon as I know. C. says it will be two days more after the day it flies. I say three or four. After we leave here we expect to stop one night in Kansas City and, if we have good weather, one night out west in, say, Kingman, Arizona, and then the next day Los Angeles.

I hope the plane will be all right. I always have a feeling that with a new plane—never flown—there is a chance of its falling to pieces in the air! Though this isn't really experimental.

I have been reading Hakluyt's voyages again, about Frobisher and the Northwest Passage. They are thrilling about Greenland and the coast of Labrador and Baffin Land. But mostly the spirit with which they are written: ". . . the rude Indian Canoa halleth (*what does that mean?*) those seas, the Portugals, the Saracenes, and Moores travaile continually up and downe that reach from Japan to China, from China to Malacca, from Malacca to the Moluccas: and shall an Englishman, better appointed than any of them all (that I say no more of our navie) feare to saile in that Ocean? What seas at all doe want piracie? What navigation is there voyde of perill?"

Also, I have been reading *War and Peace,* for the first time. You must have read it. I would rather sit and read it than do anything else—*even in the morning* (there's something wicked about reading a novel in the morning). I can't put it down. I can't remember when I felt that way about a book.

Only it is frightfully romantic, overwhelmingly romantic—16-, 17-, 18-year-old romanticism. I should have read it five years ago—or longer. Those Prince Andreys, those court balls, those duels—you know, they don't quite fit with me now, I'm a little too old!

This is a long, long letter. I wonder if it will get to you tomorrow? Has Aubrey read *Revolt of the Masses* by Ortega y Gasset?

Everybody on the route looks at me carefully, helps me carry bags, lift things, etc., and I'm already getting presents for that baby I'm not having![1]

Saint Louis, Tuesday, August 28th

Darling Elisabeth,

Two days more. Today and tomorrow, and I suspect even the day after. That makes it Friday before we start. I am discouraged and cross.

I have washed my hair, my handkerchiefs, underwear, taken bus rides downtown, bought toothbrushes and magazines, and even started on some knitting, teaching myself from *Vogue*'s first book of knitting, and in between times trying to rewrite parts of the book. And I am bored to extinction. Also I worry about our precious time slipping away. C. says we must be back before the end of the month (September) but we can make a fast trip back. We have given up our lovely apartment. C. hates New York and they raised the rent, which was too expensive anyway. That leaves us in Englewood again. Though I love being with Mother and having Jon at the Little School, I don't think we can live there a winter. It doesn't work. I am hoping C. will come to some decision out west.

C. says he expects to be about two weeks out west. I should

[1] Reference to newspaper reports that Anne Lindbergh was expecting another child.

think we could spend practically all that time with you, with the possible exception of a night or two.

Saint Louis, Saturday, September 1st

Darling Elisabeth,

I felt so awfully last night to have to call up. But you were so much more cheerful about it than I was.

The delay is a trip back to New York for something. I don't know just what it is but we got an urgent telegram and then a phone message from Harry Guggenheim.

C. says he can get it all done in three or four days but I am doubtful about his guesses. I can hardly believe we'll be through that soon. He said we'd be in Los Angeles in almost a week to the day—take it for what it's worth!

And he will *not* have to get back before October 1st (as he had to before), and I won't either (to shut up the apartment) so I think it will work out better.

DIARY   [*Englewood*], *Saturday, September 8, 1934*

Down to Elberon to Dr. Scobey to have my tooth filled—a horrible day, rainy, increasing to a bad storm. Got back in N. Y. at 8:00, sheets of water shifting across the streets. Find Con all dressed to go out with M. Monnet. The storm is getting worse. C. is already in Port Washington, as I told him I could not get back in time for supper. Con, M. Monnet, and I go out in a taxi to the Waldorf roof for supper. It is great fun and unexpected. Good music, lights, people dancing, and Con and I on a lark. M. Monnet orders the meal in French. Champagne. The storm outside. "Can it be the stars—tum tee."

We talk about China and Russia, M. Monnet on communism. About the trip (I probably talked too much), about danger, and fear, and youth, about happiness and its unconventionality. And I thought, "It is *this*. This is the kind of thing that makes happiness"—though I wouldn't dare say so. It would spoil it. It was perfect. If we had planned it, it would have stiffened. If there

198

PHOTO CHARLES AND ANNE LINDBERGH

Kayaks following the plane after landing at Copenhagen,
August 26, 1933

Flying over Stockholm

PHOTO CHARLES AND ANNE LINDBERGH

PHOTO CHARLES AND ANNE LINDBERGH

The farms of Skåne

The Lindberghs arriving at Moscow, September 25, 1933

Portrait of Elisabeth Morrow Morgan
by Elizabeth B. Van Dusen

PHOTO CHARLES AND ANNE LINDBERGH

*The Morgans' sitting room at Tynewydd, Glamorgan, Wales.
Portrait of Elisabeth over fireplace*

WIDE WORLD PHOTOS

*The Lindberghs
with Theodore Marriner,
American Chargé d'Affaires
at the United States
Embassy in Paris,
October 26-November 2, 1933*

PHOTO CHARLES AND ANNE LINDBERGH

*The Sirius tied to a bank of the Rio Minho, Portugal,
November 14, 1933*

*Spanish fort and Moorish camp at Villa Cisneros,
Rio de Oro, Africa, November 26-27, 1933*

PHOTO CHARLES AND ANNE LINDBERGH

PHOTO CHARLES AND ANNE LINDBERGH

French flying boat base at Porto Praia, Santiago,
Cape Verde Islands, November 27-30, 1933

Anne Lindbergh at Porto Praia

PHOTO CHARLES LINDBERGH

Charles Lindbergh doping down fabric edges on the wing,

PHOTO ANNE LINDBERGH

The Lindbergh plane circling S.S. Westfalen, South Atlantic, December 6, 1933

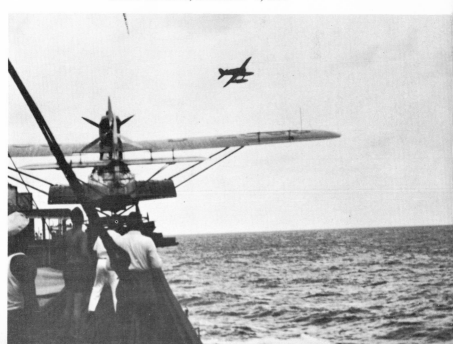

WIDE WORLD PHOTOS

The Lindberghs arrive at Miami, Florida, near the end of their five-and-a-half month flight around the North Atlantic, December 16, 1933

had been only two, there would have been constraint. The insulation of a third person makes for complete ease. There was ease because we three knew and trusted each other, and there was surprise because Con and I do not know M. Monnet too well, and there was delight between Con and me because we understand each other so perfectly and knew each was realizing what a rare evening it was. And M. Monnet was gay, perhaps because he was giving us pleasure, perhaps because he knew we liked to hear him talk, liked his mind and his wit. Perhaps it was the best for me, because I snatched it from the teeth of a bad day and I felt suddenly gay, like a young girl at a party. We didn't get up from the table until 10:30. I called C. and drove out to Falaise. The storm was over, but live wires and trees down, and detours. I got lost, but I sang all the way out.

Monday, September 10, 1934
Got up early. Mist, or ground haze. Took off more or less blind and climbed blind. Sky clear above and clouds slanting diagonally down the sky (we were on one wing). Then clearer, through scattered low clouds. Land at Cincinnati and on to Saint Louis. C. has cowl more securely fastened.

Tuesday, September 11, 1934
Leave Saint Louis for the west. Land at Kansas City. On to Wichita—very strong wind—we ground loop. The landing gear folds up underneath us and the wing is on the ground. Get plane in upright position and hauled in.

Night at Wichita. C. worried over ground loop.

[*Beverly Hills, Will Rogers' Ranch*[1]], *Wednesday, September 19th*
Mother darling,
We arrived day before yesterday but I haven't had a moment to write because I have been talking to Elisabeth every moment. I know that sounds as if I've worn her out, but I haven't. Her pulse

---

[1] Will Rogers, "cowboy philosopher," columnist, and friend of the Morrows, had lent his house to the Morgans for several weeks.

has not gone up and she's slept well. She looks very well to me (marvelously since the last time I saw her, in Wales). She hasn't much color because the last three or four days it has been very hot and she has been sitting in the shade. The most encouraging thing to me is not the way she looks but the way she does *not* get tired. Talking is tiring—at least to me—but she is not nervous or high-strung or keyed up or too excited. She remains on an even key.

Also they seem quite happy. I saw them just a year ago when they had made the forced decision to come here. But they are really contented about this. Elisabeth is busy planning about Mexico and Wales, happily and enthusiastically. There does not seem to be any looking back or any strain about the decision. She has the kind of peace you get when you take stock of things and know where you are.

When I look back at my winter in New York—hurrying along without ever taking stock—I realize how much more she has done in this year than I have. She knows what she wants to do with her life and just how she can do it. Also she seems young—so many ideas: "Someday I am going to write a book," "Someday I am going to organize . . ." and yet it is not the fretting desire of a young person. It is an older person who knows what power she has, and what limitations.

This is a heavenly place. Do you remember it? Way up on a hill overlooking the sea, and those islands, floating in mist and a curve of lights that is Hermosa and Redondo Beach. C. and Aubrey played golf last night and have talked politics incessantly, world politics. We eat outside in a patio with plants and vines around the walls, and a tree in the center. It reminds us both of Cuernavaca. The place is quiet and miles away from the road so no one can get in. No one knows we are here.

We had a somewhat tiring trip out. Our own ship ground-looped in Wichita. Not dangerous, not serious, but *very* humiliating. C. was worried about it. I told him I knew exactly how he felt—the way I feel when I have bought a beautiful new dress that I think is going to be practical, one of those dresses you wear and wear and wear. And you pack it once and you find it crushes badly—in fact the pleats come right out and look as though you slept in it all night—and then you realize sadly that it is one of those dresses that are going to spend their time on the road to the Cleaners and Pressers. "I'm afraid," said C., "we've got a ground-looper." However, we discovered the brake was put on backwards on one wheel, which would tend to make it ground-loop. So C.'s self-respect was restored.

Well, anyway, after a two-day wait in Wichita we start out in our old friend the Monocoupe we had in Maine. We go an hour and a half, over Oklahoma (just past Waynoka), and a most terrible noise—the way a steamer rattles when it stops or starts and the vibration is wrong, just a horrible shaking rattle. "What is it, Charles?" I said, thinking a wing had come off at least. "Just engine," he said, and we turned and floated down practically perpendicularly against a strong wind and landed *beautifully* on a slope in a plowed field. C. said, talking of the two landings, that it was humiliating in the middle of the Wichita airport to smash a landing gear and damage a wing, while here, with a forced landing and engine failure, landing in a furrowed field where he had every excuse for damaging the ship a little, he didn't do as much as blow a tire!

Well, out came the family that owned the field, the farmer who was plowing, his son, also plowing, the son's wife, and his wife. They were terribly nice and it was really great fun. Of course they had been through hard times. Bad year? Oh yes, it had been a bad year, but then it was the third bad year. Drought? Yes, of course there was drought, always was in farming and especially in Oklahoma. They didn't talk politics *at all*. It just wasn't a vital question to them. In fact, they didn't talk much. Never asked us a single impertinent or curious question and were indignant about the curious crowds that soon came up, plus the reporters. When one reporter asked the farmer what they gave us for lunch, he shut his mouth and clipped out dryly, "Oh, I guess the old woman fixed some dried bread and beans!" She had given us a marvelous meal, killed a chicken for us. She ran out in the yard to catch one. "Don't squawk *now*—you're Lindy's meal!"

We were there about three days waiting for the third Monocoupe. C. took the whole family up for a ride. Then on to Roswell, New Mexico. He landed in the desert, getting some cacti in his tires, which kept going flat on our way west.

There were piles of mail here—a wonderful orgy. We read Harold Nicolson's letter the first evening.[1] He does seem fair and wise in what he has decided to do. It is wonderful talking to Elisabeth about Daddy. It is almost the same person (my picture and hers) which is not true of C. or you or Con, or even Dwight. Though of course I suppose no two people ever see the same person. It is clarifying to talk to her. She has our whole life in her mind.

To E. L. L. L.   *Englewood, September 28th*
Dear M.

Things have been happening so fast, it is hard to keep up with them. This is just a note at midnight to tell you that this man you read about in the papers is beyond doubt one of the right people.[2] What may develop we don't know. The most positive proof is the identification of handwriting and then the finding of the money, and other bits of evidence mounting up: wood of the ladder coming from the yard where he worked, some nails in his garage, etc.

It really was the persistent dogged hard work of the New Jersey State Police (and of course the other police too) that succeeded in tracking down the man, though they have got very little credit, chiefly because they do not talk freely to the press.

We had a hectic month of traveling—out to Saint Louis for

[1] Harold Nicolson was planning to write a life of D. W. M. which was published by Harcourt, Brace and Company, 1935, as *Dwight Morrow*.

[2] Bruno Richard Hauptmann had been arrested by the police and charged with the kidnapping and murder of Charles A. Lindbergh, Jr.

our plane—a wait of two weeks. Started out again for the West. We were four days in California when we were called home on this case. We are in Englewood temporarily waiting for publicity to die down before deciding where or what to do. Will write soon again.

Thursday, October 11, 1934

Elsie's day off, and not a stroke of work done on my book. I never seem to manage it. (1) I should take my work downstairs immediately so as not to be disturbed by C.'s telephone calls. (2) I lost a good part of one of my two morning hours in a walk with C. and Thor and Skean in which Thor was given a lesson in obedience. (3) Down to the school for Jon, who got sand in his eyes just as I appeared, so I had to wait till he was serene again. (4) Stopped to see Uncle Jay to tell them to come up tomorrow. Jon sits in car.

Out to the kitchen to get Jon's lunch. Carry Jon upstairs. Jon eats bacon ravenously and refuses everything else. Goes right to sleep. I, exhausted, can't eat any lunch and just sit reading magazines until three. All afternoon spent making the pen attractive for Jon: swings, steps, doghouse.

[Englewood] Tuesday

Darling Elisabeth,

I can't do anything but typewrite. Very restful—and you feel as if you were being efficient! Also, I am enjoying myself writing you. I have been awful about it. I don't know why exactly except this general air of emergency and excitement that has prevailed ever since Harold Nicolson appeared on the scene.

I think Americans have a terrible inferiority complex about English people on the whole, don't you think so? What is it? I don't understand. I suppose it's because they are so much like us and yet different. They are older and more assured—real assurance, I mean. We can't help comparing ourselves and feeling country-bumpkin in the comparison, young and inexperienced.

It seems impossible ever to catch up. You know that impossibly inferior feeling that you have toward an older boy at school? We are still so young that we can be terribly hurt.

All this isn't quite to the point but there has been a lot of fuss—rather inconspicuous, hushed-up fuss. In the first place, all the furniture moved up into Dwight's room. Of course there was already furniture up there. Presumably that was why H. N. had liked those rooms, but still, there seemed to be a lot of moving. You know, Tom, George, Burke, Banks, up and down the attic stairs, Jo calling back and forth, men wheezing and panting, Mother running up every little while "to see what it looks like *now*," until I lost my head about it and very inconsiderately said that we would *have* to move over to the new wing (all Dwight's things having just been moved over there).

So we move: hundreds of trips up and down those stairs, carrying clothes, scrap baskets, books, etc., to say nothing of the things taken out of the attic so that we would not have to disturb H. N. when working. On one of the trips to the attic Mother showed me the bathroom. A large antique chair, maple, rush-bottomed, stood where the scales used to be. Mother: "Look, Anne, that nice chair Jo has put in his bathroom."—"But, Mother, why does he want a chair like that in his bathroom?"—"Oh, you don't know, Englishmen wrap themselves up in large towels and sit for hours." Marvelous picture! More of this English myth.

I don't think I like writing letters in type. It is slow, and then it seems so terribly public. I am shocked at what I put down, as though it had appeared in the newspapers. Also, it looks too permanent, too definite and irrefutable. It embarrasses me, too, like talking over the long-distance telephone.

I should be writing on the book—that is, correcting—but it is discouraging. I have been, up to last week, working hard. I wrote two new chapters—one, a preface, and one an introduction —"North to the Orient." Then I read them over, having glued them onto the old third chapter. It was shocking, the glue showed so. The book is already in two badly glued sections: One—

humorous, slightly slapstick, setting-out-to-be-a *Geographic* article (about five chapters). Two—more serious, more pointed-up, more or less "theme" chapters (about seventeen). Then my new beginning—still more serious and vague and pseudo-philosophical than the "theme" chapters. Everything new I write throws the rest out of kilter. It is just like a room decorated at different periods. You decide to put new chintz on those two worst chairs— "The rest aren't so bad." And then, that done, the others look shabby, and by the time you've recovered *them,* the first ones are faded again . . . ad infinitum. It all comes of being lazy. I grow faster than I write.

I have read over the three chapters[1] you sent me. I still think they are very good. Perhaps the "Green Sofa Sunday School" is the most complete, though "Reading" is excellent. The "Even Daddy listened" part is beautiful. I think perhaps you do not let yourself go enough. Perhaps the Puritan or the Welsh or the Swede in our family puts a restriction on us. I feel at times that you have tried so hard to be objective that you have held your-self in.

The "Even Daddy listened" piece is like an opening of the gates, and I think you should do it more often. "Reading" is very well done and quite complete. It will be the most useful one for Harold Nicolson to read. You *will* let him read it, won't you? He is terribly appreciative of those small details that make such an important part in a picture. I think "Reading" is a big detail, really, and extremely important for him to see.

I think "Family Prayers" should be added to the "Sunday School." Do you remember Con and Dwight fighting over who was to be next to Daddy? And Con's suppressed indignation at being prayed for, learning to read? She would almost explode be-fore the prayer was over. Also the embarrassed silence when we got up that Daddy always broke by kissing us heartily or by con-tinuing to tease Con.

[1] See note on p. 192.

Well, I know this is coming just at the wrong time. You are moving, and restless, and no time to write.

I am so happy about Mexico.[1] There is just a chance we might get down, perhaps not for Christmas but later. C. wants to go, if there are no parties. I haven't the excuse of having a baby. I must stop thinking about that and try to work hard on the book while I feel well.

Darling, those days at the ranch were wonderful—that talking. It sets me completely right. I feel that if I can talk like that with you from time to time in my life, that is all that is necessary. It's worth living for. Life becomes suddenly visible, clear and sharp and bright. Aren't those the most wonderful moments? It is always the same experience, like looking through the ruffled surface of the water through a glass-bottomed bucket to a clear, still, perfect world below. Several things do it—sometimes music, sometimes pictures (Hopper's *Twin Lights*), Virginia Woolf. Sometimes flying does it, on a still morning, and, very rarely— talking to people.

The trouble with growing older seems to be that life becomes more and more precious—unbearably so—if you really start thinking about it you can't go to sleep. Charles is a great help at times like this. He says, "Oh, rats! If you don't go to sleep I'll spank you." Oh, I am glad I didn't marry that "blind poet"!

However, C. does not approve of long letters. I should be writing something worthwhile—the book. I suppose he is right, really, as I am the most dissatisfied if I feel I haven't accomplished anything. But what is difficult to explain is that writing letters is *thinking,* just as talking to you is thinking. Every once in a while, one must think!

I have rambled on and have not told you how exciting the box of trousseau things was.[2] Con and I are sharing it. C. says, in

[1] E. R. M. M.'s health had improved, and the doctors felt she could visit her mother in Mexico during the winter.

[2] E. R. M. M. had sent her sisters a box of her clothes that she would not be wearing during her year of convalescence.

that very male way, not annoyed at all, but rather un-understand-ing: "Can't you buy your own clothes? If you *need* so-and-so, why don't you *get* it?" Why should I be so pleased at having an unexpected box of pretty things? He can't understand it. If I *need* things, I should get them. There is no conception in his mind of the pleasure in getting pretty things that I *don't* need.

Does Aubrey feel that way about the things I send you or does he just take it as part of feminine illogical minds? Anyway, I am going to get you two tunics this afternoon. If the men object, they can just cross off their grievances together—cancel them.

I read the last chapter of the G. Lowes Dickinson.[1] It is too beautiful. I shall read the whole thing. If he had never written the rest, that ending would be enough. It is justification of a life, and in a way of all lives whose values cannot be weighed in accomplishments. It is wonderful, as it gives one a new measuring stick. I think that's what you do for me—give me measuring sticks, other values to weigh things with than the obvious iron-weight-subway-stations ones I have been using.

I must finish *Lord Carnock*[2] before I begin another book, though. He [H. N.] seems to be worried that we will not like the book [on D. W. M.]. I think you will be a great help. You are more natural than any of us, and independent, and it will help him to talk to you. Also Aubrey. I *know* they are going to get along. We are all miles behind when he talks about the new Disarmament Conferences, the difficulties. It was terribly interesting, even for me, who never reads the newspapers. He said a wonderful thing about the conferences, about the futility of superficial friendships, hands across the sea, or the table, or whatever it is. He said he did not believe in stressing superficial similarities between nations but rather in stressing their *differences*.

[1] *Goldsworthy Lowes Dickinson,* by E. M. Forster.

[2] Harold Nicolson's biography of his father, published in the United States as *Portrait of a Diplomatist.*

The differences must be clearly defined before any understanding is possible. The real nationalists are the people to deal with; the others are just wishy-washy. Of course he said it much better. And I kept thinking all the time how true it was of marriage.

He was wonderful about pacifism too—real pacifism and the fake namby-pamby kind that is just sentimentalism. He said he was a terrific pacifist. It was quite thrilling. All women, of course, feel that way, only they do not see through to the logical conclusion of the argument.

Do you remember Prince Andrey (ah!) before the big battle, talking to Pierre about war and the sentimentalists' trying to make humane rules about war? He (Prince A.) said it was like the sensitive woman who faints at the sight of the slaughterhouse but enjoys roast beef without a qualm.

Well, anyway, it was all so exciting that I shall read *Peacemaking*[1] next.

I forgot to end up my story about the fuss of H. N.'s arrival. Of course Mother was out, so I had to be there to receive. Panic of shyness, but he is a quiet man, a little hard to tell whether he is shy or bored—perhaps a little of both. However, he has turned out to be kind and understanding. He is considerate of all Mother's plans and sorts out the relatives with insight and understanding, is sweet to Jon, asks Jo about her sinus, doesn't mind when C. tells risqué stories of the [Chicago World's] Fair, asks Elsie about Wahgoosh and altogether gets on with every member of the household with the utmost tact. I think he is getting a little tired of the intensity of the household. C. is the only person who is not intense.

Jon is a joy. He is greatly improved lately, is eating vegetables again and is generally more independent and reasonable. He is so terribly precious. Do you think I should not call him "Darling" and try to be restrained? Of course, both losing a child and not

[1] Harold Nicolson's book on the Paris Peace Conference, 1919.

having another tend to make me overloving. But it sometimes seems to me that restrained love only comes out in a kind of intensity of annoyance or irritation or nervousness that is worse than the perfectly natural expression itself. What do you think?

The new wing is working out well, and Jon has a good regular routine and seems much calmer. I do not think now we will move this winter, but perhaps next winter get a place in the country near the Guggenheims.

C. is again at the [Rockefeller] Institute and also enjoys having H. N. in the house—not only because he is another man in this harem but because he likes talking with him.

Mother is doing *much* too much but is very happy. Mexico will be a rest, I think. She is trembly with terrified happiness about it.

DIARY   *Saturday, October 13, 1934*

At lunch Mr. Nicolson asks Mother again for the *Geographic*,[1] so C. says I must give him one, and we do. I do not go in for tea, thinking perhaps he would feel he must say something about it. But C. comes for me with a cat-smile on his face: "Don't you want tea? Mr. Nicolson is there," and pulling me up. We go in. Mr. Nicolson starts out: "That was an excellent article." I thank him and try to turn it off (very pleased). "I didn't intend to read it," he said, "but I got started . . . No, but it was well written. . . . No, seriously, I mean it, you really ought to do more of that. I'm not just saying it to be polite—I really mean it." He looked quite earnest, then, smiling at C., "You should take another trip so that she can write another story, for the writing instinct, once it is started, is much stronger than the flying one!"

Then he talks of the photos and various parts of the story he liked. The take-off at Bathurst the best, the radio over the icecap, a light at the end of the hall. I cannot remember it all. He said I seemed to have held myself in, tried to be technical.

[1] *National Geographic Magazine* article by A. M. L., "Flying Around the North Atlantic," September, 1934.

I felt so excited, elated—at the praise and even more at the understanding—that I felt absolutely released, as though a great deal dammed up in me for years I could let out, though luckily for Mr. Nicolson I didn't. (C. very sweet, smiling at me with pride.) I did burst out: "Of course I had tried to hold myself down. I had written twice that much and cut and cut and cut. Almost all the parts that were really me I had cut." He said, yes, it sounded clipped. And when C. went out, he said again "Seriously, you should go on."

I was so extremely happy that it is hard to analyze. I suppose it is vanity, but it wasn't what he said. Far more than that, it was being treated *seriously*—a kind of recognition, or respect. A spiritual counterpart to the physical recognition when a man tells you, for the first time, that he wants to marry you. That sudden realization, It is I he is talking about, *I*. My eyes—*I*—here in my pink dress—I exist, then—I *am!*

It was a sudden recognition of something inside of me that I have believed in, from time to time, that has sometimes been coaxed out, often crushed, raised its head in rebellion, been forgotten about, hurt, smothered with false attention, that I have tried to ignore for fear of being hurt. "I can't write. Someone should kill this thing in me. Someone should tell me bluntly I can't write, send me back to children."

But Mr. Nicolson said—implied—that it existed, that I should go on. And the Thing rose up inside of me and possessed me. For twenty-four hours I felt young and powerful. I felt life was not long enough for all I wanted to do, and I lay awake all night, my mind racing and my heart pounding.

Sunday [*October 14th*]

Not having slept, I felt rather tired but still, in spite of the night, a giant! I began to be worried about it and tried to take myself down. After all, he didn't say very much. Perhaps he was just surprised—after all, you express yourself so badly and seem so young and halting when you talk—he was just surprised that you could express yourself in writing. Also, he does feel sorry for you and is trying to help you. Nothing justifies your being as elated as this. Even if you *did* learn to write and write well, what of it?

Tuesday [October] 16th

A simply crowded-with-people day. Mrs. Curtiss[1] and Joe Auslander[2] for lunch. Mrs. C. was very charming and witty. We talked about Con. Con had gallantry and common sense. Mrs. C. said the outstanding quality of our family was gallantry, but Con is wise and gallantry is always a little mad, a little off-balance.

Wednesday, October 17th

Into town. On the way home I see a dog crouched in the middle of the road, right where the cars rush by. I leave the car and run back. First tell him to get up and then see he has been hit and is absolutely stunned. Blood on the road, out of his mouth and nose and in his eyes. I lift him by the scruff of his neck and carry him off the road and put him in the soft grass and leaves, under a light. Then I go back to get C. The dog just lifts his head and looks at me as I go. C. is not home; when he comes we go back. I find the mark the dog made in grass, blood on the road opposite, the dog is gone. Probably he came to and walked away. C. takes me out for a ride in evening. Feel low for no reason—just tired.

Thursday, October 18th

Spent the day taking care of Jon—a terrible day! After school we go for a walk. He throws things in the pool and wants to get them out. I tell him we can't and suggest going to see the pumpkins. We take a long time—too long. He gets a little pumpkin and immediately throws it in the brook. "No, we can't get it out

[1] A. M. L.'s teacher of creative writing at Smith College, friend and author.

[2] Joseph Auslander, poet, friend of E. C. M.

again, Jon—you threw it away." It does not seem to bother him.
"We get some more tomorrow," he says gaily!

I get some liver for his lunch ("wubber" he calls it)—"Don't
want wubber." He only takes what I feed him. He does not sleep
in his nap but just chirrups the whole time.

At supper I leave him with his cereal and come back to find
he has stirred it all to a brown pulp and has got his hands in
it and is squishing them with pleasure. I am angry but simply
take it away. He only says, "We hab some mowah tomowow!"
(The adults' favorite phrase!) He gets himself into a froth of
soapsuds washing but that seems an innocent enough pleasure.

At the time when we generally read, he says, "No mowah
Tom Kitten," and so I put him at his white table with crayons
and I lie down exhausted on the bed. He goes to bed quite
nicely, saying, "Who goes to sleep?"—a lovely game. I: "Peter
Rabbit goes to sleep . . . and a, and a, Mrs. Tiggywinkle goes
to sleep . . . and a, and a, Ola goes to sleep . . . and a . . ."
At each "and a" Jon's face is aquiver with twinkling excitement.
He lies down under the covers and looks up at me. I end with
"And Mother goes to sleep, and Father goes to sleep, and Elsie
goes to sleep . . . and *Jon* goes to sleep."

I take a hot bath and get a little rested before C. comes.
I lecture to myself: it is absurd and wrong and weak and
inefficient to get so tired. Try to make rules for taking care of
Jon: (1) Never plan to do *anything* else when you are taking
care of him; it is impossible, physically and mentally. (2) Lie
down on the bed and rest as often as you possibly can for
snatches. You don't realize how physically tiring it is, trotting
up and down the stairs, carrying Jon around, carrying his toys
back and forth, scrubbing his table and chair and mat after
each meal, leaning over the bathtub, standing to prepare his
meal, making his bed, lifting him, etc.

Oh, the feeling of *impotence* one has with a child!

Friday [*October 19*]

I feel like those ads for yeast: "Do you feel tired in the morning, nervous, lack of appetite, sleep badly? Try our . . ." C. says it is imagination and I should try Christian Science. I suppose I am poisonous to live with.

[*Englewood*], *Tuesday, November 6, 1934*

Cocktail party in the afternoon. Agony on the stairs. I can't go in. I *can't* go in. Then I slip in quickly, like going timidly down the ladder into a pool, not diving courageously into the cold water. A rush of smiles—people—trays—catching someone's eye over a shoulder—never really talking to anyone because you are always watching the next person over their shoulder. And yet, the heady excitement of it, the make-the-most-out-of-this-moment feeling, which can sometimes lead to a moment of great intimacy. I wonder why—even in the midst of that superficial open chatter, as though the contrasting unreal background were a setting, the perfect setting for the real gem of a sincere moment. And it is partly that emergency "gather ye rosebuds" pressure that makes you seize the moment. I may never see you again, tomorrow may never come, quick, tell me . . .

Why is it so easy to talk to people you don't know at a party? Partly that *you* are new and different: beautiful clothes, wine, glitter, like wearing a mask—a Cinderella feeling. It is the "just for tonight" feeling really, the "tomorrow will never come" feeling. I think Americans have this particularly strong because, like the men in the early days of Aviation, they are living in a world that is always an emergency world, a world of haste, change, and pressure. You never *do* see people again. Tomorrow never does come—for that situation. Life is made up of quick intimacies which do not last.

Sunday, November 11, 1934

Elisabeth . . . appendicitis. All the time underneath: Elisabeth.
Good news at night.

Monday, November 12, 1934

Telephones ring all day. Dogs bark all day. Jon cries most of
day. Very cold and the wind howls. Jon says, "The twees are
cold!" I'm sure they are, poor trees. I work on the preface,
think I have a good idea—reread—very poor.

Feel terribly a failure today. I have been thinking much too
much about myself. It is a constant fight, or should be—an
old puritan fight against egotism, self-consciousness, pride. How
lovely natural people are, people who don't have to hold themselves in all the time but are tempered within themselves.

Tuesday, November 13, 1934

First snowstorm

The dinner party—rather stiff and metallic. Cloth-of-gold
dresses moving slowly, swimming about with great dignity
and no haste. The Mexican music should have been rowdier,
more passionate—still, it was reminiscent of Daddy. C. shakes
hands with the musicians and then goes out and drinks a cup
of champagne with them. They were thrilled—C. always does
the right thing—gives happiness extravagantly just where it is
needed. He loved the music too—I was very happy.

Wednesday, November 14, 1934

Elsie's day out. The big room is being cleaned up, so I cannot work there. They are getting it ready for something: gilt
chairs, furniture moved, etc. *What?* A hundred college women
from the Northern Valley. I am irritated, then think, No, it
justifies this big house (not that Mother needs any justification
—she has done enough to be past that. If it makes her happy
it is justified), but looking at it from a point of view of social-

ism, if you have a house as big as a hotel you should *use* it like a hotel. Only I don't like living in a hotel!

It is cold working upstairs, and Novembery. Go for Jon. It is terribly cold out. I plan to get in early for lunch. Then I forget the milk; go back for it. Jon has smashed a Mexican fruit. I go for milk; stumble over dogs and drop it on tile floor. Jon is stunned with the excitement. The dogs delighted, lap it all up, while I futilely try to pick up the pieces and keep the dogs out. Cooking the dinner, the egg goes to pieces; I have to cook another. Jon will not sleep. Washing dishes. The college women begin to drive up. Thor thunders. If I can get out by 3:30 . . . We clatter downstairs while the women are opening the meeting, I carrying the slide and a paper to keep Thor quiet. Once outside all cares go; we sit in the leaves.

I don't dare go back in our wing for fear of noise. People swarming downstairs. Finally I carry Jon upstairs—very late. Jon puts a wooden scotty in his cereal and the black comes off! I fix new cereal and finally get him to bed.

I take a bath and get ready and come down to supper. C. is not there. The evening paper headlines: a little girl kidnapped, body found, skull crushed, shallow grave. I don't mind the columns about us and the case, it is dead sorrow, but that was living anguish. I felt I could not bear it. I went up to Mother's room but could not get over crying—couldn't stop. Cold water. I threw away the paper that was on Mother's desk. How awful to come home at night to that! Powdered my face, but still no control. Once you start, it is not connected with the original cause, you just cry. Everything starts you crying. Everything. I sat supper out, trying to read *Anna Karenina*. Banks: "Is your cold worse?" (But I think he was just making an excuse for me.) "I will fix you a hot toddy for tonight." I go out to walk and look at the stars. Thor follows me round and round the garden. It is much better. C. comes home. He does not notice, thank goodness, only my eyes are swollen.

Thursday, November 15, 1934

A lovely clear day, when the sun stays on you for a while and warms you. I knew it would be a good day, that I could take things in my stride today, and nice things would happen, just as yesterday was the other way around. I *would* drop the bottle of milk and spoil the egg and miss an appointment and see that dreadful thing in the paper. So today the writing was good and Jon enchanting: "Jon catch the leaves!" (falling down) and then, running under them, "The leaves catch Jon!" and of Thor's misty breath, "Thor makes smoke." Then lunch went fairly well and I was not shy. Harold Nicolson said she [V. Sackville-West] liked the article. Something about "literary merit" and about being too shy and not letting go. I wanted to argue it and was a little ridiculous taking myself seriously.

I can't help taking writing seriously. I suppose real writers don't because writing is life, and must be laughed at. I must take it out of the sacredness I have put around it, or if I can't do that never let people know I think it sacred. I care about it more than anything else, but never never never let anyone know it, never let anyone fool you into talking. (It is so easy to be tempted by praise or understanding.) How terribly you feel when you've given your secret self away. Nothing is worth it.

TO E. R. M. M.　　　　　*Englewood, November 19th*
Darling,
You have had it a week now,[1] or *not* had it. I know it is no laughing matter, and certainly not yet when you are in the middle of all those nasty, uncomfortable, ugly, disagreeable things they do to you—little things that are always an accompaniment to the large discomfort of a big thing. But you don't want to hear about them.

Everyone has called up about you. You should have seen the party—all the old guard—asking about you. Mr. Leffing-

---

[1] Elisabeth Morgan had been operated on for appendicitis.

well's[1] shout of admiration when I told him your message to Mother [after the operation]: "I fooled them again!"

Did I tell you Harold Nicolson felt he was one of the best people he talked to? It is strange and almost shocking the way H. N. sorts out the sheep and the goats: "So-and-So—I don't think he was a good influence on your father. . . . So-and-So, rather an old bore." It is not the criticism but the *impersonal* attitude. Then it is nice to have him appreciate Mr. Rublee,[2] Mr. Leffingwell, M. Monnet, Judge Hand, "Steve" Birch and Mr. Prosser.[3] But the impersonal attitude toward those people who were all on a shelf together is the shock, though rather pleasant—a breath of fresh air.

For this house has had a return to the rather hothouse-living-in-the-past atmosphere of just after Daddy's death. All the old friends talking about Daddy. "He used to do this, that, etc." It has been a little overwhelming, though H. N.'s impersonal and keen analysis rather blows through it—a great relief. Of course Mother, as usual, has been swinging three or four things at once: Community Chest, William Allan Neilson [Chair of Research], outside speeches, so she has not been too wrapped up in the past.

Your Christmas present came but Mother grabbed it. It makes me sick, your thinking of Christmas presents in all that confusion of leaving.[4] Have you read *Not I, But the Wind*?[5] Lovely in the beginning but it doesn't hold. It was rather a Katherine Mansfield life, moving and moving. I'll send it to

---

[1] Russell C. Leffingwell, Assistant Secretary of the Treasury 1917–20; later partner in J. P. Morgan & Co.

[2] George Rublee, Washington lawyer, legal advisor to the United States Embassy in Mexico, 1928–30.

[3] Learned Hand, judge and author; Stephen Birch, president, later chairman, of the Kennecott Copper Company; Seward Prosser, president of Bankers Trust Company, 1914–23.

[4] The Morgans were about to leave for Mexico when the appendicitis attack occurred.

[5] Frieda Lawrence's biography of D. H. Lawrence.

you if you'd be interested. She (Frieda) says a nice thing about "sex": people talk about "sex" as though it hopped about by itself, like a frog!

I think about you a great deal. Do you want some colored beads to play with on the pillow? [As we did as children having measles together.]

DIARY   *Friday, November 23, 1934*
Shopping all day. Come back to find bad news: Elisabeth has bronchitis—bronchial pneumonia? A rush of finding out about planes, trains, etc. Packing, errands for Mother. Will the planes go? We take Mother to Newark. A terrible night, drizzle, cold. Crackers in the car. Mother writing down errands for me. The plane is going. She steps alone into the plane. I long to go with her, just for that night. We watch the plane go off into the drizzle—just a light. I feel terrified and yet feel that fate *couldn't* strike at her—such a courageous figure. She *will* get there all right.

We drive back in profound gloom. Elisabeth has been struck, I feel, and this is the end. It is already over. It has happened. I have been waiting for it for years and it has happened. I hope she does not suffer or fear.

We wait up till we hear Mother has left Cleveland. C. is a rock of strength to Mother and me. I do not sleep.

Englewood, Friday, November 30th
Mother darling,
I don't dare write about you and things out there except to say your letters are wonderful. They are not medical but they give those things that sound terrifying in a report. You describe them as I would see them and it makes it less terrible—the oxygen tent, etc.

Englewood, Sunday night, December 2nd

Mother darling,

I can tell so much more from your voice than from the reports, and it affects me in proportion. It is a strange false atmosphere to be living in here, for I cannot help, when I get good word, being elated. It doesn't do any good to be told, "You must not get your hopes up," because with anyone you care so about, when you let hope in, it simply fills the whole of you. You can't half-hope. And when the word is bad, you are afraid, and you fear the worst. It matters too desperately to have half feelings about.

Of course people want to save you from going up and down with the fluctuations, but you can't help it. You are not down today *because* you hoped too much yesterday. No, it's because any good news *may* mean so much, and any bad news *may* mean so much. I do not mind going up and down, I only mind the false atmosphere, for when we're *up* I go out and continue with things and when we're *down* I sit and do strange things feverishly. But I mind terribly if I have been fooled by some false impression and I have been gay when you were desperate —I mind that very much.

I don't know if all this isn't perhaps just what you don't want to read. I thought perhaps the guarded atmosphere of doctors might be getting on your nerves. It would for me. They seem to think when you're happy that you don't realize the seriousness of the situation. They don't realize that you are at such a pitch, so delicately balanced, that the slightest dram of hope or discouragement will tip the whole weight of your emotions one way or the other.

I wish something could be done for you. Do you want someone out there to blow up to or can't you afford to now? I could come. I meant to say that on the telephone but then thought you'd understand. The only objections to my coming (it could be kept from Elisabeth) are that I think it would draw publicity and pressure to an atmosphere already under tension. Perhaps it would not if I went straight to the house and never approached the hospital. Well, you know about that. I'll do what you want. I could take the TWA plane early in the morning and get in late at night.

Amey and Chester[1] were here tonight. I'm glad they were here, as your call came in the middle of the evening. Would you like Amey out there? They are so understanding.

Friday Harold Nicolson left. The last day he saw Grandma and was enchanted by her, "the most beautiful, most fragile, most lovely old lady." She told him (reported to me by her) that it was going to be very difficult to write the life because Daddy did well at everything he touched and it was going to be difficult to write a book without criticism (hitting the essential point, as she always does!).

He got something from the movies, had a talk with C. about Aviation and Daddy. I read him my things about the old house. Con and Dwight talked to him. I told him about your getting the letter when you needed it and he was pleased. I tried to give all messages. Of course he thinks you are wonderful. And he signed the guest book! You thought I'd forget that, didn't you?

I will write again. I am thinking of you all the time. "Suspense is hostiler than Death"—do you remember? [Emily Dickinson]

DIARY   *December 3-5, 1934*

A long long week, so strange and unreal and artificial now, and suddenly dropped into the past. A week of false hopes and false dreams; all kinds of plans and schemes that now seem irrelevant—because Elisabeth died. Roads that set out and never got anywhere, half-finished sentences, half-drawn sketches of the future—and the whole thing insubstantial pasteboard to be

---

[1] Amey Aldrich, college friend of E. C. M., and her brother Chester, architect in the firm Delano & Aldrich.

knocked down in one breath. The future which had started to grow, like a young crop (we had to plant it with just as much faith as we always have), burnt down to the ground.

It is hard to remember. It seems so long ago.

And not that we were fooling ourselves. I don't think I fooled myself from the beginning. Charles trying carefully to keep the scales balanced in my mind: "Don't be too encouraged. . . . Don't be too discouraged." What they don't understand is that you have so much to balance on the scales. It isn't that you count too much on that straw, but that you are looking beyond. Your mind leaps to the final mark. It is the door opening down a long corridor. You look all the way down to the final defeat or success. It seems too silly anyway—to try and save yourself by such straws as "I always thought . . . I never believed . . . I never let myself hope"—like saving out a few coins when you are betting a whole fortune. They won't help you if you do lose. Small change.

We went up and down. Better—and I could sing my heart out. Worse—and that old, old weight back on the same place on one's chest. Those long-distance telephone calls, steeling one's voice to make it ordinary, harsh, matter-of-fact: "Yes, Aubrey, yes." Those doctors' reports: "Oxygen tent . . . pulse . . . respiration . . . condition virtually the same." That awful day: "Profoundly prostrated." Mother's voice telling me so much, sometimes buoyant, sometimes harsh and breathless with emotion. Telephoning the news to other people, trying not to give too much hope. C. translating messages, C. telephoning Dr. Cohn.

And then that strange heady excitement of being the person in the house that people came to. How about this . . . that? At least, there was a superficial taking over of Mother's place that seemed to be a great help to me. Here is something I can do, how wonderful this is—freed from self-consciousness, freed from that eternal struggle of what I must be for C., and what I must be for Mother, and what I must be for myself.

I was freed from my shyness in a peculiar way. But it was a suspended life, like the one on a boat or a train or in some emergency, when you drop the conventional pattern you have been walking in. A dangerous state to be in, for having lost one's usual restraints one is quite without standards. And it was more than usually difficult, as all emotions are so near the surface when you are in anxiety. Your heart is right behind your eyes. So that it was easy for Miss S. to annoy me, or for me to hurt Jo's feelings. She was on edge too.

It was a crowded week, from the point of view of activity. [All planned by E. C. M.] The Community Chest dinner after the first long day (and Mother *still* on that plane!). The Kerrs for lunch Sunday. The Cosmopolitan Club dinner—seating and planning. Dwight and Con down.

Thanksgiving and Grandma. A keyed-up feeling all day, an emergency feeling: "get through this . . . keep in readiness . . . keep yourself under control." And at night, finally, one's body and hands still, the mind racing racing racing, talking feverishly, arguing, explaining, the things one could not say during the day. One's mind, relentless, pent up, breaking down the dams and running away at night, working out problems of living, marriage, children, work. And no sleep until the half-open door began to blur with a vague light, before day. I could see it like a column at the foot of the bed.

There were some nice things during the week, too—pleasure which seemed really to have nothing to do with the rest of my life but suspended without connection, like a child's joy at being given a present. It seems strange that I could have enjoyed them, with such big things going on underneath. But I did. That afternoon when I went over the notes about Daddy with H. N. In the first place, I did not think they would mean anything to him, and they did and of course that was exciting, because then I knew I had got truth down on paper. But not only that: I could talk, and felt natural. I told him what I thought of *Lord Carnock* and *Tennyson*. He talked about what he was trying to do in Daddy's life—about the absent-minded phase. A beautiful sharp illustration of Daddy's mind "like a pack of hounds."

Then the intense pleasure of talking to Con about everything. Our joy when we got good news, our profound gloom at bad, our sense of false security and false hope, our sense of suspension and finally sheer exhaustion. Con said, "I feel like a tennis ball that's been bounced too much."

We woke in the night [December 3]—the early morning. I was very chilled and C. called from sleep: "What is the matter?" I got up and took some aspirin and put on a warm wrapper and got back into bed. "What's the matter?"—"I'm so cold— still so cold." And then, very soon after, we heard a knock on the door, or the telephone bell, and Marshall's voice, "Colonel, Pasadena calling." We were stark awake, and struck, knowing what it was.

"I'm afraid that's bad news," C. said. We jumped out of bed and into the study. It was half dark and still outside. C. took the telephone and just nodded at me to tell me what it was and I think asked the time. Then I scribbled on a pad, "Tell her I'll come out." But C. shook his head. I think he did tell them about being ready to do anything.

Then we went back to bed. C. worried about my being cold and wanted to comfort me, but I did not want to be comforted, I only felt completely stiffened and hardened and aware of a great many things—of what I must do the rest of my life, and how I must be good to Charles and love him always, and the things I must cherish and the things I must crush.

All life ahead of me telescoped. I would fill it up with things. It would pass quickly. In that leap of the mind I seemed to jump to the end of my life and not even fear death. Oh, I prayed Elisabeth was not afraid. After all, I felt, the big things in my life had happened. Nothing important was going to happen to me again. Elisabeth had been with me through all of them: love and marriage (though that is still to do) and birth, children, and death, and evil, and now the loss of Elisabeth herself. There did not seem to me anything to fear in life any more, or anything to want. And I decided that I must write. I must write about Elisabeth, all of her I had—all I remembered. I must write about her as long as I lived. I must write her in many, many ways.

And I thought of Mother. It seemed incredible that anyone would ask her to suffer this. It seemed that it must crush her, for Elisabeth meant more to her than anything else in life after Daddy, and was part of Daddy, and was the young girl in her. And I realized I would not be able to help her or comfort her any more than C. could comfort me. Only Elisabeth could comfort her for the loss of Elisabeth.

But of course I could do the things she wanted—all those things like sending telegrams and seeing relatives and letting people know—and I felt bad that I did not know Aubrey well enough to help him, as Elisabeth wanted him helped, and then again that I could not tell him how grateful, how terribly grateful we were for what he had done for Elisabeth.

I did not feel that I had lost something that was *mine*. I just felt that life wasn't going to be worth much without her, as the world might be without sun or fire. I did not think what I would miss in talking to her or her letters or her understanding. I just realized in one gulp what life would be without her and tossed it away as unimportant, as though I had already lived it in that moment of realizing it, and it was behind me.

I think we lay there half an hour, I testing things in the heat of that moment of realization. Then we decided—C. helping me—that we must tell Con and Dwight and Connie Chilton.[1] Telling Con was worse than hearing it myself, as though physi-

---

[1] Constance Chilton, college friend of Elisabeth Morgan and co-founder of The Little School.

cally it just became real to me in that moment, and I could not speak. But she knew without my telling her. C. told Dwight. Then Connie Chilton and Aunt Edith. It was hard meeting her understanding. It was hard first speaking to Banks and Elsie.

I decided to take Jon to school—there seemed no reason not to. I would have to go on, not with the old life, as people always say, but with the new. It was going to be like this the rest of my life—I might as well start. It was so strange walking out—an entirely different person, as though I too had died, or been born.

It was cold and clear and still, with bands of cloud across the sky. But everything was new and different and came to me sharply, as though I had been allowed to see for the first time, as though my ears had become unstopped. It was painful, as breathing and sight and sound must be to a newborn child. Things seemed unrelated to the former life—trees and sky and gravel under my feet. I would have to learn the laws about them all over again. That plane that passed quite high over the garage seemed purposeless, boring a hole through a vacuum.

I don't remember even looking at Jon. But at school: Connie was in her blue sweater at the door, as usual. She came running out and put her arms around me. It seemed to me glorious to have her going on, just as Elisabeth would have wanted. I will always love her for it.

Englewood, December 5th

Darling Con,

It seems incredible that I have not written you but there have, strangely enough, been things to do—telegrams the first day, lists, people, planning the funeral, a whole load of unreal strange conventions, with now and then a flare of intense feeling—love, anger, sorrow—to show you still feel underneath the numbness.

She died suddenly and easily, which I am terribly grateful for. They got on the train that night and will arrive about eight in the morning Friday.

I feel I must tell you something about the service. I spoke to Mother once. She was militant and wonderful about it: "I want it simple, but I don't want it casual or badly planned. It must be perfect. It must be beautiful." She wants the same service as Daddy's, but it is to be in the big room. Pitney Van Dusen and Dr. Elmore[1] are conducting the service.

We don't know who is coming yet—we haven't asked anyone. I wish they would have it in the drawing room, where you could look out on the trees and the sky. I wish the flowers could be natural, as though off the place—young and fresh and beautiful, like Elisabeth. I wish it did not have to be in that big room where they were married.

I think this is worse for Mother—almost—than Daddy's death. There is nothing to pull her out. It's a blow at the roots.

DIARY   [*December 11th*]

Then started a long week of unrealities: arrangements, telegrams, flowers, letting people know, telephone messages; relatives coming to call; things that had no connection with Elisabeth at all, and that she would laugh at and that I did laugh at, thereby shocking everyone. Except for the reality of Amey and walking around the garden with her when everything lifted into another plane of spiritual realities, and I felt that I should never lose the spiritual reality of Elisabeth. Amey helping practically, too: lists, flowers, the "blanket"—horrible word!

C. taking a whole load of problems (cemetery lots, undertaker, etc.) on his shoulders. There was too the reality of seeing the Leffingwells, as Elisabeth loved them. I could not speak to

---

[1] Henry Pitney Van Dusen, clergyman, educator, and author, President of Union Theological Seminary, New York, 1945–1963, friend of E. R. M. M. and E. C. M. Dr. Carl Elmore, minister of the First Presbyterian Church in Englewood.

them. And the comfort of Connie Chilton coming up in the evening, talking to us on an eternal basis; Elisabeth was real again. Then the night Con and Dwight came home—the joy and relief of seeing them, of being together, of being able to slough off our conventional emotions (that people expect you to have), to laugh about Elisabeth, to remember, as Dwight said, "How she cussed me out."

One of the strangest things about that week was the amount of feeling that could be poured out on trivial details—the anger, the hurt feelings, the pride, jealousy—caused by the blanket of flowers, the list of people at the service, the singing, whose suggestions to follow. I was the worst offender, feeling passionately, "I can't *bear* a *blanket* of flowers. Couldn't we have something natural, like Elisabeth?" Or, *"Why* should we have to have So-and-So? Elisabeth didn't like her."

It seems strange that one should fight passionately on details at such a time. And it's all a question of superficial words, symbols easily misunderstood, having different meanings to each. All one's emotions are rushed to one spot. You are in readiness, the troops just held back, and any chance cry will precipitate a battle on any pretext. Unless you have real discipline in the army.

And then the morning they came. Con and Dwight went in to meet them. C. and I stayed at home. I dreaded the impact. I wanted so much to be controlled and I was afraid to see Mother crumpled—why, I don't know, as it is impossible to think of her crumpled. But there she was, just the same in the little gray suit, the soft gray hair, the face drawn in a mixture of strength and wistfulness. She had come and everything was all right. She would carry us all along. It was hard to see Aubrey, and I had a strange hallucination as I looked at him. I saw Elisabeth's face and not his—I suppose our combined thought of her.

We swept upstairs and Mother and Con and I sat in her sitting room. Mother talked to us. We all cried, but Mother was not pent up as I was afraid, for she had talked herself out to Aubrey. There is a wonderful bond there and strength in it for both.

The arrangements: the undertaker in the library with Aubrey, C., and me. The sudden relief when we are left alone (Con and Dwight come in too), and we laugh at the falseness of it. We feel elated—it is like the presence of Elisabeth among us. We have a secret community, a secret bond. We shut everything else out. The outward conventions do not bother us. And we are on that keyed-up plane the rest of the day.

The big room, lots of chrysanthemums. Con and I moving a bowl into the sun. I spill the water all over me and on the floor and giggle. People are afraid to laugh. Elisabeth would laugh. The room looked lovely—chrysanthemums and sunlight. Up in Mother's room before the service, still in that mood of elation. Mother understood it though she was not part of it. I keep thinking all day of Elisabeth's letter to me about Daddy's funeral.

We walk in the back of the room [for the service]. The gardener, the old man with a bowed head and hat in hand. I see Vernon; he loved Elisabeth and she was very fond of him. The service was beautiful—Daddy's service, which Elisabeth had picked out. Everyone in the room was quiet and natural. No one wanted to cry but to sing the hymns gratefully. We did not face anyone but went out and waited upstairs for everyone to go.

That night we were happy, all together, talking of Elisabeth and thinking of her and finding her again in each other. We felt—unspoken—that we could never lose her. Aubrey brought down their Christmas present for us, that he had found, Elisabeth had written the card. An old globe in a case and an old ivory navigator, like a little sundial but workmanship like a gem, and the card in Elisabeth's writing: "The Heavens and the Earth for Charles and Anne..."

Later we went out to the pantry to drink milk and talk and

laugh. Mother (who had gone up earlier) came down like a girl, in a wrapper, with her hair in a little crooked braid down her back, and sat on a stool and Dwight was gallant and sweet to her. She sat rather wistful but pleased among us, and we were happy, thinking, talking, feeling—about Elisabeth.

"But gathering as we stray a sense
Of Life so lovely and intense—
It lingers when we wander hence

That those who follow feel behind
Their backs when all before is blind
Our Joy, a rampart to the mind."

[JOHN MASEFIELD]

Wednesday, December 12, 1934

I must write it all out, at any cost. Writing is thinking. It is more than living, for it is being conscious of living. At this moment I do not worry about losing Elisabeth. I shall never lose her; I have the rest of my life to think about her, to realize her. No—what I must work out is my life without her, going on without her. The person I was with her I must keep intact, because it is a denial of her to let it go. It is failing a trust. I must be what I was with her, for, as always and with everyone she touched, the truest clearest person came out at her touch. She had the gift of clarifying you, a creative sympathy. So it is not she that I lose—I cannot lose that. It is the only reality. It is as complete as a piece of music, and as timeless. She is reality. It is what is *left* that is no longer reality—myself, of course, the real self I was with her.

But also Jon and Charles and Mother—they are unrealities too, in a strange way. I will be a poorer wife and a poorer mother and a poorer daughter without her.

There is a pattern for me to follow. I know exactly what I must do. It is quite clear—only I lack the heart to do it.

The incredible thing seems not so much that she is dead, but that she is dead and I am living.

Saturday, December 15, 1934

Looking at the magazines—little advertisements: bed jackets, breakfast trays, nightgowns, sunbonnets, sandals. And I cannot give them to Elisabeth!

Wednesday, December 19, 1934

It is wonderful talking to Aubrey. We talk Elisabeth constantly, completely. I do not feel I am burdening him by talking to him. It is being with Elisabeth to talk to him. He is Elisabeth and the person who fulfilled her. And I feel Elisabeth backing me up, as though my appreciation of him would make her happy.

Why couldn't I tell her, before, how wonderful he is, and only realize it completely now she is gone? But still, she was always certain of my liking him.

Friday, December 28, 1934

Talk to C. about writing. Down in that awful pit again. No one can help me—I must do it alone.

Thor gone. Terribly depressed—security shaken again. I walk to look for him. The atmosphere of insecurity, the pit of "something lost." That horrible mood. Strange how a relatively small thing will throw you deep in it again. C. is very sweet —just as miserable as I. We don't dare leave the baby alone. In our bed he howls and kicks! Elsie is late, Jon sobbing, "Jon wants to go back to his own bed."

Saturday, December 29, 1934

Wake up very discouraged about Thor and tired from not sleeping. A scratch at the door—Thor! He jumps all over me, is terribly happy. C. comes up. We are all sentimental about him.

Con has Margot Loines[1] out—an extraordinarily alive, independent, free person. She makes my mind work hard and jump over the grooves. It does seem to me that she has come early to the stage where I am now, where one realizes that it isn't being "understood" that matters, or being "appreciated," or being "expressed." That, really, is adolescent. It is necessary to have a little of that—just enough to keep the thing inside of you pacified and quiet. It must not grow hungry and lean and martyred; then it is dangerous. Keep it pacified with morsels of praise and attention, but never let it grow fat and demoralizing. Because I think that what is really *you* cannot be expressed, or understood, or appreciated (those things are irrelevant anyway). It can only be given—given as Mother gave to Daddy—without sacrifice, without martyrdom, without self-consciousness—given as Natasha gave to Pierre.

It does seem to me more and more that love has no value in itself or by itself (except perhaps first love, to the young). People talk about love as though it were something you could give, like an armful of flowers. And a lot of people give love like that—just dump it down on top of you, a useless strong-scented burden. I don't think it is anything that you can give, or if you can, it is valueless.

Love is a force *in you* that enables you to give *other* things. It is the motivating power. It enables you to give strength and power and freedom and peace to another person. It is not a result; it is a cause. It is not a product; it produces. It is a power, like money or steam or electricity. It is valueless unless you can give something else *by means* of it. It has taken me a long time to learn. I hope it will stay learned and that I can practice it.

[1] Margot Loines, friend of Constance Morrow, later married to Dwight Morrow, Jr. Now Mrs. John Wilkie.

I seem to have learned so much in the last month, so fast, that it will take me years to assimilate. I have been so busy learning that I haven't done anything else, jumping from day to day and from hour to hour, up one more step. If only I can hold it, if only the thing has time to harden, to *set,* before another emotion rocks it or before the small vanities rise up again. All I can say, over and over again, is "Let them not have dominion over me."

You can't count on anything, but there is next week and next month: not to disappoint C. at the Trial,[1] to finish the book for him, to give him a home and a sense of freedom and power and fulfillment.

[1] On January 2nd, the court trial relating to the kidnapping and murder of Charles A. Lindbergh, Jr., began at Flemington, New Jersey.

1935

January 9, 1935

Yesterday I wrote all day long in my diary because I felt I must know what had been happening to me and couldn't know without writing it. It was such a relief that I felt fresh at the end of the day and started to work with pleasure on *North to the Orient*. And I have worked all day today and only in the last half hour did I write something I thought was good.

Dr. Condon[1] on the stand. Evidently he made a wonderful witness. Aubrey and C. back late.

We go out for a walk—bad fog—C. tired but satisfied.

C. asks about my work and what is done; is pleased I have been working, tries to read the newly typed chapter to show how important he feels it is, but is too tired. I have to hold myself in terribly when he criticizes it—picks out words. I know there are lots of things wrong but I resent the criticism. Am I so small-minded that I resent, would resent, all criticism? The anger I feel when I see a hard black line drawn right through something I have written, the frustration! And yet it is good criticism and deserved and he shows infinite patience in going over it and caring about it.

TO E. L. L. L.   *Englewood, January 9 and 10, 1935*
Dear M.

This is just a note to say that Jon is well and C. also, and I. C. goes down to Flemington every day.

He was a wonderful witness—as he would be—natural, perfectly clear, and of course sure of the truth of his statements, which withstood any test of cross-examination. In fact, he

---

[1] Dr. John F. Condon, a retired teacher, who had offered himself as a neutral go-between at the time of the kidnapping, and through whom the ransom money was passed.

made such a positive impression of integrity in the courthouse that one reporter remarked, "I think *Reilly*[1] withstood the cross-examination very well."

One outstanding impression everyone gets is of the dignity, wisdom, integrity, and common sense of the judge.

I do not know what our plans are, though I hope after this is over we can go off for a rest. They do not know how long it will last—a month to six weeks, perhaps, in all. Both Elsie and Betty[2] came through a difficult ordeal very well. It was cruel on Elsie for they insinuated dreadful things about her husband who, as she said, was not there to defend himself. However, she defended him loyally and gave everyone the impression of her absolute honesty and devotion.

I am afraid this publicity is hard on you, besides the strain of watching the trial.

I had the Madonna on the mantel in the living room all Christmas week.

DIARY   *Thursday, January 10, 1935*

Patched up *North to the Orient* until 4:30 when Corliss [Lamont] came to tea. We talked until about six. It was very nice, though I felt incredibly old, as though I were talking at the end of my life to someone I had known aeons ago. We talked about Elisabeth and argued about immortality and we read out of Elisabeth's *Spirit of Man*.[3]

Then we talked about how foolish we all were eight years ago, and Corliss told me about an essay he had written one Sunday at North Haven, with Elisabeth helping him, laughing, about "the one and only theory"! Marvelous—"the one and only theory" we deluded ourselves with for years. The falsity of the romantic pattern in life that you go on applying to every

---

[1] Edward J. Reilly, Chief Defense Counsel.

[2] Betty Gow, Scotch nurse of Charles Lindbergh, Jr.

[3] *The Spirit of Man,* anthology edited by Robert Bridges.

relationship no matter how slight. I read some of Rilke and we argued about woman's "place," Corliss taking exception to my saying "a woman's mind" (Elisabeth had "a man's mind," I said). And yet I met sympathy and understanding and a kind of respect and acceptance of me and how I was trying to live and what I was trying to do, without the unrest of trying to change me, reform me, that if he were nearer to me he would probably feel.

Why can't one keep that admirable distance when one is married, that respect for another person's solitude, that withdrawal before what they are doing and being? Is it incompatible with a real and powerful love or is it the result of one's preconceived ideas of marriage, one's preconceived standards?

It was pleasant. Why don't I do it more—why do I make life such a difficult thing? It is normal to see people, and I would be better for it.

Saturday, January 12, 1935

I have slept rather badly the last nights, waking in the early morning confused and full of dreams. This morning again I dreamed with that peculiar vividness that I have sometimes —once about Daddy. I dreamed of Elisabeth. It started out a kind of nightmare: Elisabeth carrying me through strange temples, down long hallways. Finally I noticed how tired she was—frightfully upset to think I had let her carry me. Then we went through a door and were on the enclosed piazza and I was reading a story in a magazine. It was about her.

"Do you know So-and-So?" I asked; "there is an article about you."—"What does it say?" She was childishly curious and amused. She sat in the chaise longue and dangled her foot over the end. Then somehow she was in my arms—crying and crying, sobbing. I had my arms about her and could feel her and I begged her not to cry and kissed her and told her how much I loved her. But she went on sobbing and I, realizing, although I had her in my arms, that she was gone, I cried to her, "Elisabeth, you *will* come back, won't you?" and she said, "Oh, yes, I will come back," and she went out of the door and I woke up crying. Losing that physical reality was so terrible. I had not felt it before and realized something of Aubrey's pain.

Colonel Henry [Breckinridge] and Aida for lunch. C. gives Colonel Henry my chapter about fog flying. He says very little, but I am sure he does not like it. He objects only to my saying "God" so often, but in reality I think he objects to much more—to the whole thing. I think he feels it is not courageous —that we all feel fear but we should not admit it, that there is something cowardly about my stripping my feelings bare like that—something indecent. I wonder. It did not seem so to me when I wrote it—what else can I go by?

Monday, January 14, 1935

Typed all day.
"Jon, look at the snow on the ground."
Jon: "Who makes it?"
"It falls from the sky, like rain."
Jon: "Who makes the sky?"

Tuesday, January 15, 1935

Thelma[1] comes out for lunch and we talk all afternoon. It is such a relief—a feeling of freedom, power, release. Thelma gives me some of her own coolness and detachment. And not only that, but in seeing me—the real me—suddenly I exist. Thelma thinks I exist—then I must exist. We talk all afternoon and go out for a walk in the flurry of snow, with bandanas over our heads. Thelma seems to me such a remarkable combination of a person who has detachment and clarity of mind and also sensitive emotional perception. And she is remarkably free of conventional

---

[1] Thelma Crawford Lee, a friend of Elisabeth Morrow Morgan and A. M. L.

ideas of people's relationships and emotions. It is possible to be completely honest with her. Life does not seem so difficult. Very happy—wear a new hostess coat for dinner. Talk—Thelma, Mother, Aubrey, and I—about Harold Nicolson's books, about Gertrude Stein, about Virginia Woolf, about H. H. Richardson, about fitting art to the form. C. calls me away from time to time to make corrections on the "book," which he corrects earnestly.

Friday, January 18, 1935

In to Dr. Scobey. As I feel very tired after a night of nightmares, I decide to play the "well, what *do* you like?" game. All the way going into town I live entirely in the top layer—sight and sound and feel: George Washington Bridge, the river spreading out into sunlight; the cakes of ice on it against the cold blue of the water. Triangles of sunlight wedging across a street through city blocks; blue puddles where the ice has melted; trees waving at the top, their trunks firmly rooted. (If one could only feel that security in life!)

Through the park, the sun was behind the buildings at the south end so they all looked one-surfaced, bluish and distant, a bloom on them like the Camden Hills, only they were angular, hard, terraced; and against them, those Japanesey pines, drooping, pagodalike, soft.

The whole ride was made thrilling by this surface living. How stupid I have been—"Chooseth to sit upon his little handful of thorns." I should take all these things and many others —small and big physical pleasures—take them for what they are in themselves. Hot baths and eau de cologne on one's body, and the heat pad at one's feet at night. And things to eat, too, toast and sherry—take them and *use* them deliberately, fiercely.

Saturday, January 19, 1935

I read Elisabeth's journal given me by Aubrey all morning, going way back to the trip we took abroad together—the motor trip to Mont-Saint-Michel and Paris, the day in the park and at the Russian restaurant![1] Then that time in Mexico before I was married, and Nassau. It was so spontaneous, true, and clear—all Elisabeth's goodness and beauty and spirit. The journal is intensely her—far more than the things she wrote. It burns with life.

I want to get all her letters and my diaries about her, for I was much more conscious about her than she about me. I knew what I had in her, and what I would lose. But when she talks of me, there it is like the quick touch of her hand, that birdlike little hand, small and delicate but quick and deft and hard, as though one felt through to the beauty of her small firm bones.

Mother and I talk of E.'s diary. Mother said, "How she *understood* me!" It was heartbreaking. And I cannot help her, though I think I understand her too, but I can't give it to her.

Sunday, January 20, 1935

Con home. We talk about going up to Boston to see *Yeomen of the Guard*. I leap at it, but later, talking it over with C., I realize that it is a bad idea. He says I could not possibly get up there without publicity and that the appearance of going off to a theater while the trial is on would look disrespectful and light. Of course I never thought of it that way. God knows I don't take it—or life—lightly. C. so rarely cares about appearances, but this is different. It would give an utterly false impression.

And yet the whole thing discouraged me. I feel completely frustrated. This is just a little thing but it is another clamp; I am hemmed in on all sides and pounding against the walls. And yet I must do it alone. No one can help me. I can't spill my troubles out on Mother or Aubrey, or C. They all have enough of their own—more than I—to carry.

I must not talk. I must not cry. I must not write—I must not think—I must not dream. I must control my mind—I must

[1] Described in *Bring Me a Unicorn*, pp. 39-43.

control my body—I must control my emotions—I must finish
the book—I must put up an appearance, at least, of calm for C.
I must force myself to be interested in plans, in work, in Jon.
I must eat. I must sleep.

But last night lying in bed, shrinking over into my corner,
trying not to cry—or at least to cry only inaudibly—not to
wake C., trying not to toss or turn, trying to be like a stone,
heavy and still and rigid, except for my tears, except for my
mind. And even the mind wasn't running free; I don't dare
let it. Say poetry—think clothes—don't let it run away.

I felt I could understand insanity and physical violence. I
could understand anything.

Monday, January 21, 1935

Monday went pretty well. I felt relieved and could work in the
afternoon.

G. here. My idea of complete disillusionment is to wake up
and find out that the world really is what G. makes it seem
when she talks to me. Anything she touches is suddenly tainted,
cheapened, brought down to back-stairs gossip, indescribably
vulgar and somehow bawdy. She coats everything with it and
yet it is done with the air of a lady, so that I am appalled and
sickened.

As I look back on my life, she was always there, like a bawdy
Juliet's nurse. The night C. proposed to me (half-winking in the
background); my first baby, when I knew I was pregnant ("Well,
after all, dearie," smiling knowingly, "what did you expect?").
Those awful days when I minded so much being big and ugly
("You're eating for two!"). All through the kidnapping repeating
people's gossip ("Why wasn't the shutter locked? Of course *I*
would never leave *my* child alone in one part of the house").
Even my relation to Mother is spoiled, made material and gross under
her eyes ("You oughtn't to fuss: you're getting your meals and
beds free").

I think of Juliet's nurse telling Juliet after Romeo is banished to marry Tybalt—"O, he's a lovely gentleman"—and Juliet turning on her bitterly: "Well, thou hast comforted me marvelous much!" And she is the waiting-woman in Grimm's story of the Goosegirl. "Alas! dear Falada, there thou hangest! . . . Alas! Queen's daughter, there thou gangest!" Why do I let these people and things bother me, shake me?

Tuesday

Lovely snow. Walking with C. at night—snow and moonlight. The surface game—enjoyed it. A pine tree bent down with the soft weight of snow: a girl in love.

Wednesday, January 23, 1935

Amey in the morning, to watch Jon at school. Mother gets Harold Nicolson's first five chapters [of biography of D. W. M.]. She reads them and gives them to me. I read all morning and afternoon. There was a blizzard outside. I cried and cried. I don't know why, exactly. They are *terribly* good—much better than I dreamed they would be. The story itself was so moving that I felt humble in front of this person I had never really seen before and never appreciated. I was thrilled, too, by the clarity of the analysis, delighted by the humor and charm—and oh, longed for Elisabeth. All the time I read, my mind ran in parallel lines, writing letters to her. And then reading the phrase—*"creative confidence"*—I kept feeling, Oh, it is Elisabeth! I began to realize what Mother had lost twice.

Mother and I talked about the book. She is very happy about his point of view. She feels too strongly about Elisabeth to talk. But I felt nearer her, and purged, last night, of myself. C. and I walk in the blizzard. It is beautiful but such hard work. I am pulled up the hill by his hand, nice.

Thursday, January 24, 1935

A wonderful day—alone all day and night.

Today I went into town and met Margot Loines for lunch. It was wonderful. We jumped all the fences and started right in at the bottom. Things grew inside of me as we talked. About poetry first (Spender), about acting and writing, about Rilke, about sculpture, about marriage—all rather breathlessly. We talked of contacts, too, and that flash of understanding. I used to be afraid of that swift impatient flash of understanding, of making friends too easily. I'm not any more. Partly that real understanding comes so rarely and is so wonderful; one should just take it and give thanks. Partly because I don't think I make mistakes that way any more. She is aware (if they are not aware they don't interest me); she is absolutely honest emotionally; and she is honest intellectually. With people like that, *if you can keep up to the same standards,* you can't make mistakes—real ones. You must be courageous, but it takes wisdom as well as courage to be honest.

Oh, but the fun of talking like that, today. It is like playing with a rope. You let out more and more—cautiously. (How much will they take?) Your hand on it the whole time to jerk back the slack. No—there is a steady pull. All right, then—another loop. Try this, see if they can take it, throw it out. It was all taken—the rope still taut!

I feel as if I were learning so incredibly fast (only it has taken *frightfully* long to get here), that I am going to burst with it. I can't hold it all. I want to give it, to put it down. I want to make something of it.

And C. will come home after two days and ask me tonight what I have done on the book and I will say *Nothing.* I am right, though. I am. I can't deny this growing, only I should be strong enough to do both.

Saturday, January 26, 1935

Wrote all afternoon: "Preparation"—difficult. C. reads it at night —very kind and helpful. C. said something beautiful: "Icarus is only the first *expression* of man's desire to fly!" Thrilling. I am going to use it and he is pleased.

Sunday, January 27, 1935

A lovely day: still and clear, and dazzling snow. Outside most of the morning with C. and Jon. C. builds a snow house for Jon and pulls him around on a sled. I get skis. Jon is very happy: "Want to go wid' Fader." We make a ski path behind the house and go down all morning. Thrilling: speed, control, balance, and icy tingling air burning your face. C. gets a shovel and pounds the path flat, enjoys seeing me the active athletic one. Come in glowing; feel healthy and "Norvegian" carrying my skis over my shoulder.

Work all afternoon; slow plodding on "Preparation" and then can't do any more. Only *really* write about one page. So slow it hardly seems worth it (and after that one page my mind is fagged out!). C. makes out marvelous lists of equipment. They will take up a whole chapter in the book!

His lists are much better than my chapter.

At night he talks about his work in the [Rockefeller] Institute, about Aviation, about approaching a great change in his life, about wanting, when he was still a boy, to study life and about life, about political changes and scientific ones, comparing their contributions to the world. Which is more? What political contribution would you exchange for *anesthesia* or *vaccination?* Very interesting. It was easy today to live the new life I feel I've taken on.

Monday, January 28, 1935

Worked "hard" all day—at least, the afternoon. Got four pages typed and smoothed out hitches; not much new material. Just the technical business of getting out what I want to say (after I *know* what I want to say) takes so long. I struggle and struggle, and it comes out a platitude that everyone knew all along! Also that peculiar way that one of your points•(neatly tabulated under

A, B, or C in the outline) runs away with the whole chapter. You start out with four horses pulling evenly down the road, and one turns out to be stronger than the others and veers off to the right and pulls the whole caravan across the field.

At night Mother gives me two of H. N.'s letters to read, businesslike, competent, assured. Yes—he has written five chapters. He will have five more chapters written by the time he gets here, the book done in May. O God, why try if I'm so far behind the standards.

Tuesday, January 29, 1935

A wonderful day. In to see Margot Loines and Lincoln Kirstein[1] and the Lachaise[2] things in Museum. I cannot understand the big blossoming things, but the portrait heads are beautiful and moving—something dynamic in them, far more than in the blossoming "full-blown roses." A young and bitter head of a girl ("For this I starred my eyes with salt"). A head of a child—narcissus quality; a mask of a woman, yearning; a silver head of a woman, all patience and tiredness. A woman who does not want things any more because she knows better. And the nervous tired hands of a woman, heavy by her side.

Then lunch with Lincoln and Margot. He asks questions, so I talk too much: Russia, Aviation, our trip, Sweden. Then we went—Margot and I—to her apartment and sat and talked. It was a great release. I could throw off all those cramping emotions that bind me. I was free of them. I could tear them off, as Margot did in imagination when she made that beautiful gesture in her room, with her hands, her arms, her whole body, to show me how she threw off emotions. I would like to see her act. She is perfectly natural, but vivid and courageous, nothing

---

[1] Lincoln Kirstein, established School of American Ballet in New York City. Director of New York City Ballet Company; brother of Mina Curtiss.

[2] Gaston Lachaise, French-born sculptor, naturalized American; did the sculptural decorations in Rockefeller Center, New York City.

cramped, and yet precise, emotion within form. I understand how acting can be creative, how it can give. I never have before. She showed me her book on Italian painting she was looking at to find the feeling of a nun, for her play. Then the Botticelli book. We talked about Elisabeth too, her directness like a bird, her Botticelli beauty, of losing her and of not losing her.

I went home feeling braver and freer.

All this brings me Elisabeth vividly. She never said it, but she *was* it—truly appreciative, courageous, and honest. It is as though I couldn't learn these things from her, living, only from her loss. If I could only tell her—I have learned so much since she died. It is all pouring into me.

It is strange. I change so much from morning to night, from one day to the next, that time is stretched out. I live years and years and suffer and learn—all in a day.

Friday, February 1, 1935

Dancing with Jon—swinging him around in my arms and then throwing him on the sofa. He staggers up again and runs toward me with arms out. "Want Mudder to pick Jon up. Want Mudder to make de music go. Don't want Mudder to sit down."

Skiing in the afternoon—Thor thundering down after me in the snow.

"The bright face of danger!"

Saturday, February 9th

Get up early. Mother to testify. The long drive down. The road to Princeton we took so many times, and the road to the airport where we took Mother that night. I had forgotten about the airport, and we were on it before we knew it. She had left with hope. It must have been awful to see it. Then a new road, much better, only we were so tired by the time we got there, as if we had already lived through it.

Flemington: gingerbread houses, like those cardboard sets we played with as children. "Little town": a church, a hotel, a garage.

Crowded with people, snow, and cars. We go through cameras the back way to the courtroom. I sat about in the same place. I felt as if I'd been sitting there forever. The crowded rows, the slat chairs, the fat bored-looking woman opposite me in the jury, the high windows behind; outside, the red bricks of an old building, lit by the sun. (But where was that triangle of blue sky I had kept my eye pinned on?)[1]

That sad-eyed Sob Sister looking at me every time I looked up. People breathing behind me. That pale profile of Hauptmann startling one through a gap in the heads. The pathetically bedraggled thin face—tired, bewildered—of Mrs. Hauptmann. The smart stenographer, taking down the record, stooping as she walked back and forth in front of the Judge's box. The Judge—exactly the same—dignified, unruffled.

It was a far worse day emotionally than when I testified. I was freer to feel. That long, long morning of wood testimony: tiny minute points, technical haggling, vernier scales, how marked, etc. I thought with a pang in the middle of it, How incredible that my baby had any connection with this!

After lunch, the witnesses. My rage at Reilly's snobbery in talking of Violet Sharpe[2] as "just an ordinary servant girl." Wilentz[3] always referred to her as *Miss Sharpe*.

Then Marshall,[4] white-haired, stumbling up to the stand. He seemed so personal and yet a detached part of our life that it was a chance shot at my emotions—taken by surprise. Marshall, who called Mother to the telephone that night, as he called us to hear about Elisabeth's death. "Who was in the house [Next Day Hill] at the time?"—"Well, there was Colonel and Mrs. Lindbergh, and the baby and Betty Gow, and there was Miss Elisabeth. Mr.

[1] Reference to the time when A. M. L. testified.

[2] English maid in the Morrow household. She committed suicide during the investigation period following the kidnapping.

[3] David T. Wilentz, New Jersey Attorney General.

[4] Night watchman at Next Day Hill, Englewood.

Dwight was at college." It seemed frightfully personal: "Miss Elisabeth," "Mr. Dwight."

Then Reilly asked, "Was Senator Morrow alive at the time?" —"No. No, he wasn't alive then."—"When did he die? . . . You went to his funeral?"—"Yes."—"And you don't remember?" It was awful. Why should Mother have to listen to it?

And then, "Mrs. Dwight Morrow." A stir in court and Mother getting up and handing me her bag. A rush of blood to my face and pounding in my ears. Mother, small, in black, and her wistful strong face, soft and infinitely sad and tired. Such quiet dignified little steps, controlled poise. I felt I could not bear it. Those bare and terrible questions, like empty houses that have once been lived in. "What did your household consist of then?" —"You mean the immediate family? . . . My daughter Elisabeth and myself." (I must not cry.) But Mother was firm and strong. Reilly's trap questions: "Who served you the night before?"—"The night before . . . I don't know, because I was on the train." He jumped quickly to "Who served you the night after?"—"You mean March 2nd?"—"Yes."—"I don't know, of course—I was in Hopewell!"

He dropped her quickly and we went out and escaped quietly and drove home, Mother *so* relieved.

Sunday, February 10, 1935

Today Mother says that Amey can't go to Mexico (because her brother is too ill), thereby throwing me again into a panic of indecision about Mexico. I don't want to talk to C. until I am clear in my own mind. I don't want to upset him unnecessarily at a time like this when he is hemmed in by the trial. I must think it out first. Amey was to be the one person with Mother who had been there before, who could comfort her a little—a representative of Daddy. Now with Amey not going, Mother really goes alone, with no one of the past life, who can understand what she misses, how she feels, what it was like before. No one to whom she can turn and say, "Do you remember?" Aubrey—but Aubrey was not there before and he has his own grief. I know that she longs to have me go, or someone very close. She does not ask me, but once in a while escapes, "Oh, Anne, if only you were going."

Monday, February 11, 1935

Talk to Mother, and strength pouring into me.

Tuesday, February 12, 1935

I read the papers and feel bitter to think of how they *use* C. Dangle him and his life in front of the stage for their own ends. And he has to sit quiet and watch.

Wednesday, February 13, 1935

Judge Trenchard's summation is cool, dignified, wise, and infinitely removed from petty human suffering and yet relevant, just, and true to life. The verdict: *Guilty.*

That howling mob over the radio—how incredibly horrible and bitter to realize that this has to do with us. That C. should have to bear it.

Incredible as that first night.

Thursday, February 14, 1935

"Not the old wayward child to see
But some bright-haired divinity."

The trial is over. We must start our life again, try to build it securely—C. and Jon and I. It is I, really—I must start again, without Elisabeth, with my eyes open, without confusion or fooling myself, honestly and patiently, keeping clear what matters. Charles and a home and Jon—and work.

Friday, February 15, 1935

Rhoda (*Waves*).[1]

"What amulet is there against this disaster? What face can I summon to lay cool upon this heat? I think of names on boxes;

[1] *The Waves.* Novel by Virginia Woolf.

of mothers from whose wide knees skirts descend; of glades where the many-backed steep hills come down. Hide me, I cry, protect me, for I am the youngest, the most naked of you all."

"I walked straight up to you instead of circling round to avoid the shock of sensation as I used. But it is only that I have taught my body to do a certain trick. Inwardly I am not taught. I fear, I hate, I love, envy and despise you, but I never join you happily."

Virginia Woolf has written best about shyness.

We talk about shyness at night—Mr. Nicolson, Aubrey, Margot, Dwight, Con, and I. For once, I was not shy. Mr. N. telling about his boys and the *courage tests*. I think he is wrong about that approach but I could not think quickly enough to talk, and anyway he wouldn't have wanted to know. He is a strange man. His perception and understanding provoke my sincerity, but when I attempt to talk honestly as I would with Aubrey, or Thelma or Margot, or Con or Dwight, he freezes up and shuts the door he has just opened—bang—in my face. I suddenly become young and shy and hurt. Is it just British conventionality, that training of theirs to talk *at* people and not *to* or *for* them?

Or is it possible to live in a family without ever looking at them? Is it possible to turn on your honest clear perceptive self at will: *now* I will perceive clearly and honestly, *now* I will *not*. Honest living and honest seeing and honest relations are then not necessary to honest writing. I have believed they are—that in the smallest part of your life they are necessary and that it shows in your writing.

According to this theory anyone who wrote a good book would be a good man. Anyone who wrote *about* a wonderful man would *be* a wonderful man. It is absurd—ridiculous. And yet, what then am I working for? Why try to perceive everything clearly? Why try to live clearly, honestly? Why try to analyze honestly, since it isn't necessary to good writing—just go to Columbia and be taught how to be a craftsman.

A nice day. I feel miles and miles and miles away from yesterday. C. and I go through the woods in the rain. There is still snow on the ground and one can see the tracks of animals. At least, C. can. His eyes are so quick and sensitive and he sees twice as much as I do. Sensitive to a stir in the leaves, to a scratch in the snow, invisible things (to me) speak to him, cry out, as people's emotions do to me. It is quite exciting, and he teaches me to see!

Wonderful talk with Margot. She says comfortingly to my statement about it's being so awful not to have a mask and to be naked in front of people, "But people are so stupid that they clothe you"—with their own idea of you. She, coming in to a tea party, feeling herself clothed in a pink dress with a sash!

Nice quiet evening: Jon and C. and a tricycle. C. and I happy to be alone and quiet; feel a sense of ourselves as a family that could have a home and live normally. We are both content. Write Mother.

The blank look of snow on a dull day—old snow on a hillside, unrelieved except by dull dark trunks of trees (whose darkness has no depth or quality), so lifeless that you feel nothing could waken it. It is a pool into which you might drop a stone and there would be no ripples. Some people's faces are like that!

[Mexican Room, Next Day Hill] Monday, February 18th
I sat at my desk all day and pulled myself together, like a broken pot. This little piece fits in here, and something is gone here. That crack shows badly. Oh, those two bits fit together and fill up that hole—that's good. It was such a relief, and quieting. I love this room. When I come back from my outing with Jon into this room—quiet, big, cool, and serene—waiting for me and the desk waiting for me, I feel soothed and rested and touched. The greatest release and relief, like crying, or putting your head on the shoulder of someone you love. It is almost a physical comfort, arms around you. I just sit and sit and feel strengthened. But I cannot yet write, except diary.

C. back at night. He is released from pressure, working at the Institute and here alone in this house. It is wonderful to have each other alone. We look at each other with surprise and joy and feel young and on a honeymoon. Jon is mine again, too, and runs to my arms!

Tuesday, February 19th

B. came out today for lunch. She is getting a divorce, and is terribly sad. She was not glittering at all but just honest and quiet and perceiving. I admired her and liked talking to her, but I felt humble and foolish. Why should I fuss or be unhappy? After all, I have never been disillusioned about C. Disillusioned about other people, yes, and about the world at times, and work, but not about C. There are no illusions about him. He is clear— all the way through. What you see on top goes all the way through; it is not an accidental vein. He is solid, all of a piece, pure pure gold.

Englewood, Tuesday—Friday, etc., February [*21st, 22nd, 23rd*]

Darling Mother,

I was so glad to get your telegram; it sounded happy and relieved and I felt so too.

We are having a quiet and peaceful time—the kind of life you would like but will never get here because when you are here people come and things happen. Nothing happens and no-body comes when we're here. There seems to be infinite time and quiet—almost like North Haven. The house has a summer look to it, too: all the curtains are down and most of the furniture moved out of the front hall.

Jon is in bed with a mild form of *the* cold. He is happy and not fussy—just a runny nose. I think the quiet and bed are good for him, though he is not easy to amuse. Elsie comes to me and says with complete resignation and a kind of hopeless dogged-ness, "Of course, Mrs. Lindbergh, he destroys *everything* you give him, he just pulls *everything* to pieces." As though somehow it were all my fault for bearing such an imp.

I am annoyed and want to say, "Well, why don't you *do* something about it?" He only destroys things when he is bored—and he shouldn't be allowed to keep toys after he is bored with them. Take them away when he gets to the destructive stage. He's not a difficult child to amuse but he puts intensity into what he does and exhausts simple toys very quickly. You've got to stay a jump ahead of him. Then she gets harassed and says, "You can't watch him *all* the time. I can't do everything at once. He was playing quietly when I left him, just the moment I went out . . ."

Then I look at her, rather breathless and never quite up to the mark, and I think, she's just like me. C. must be just as annoyed at me; and I forgive her. (Jon is quite happy now, hammering large nails into a cake of Ivory soap. The other successful toy has been a pair of blunt scissors I gave him and an old magazine.)

Since I started this I have gotten the most astounding letter from Smith College. Did you know about it? "At a meeting of the Board of Trustees . . . to receive honorary degree of Master of Arts,"—with Annetta Clark's[1] smooth signature at the bottom! I had to read it about five times before I could believe it. You know that feeling: "He *can't* be looking at me, it *must* be the person behind me." I must say I felt excited and flattered and pleased.

And yet I don't really think they ought to do that. They ought to give degrees to people who have done things in their own rights, on their own responsibilities—women who have held a career by themselves. After all, what *are* they giving it to me for? Flying around the world with my husband? I certainly have no career as a pilot or a radio operator. C. could have got a better copilot, a better navigator, and a better radio operator. I don't know whether he could have got a better wife—although even

[1] Annetta Clark, secretary to the president through four administrations.

so, I was only a moderately good one, I kicked a lot and was afraid most of the time.

But if they're giving degrees away to good wives, L. should have one for washing diapers and sewing on G.'s buttons. It takes a lot more devotion and isn't as much fun. I suppose being a good wife is a career but I don't think you should get a degree for it. The really wonderful people do other things as well—like you. No, I think you should give degrees for the kind of contributions that Elisabeth made to schools. (C. says she would have had one eventually.)

Oh, well, the only way I can look at it is that they feel C. has made great contributions to the world and that I have helped him. Which is a lot of hooey because he would have done all that anyway, only he would not have been quite as happy. I suppose I cannot go up to Annetta Clark and explain this—so for all my disapproval I shall stand there in cap and gown. I'm sorry for this ranting, but I can't rant to C. He just says, "Oh, rats!" and stands and looks pleased and proud and small boy and says, "Of *course* you must accept," and I can't resist him (C. says he's very proud of me. Why *now?*).

DIARY   *Thursday, February 27, 1935*

I did too much yesterday and got tired and felt scattered. Too many people, and I could not sleep at night, my mind swimming round and round. Shopping: how much money did I spend— $70.00—how *could* I spend $70.00? What did I do—where *did* it go? The dressy blouse—did I need it? To dress up Elisabeth's old suit. Yes, I think so. The white blouse—for the old tweed suit. Yes, I needed that. Then the white sweater for the old suit—yes, very expensive, but the cheap ones won't wash; and the shoes, but I needed them. And then that pink silk shirtwaist dress—lovely color. Did I need it? For the South, yes—for the spring, next winter; look at the old purple one, used it and used it.

And the people. I spread myself out too much. Charles at the Modern Art Museum. Anything for C., anything for us, the two of us and our relation. Rushing back to have tea with Margot, because I couldn't bear not to. Back to the parking lot and driving out to Englewood—dinner with the D.'s. No time for a bath.

My mind swimming, swimming restlessly, I realized with a pang that it had been an awful day because I had been so *terribly* far from Elisabeth. All that mess of things was unrelated and on top, and there was nothing to rest on, not one real moment; all were suspended. I had been so far away from Elisabeth all day long.

And then with great relief I rested on something real and sharp and poignant, like a touch of her hand: the little old silver rabbit that I stopped to look at in the store window. I had a thrill of pleasure when I saw it on its tiny tray through the glass, without realizing that it was the instinctive feeling, "For Elisabeth—how she would love it!" That moment was real. It was the only thing that stood still in the whirlpool of shops, advertisements, cars, traffic signals, people, price tags, rags of conversations. It was still, in the center, and I came to rest on it—the little silver rabbit.

Englewood, March 1, 1935

Mother darling,

The letters from Mexico were wonderful. Your first glowing one . . . A letter from Aubrey which let me see you arriving and the expression on Miguel's and Cornelio's faces, and a marvelous description of breakfast at the Embassy! Then one, through Con, from you, which made me ache to be there—on how the plants have grown and what the streets looked like, and you and Aubrey walking through the Borda Gardens. I am glad it is still unchanged—that formal beauty gone dilapidated and careless, but charmingly. And a lovely letter from Amey which gave me all those early morning sounds, and the color of the bougainvillae and a general feeling of sun and happiness.

I know it isn't happiness exactly—it's just the opposite—and some of the time it must be unbearable, and yet it sounds as though you were getting a feeling of great closeness to the peo-

ple who aren't there. Intensity of feeling is almost the only thing
that is comforting. That dulled faraway feeling when you get
burdened with another life and swallowed up in things that don't
mean anything—that is awful.

DIARY   *Sunday, March 3, 1935*
A perfect day. A long walk in the woods. C. teaching me to tell
how recent are horses' hoof prints:—the amount of water in
particles of dirt thrown up, water displaced, not yet run back.

It is springlike. Moss is green with featherlike red on top; also
the ends of twigs are red, and under the leaves and snow in
places are small green vines. Also pussywillows, pricking brightly
off the ends of branches.

After lunch, a marvelous concert: Bach especially, the chorales
—*Ein' feste Burg*. I sat curled up in a chair, completely happy.
Bach is complete escape.

Englewood, Sunday [March 3rd]
Darling Con,
Your letter was wise and perfect and to the point: we are march-
ing away from Mexico, and nothing can change that. Still, the
physical beauty of the place may tide them over into a new kind
of existence, and we can go back to that. The thing that vaguely
distresses me, while I feel myself caught in it, is the continual
pointing of everything to Elisabeth. *"She* understood this . . .
she loved this." I do it myself and it is of course inevitable, like
being in love with a person: even signs on the street point to
them. But still, there is an intensity about it which upsets me.
Can we never never again be casual about Elisabeth? She was so
casual herself. She was rarely—if ever—intense. You could laugh
with her on any subject.

And how grateful I am for her vanities. "Elisabeth loved pretty
clothes too, and unnecessary shoes"—as though it justified me! Of
course it's rather silly of me to talk this way about intensity, as
I'm the most intense member of the family. But I childishly resent

another person's intensity about Elisabeth, and I feel something being sucked out of me, something being sucked out of that real picture of Elisabeth, leaving it flabby and pale and meaningless. Aubrey doesn't do it, of course, nor do you. But there is something about this house when we are here, and Mother (I can understand —how can she do otherwise?). And I feel myself doing it too— not to be cold, not to be unsympathetic, to help a little. And, oh dear, I *do* want to build her into the future, somehow, into the everyday present.

I found in *The Waves:* "And then sitting side by side on the sofa we remembered inevitably what had been said by others; 'the lily of the day is fairer far in May'; we compared Percival to a lily—Percival whom I wanted to lose his hair, to shock the authorities, to grow old with me; he was already covered over with the lilies.

"So the sincerity of the moment passed; so it became symbolical; and that I could not stand. Let us commit any blasphemy of laughter and criticism rather than exude this lily-sweet glue; and cover him with phrases, I cried."

DIARY   *Tuesday, March 5, 1935*
I did quite a lot this morning, correcting three or four chapters. The things that make me squirm the most are the things I liked the best when I did them—"This wisdom I have gathered" sort of stuff. And yet I wrote it with honest feeling, but now that I've gathered a little more wisdom, the old is platitudinal. Perhaps only old people should put down wisdom, and until we get there the rest of us should just write on the surface—describe life very accurately, honestly, painstakingly—so that if an eager person reads it, he can draw his own conclusions and find wisdom there, as you do from living.

Englewood, Thursday [March 7th]

Mother darling,

You have sent me two wonderful letters, but when I think of your days I feel guilty to get letters. "The only quiet moment . . . was spent entertaining Mr. and Mrs. Portes Gil,"[1] and "scribbling thanks for flowers and invitations all the time." But I am so glad everything has gone well.

Yesterday I took Jon to Dr. [Philip] Van Ingen, in some fear and trembling. I am always jittery in Dr. Van Ingen's office. He was, however, very kind and pleased with Jon. I told him of all the difficult days we'd been through with him, and he said he didn't wonder, considering what the intensity of the house must have been this winter and that Jon was just the kind of child who absorbed his atmospheric environment like a sponge. "Give him six months of peace and he'll flourish!" So I look forward to North Haven, as it is the best place in the world for him.

We have seen quite a number of people (for us), and one night we went to the new American Ballet (Lincoln Kirstein's) with Margot. All of Smith was there, and lots of arty people. I shrunk into my disguise, a thick bang and bright lipstick *and* glasses. Even so, I was recognized. Why it matters I don't know, but oh, if only one could be completely invisible!

It is funny, my friends don't look old yet—not exactly *old*—but they all look tired, a sort of forewarning of age. I suppose I look that way too, and yet lots of old people don't. It isn't the gray hairs that do it. It's something else. Perhaps it's just New York and this time of year and the time of life when you're getting married or getting adjusted or bearing children, or caring for them.

DIARY   *Thursday, March 7, 1935*

Into town. How I adore the power of driving a good car. That is release, too, from the cramping mold I get in. Lunch with

[1] Emilio Portes Gil, President of Mexico, successor to President Calles during D. W. M.'s ambassadorship.

Margot. We talk about acting and the ballet and Rilke. Ideas grow in her presence, and her ideas in mine. The person you like best in yourself, and that you feel is the truest, comes out in the presence of these people. And we do not need to be intense either. That is grand—a person who can be intense but who also can laugh about everything. We are gay and silly and I go home happy.

Also I read *Lord Carnock*. It is hard for me to read as I don't know any of that history, and yet it is a great relief. It is completely divorced from my world—my personal world. Never, never does it say, "Here, this is you, or this is like Charles, or how unlike you, how superior to you." There are no comparisons, no threads to take me back to my life. I think I must read more history. Science would do it, only it would always be saying, "You cannot understand this. Charles could. How far behind him you are!" It would always be leading back to Charles and to me. But history does not do that. It seems more my world— not emotionally, but intellectually it interests me. It does not pull *me,* my emotions, at all—just my mind. And it is a door *out* and not *in,* a world outside, in which I can stand up to Charles and perhaps grow something to give, something we can join in and meet on that is not as personal and emotional as my world of writing.

Englewood [*March 11th*]

Dear Mother,

Dwight called me this morning and asked if I were "doing any-thing" this weekend. I said no, I never do anything. "Well, dearie, N. is in town and I thought it might be nice to ask her out for Sunday lunch. I may not be able to get down but I think it would be nice." Well, I said I'd do my best. Dwight, however, feels not only would it be nice for her but also for *me.* Dear Dwight—he thinks I *need* people. I really am past the period when I feel that there are new and wonderful people to be discovered right around the corner. I don't want to add any more interesting people to my life. In fact, I'd like to subtract a few.

Laura[1] and I had a grand talk the other day about it. We both feel the same way. It will always be fun to talk to people—exciting, too, as reading is exciting. But as for assimilating any more friends, hard lumps of friends, into the core of our lives, we don't want to do it. We laughed about it and agreed it was getting old and we rather liked it!

Elsie told me yesterday that she wanted to go home. She is very tired and she hasn't been home since Whateley died, and the trial, and she wants to explain everything to them. She says she may come back, but I doubt it. I do hate to have her go. She seems part of our life—she has been through so much with us. She seems part of our marriage, which is a funny thing to say, but at least part of the *feeling* of being married, for she was with us when we first started housekeeping in the little farmhouse. I loved that little house; of course C. didn't; it was so inefficient and cold and inconvenient and he wasn't happy that winter, but I really loved it and will always look back to it.

DIARY   *Tuesday, March 12, 1935*

Jay was at Mary and Richard's[2] tonight—apparently not averse to seeing us, so we went down to supper. A Russian (very anarchist) and his wife and Jay. I felt I could not stand the shock of the first contact with Jay [since the kidnapping and Elisabeth's death] and tried to make up sentences to tide me over that first contact. He had his back to the door so it was not hard. I could put my hand on his shoulder and say something (anything) silly, to cover the moment. It was fairly easy. Also the Russian was already arguing loudly and we could take cover under the force of his conversation.

Jay was moved, shy, apologetic, grunting bluffly and hurriedly, "Well, how are you, how are you." Then we could listen to the

[1] Laura Brandt Stevens, friend and roommate of A. M. L. at Smith College.

[2] Jay and Richard Scandrett, cousins of A. M. L., and Richard's wife, Mary.

Russian, who was interesting. But I could not listen to him, I was so intensely aware of Jay all evening. He looked small, tired, and worn, his eyes still shy and appealing and young and gentle. But the rest of his face has hardened into a kind of caricature of bitterness—the lower lip protruding, fiercely, when he talks. It always used to, but now it has set into a pronounced form and not only more exaggerated but also harder, as though carved in wood or responding to steel springs in his muscles. And his mind acting to set reactions. He was not domineering and arrogant (although not giving in at all) but, in a way, subdued and quiet and almost humble. I thought, Is it possible for this shy stubborn little boy to have hurt people—everyone who ever loved him?

I could not be gay with him as I used; I could only flash a quick appreciation of his sharp wit or of a bitter undertone in some quick clipped remark. Remarks were forced out of him metallically, clipped off him by pressure and resistance—a pencil being sharpened by a knife and the little slivers of wood curling out and spitting off. Picking up the slivers one could tell, "This was done by a knife." But he was grateful for those glances and tried (*so hard*) to be nice and to pick up my quips and tease me.

I would sit and watch Jay when he wasn't watching me. And his face, his bitter tired face, when I found it again in the room, answered something in me. I said, "There," with relief, as though it were a beautiful face. A very familiar, much-loved face does answer to the pattern of beauty in your mind, as though the face had left an imprint, a stamp. The mold was still there (isn't Beauty a mold that we try to fit objects into? If they fit the mold they are beautiful). And I said, There, that's the face, that's it, as though I had been looking and waiting for it, though I hadn't, and haven't seen Jay for about six years and never was in love with him—though we adored him and I was close to him.

There are so many different ways of loving people. I suppose people who are part of your life as you grow up, really part of your life—especially during adolescence—are bound up in you forever. (Elisabeth and Jay.)

I thought of Elisabeth all evening, and Jay thought of her. At times, I thought, we are all dead—Jay and Elisabeth and I. Certainly we are meeting on a different plane. We are not like the other people in the room. Perhaps we three are alive—Jay and Elisabeth and I—and no one else in the room is alive. Yet we must not show it.

C. was unreal, too, and young, as though we were still engaged and he on show. He talked very little but fitted in well, and I think Jay liked him, though shyly and against his will.

Then we got up to go. I hesitated—I could not shake Jay's hand and say good-by. I could not force him and myself to act out that hidden reality. I'm sure he felt the same way, for he went out and talked to a man in another room while we left. Bless him for such supreme understanding of me and the situation.

I did not talk much to C. about it, but the evening had been a strain and he knew it. He was security to come back to. He had enjoyed the Russian too. I realize that I avoid people because people mean so much to me. They throw me off keel so easily— anyone does. To remain steady I must keep away from them. I think Jay is that way instinctively. He hates people because they throw him off keel. He has gone much further than I and is fierce about it; he is chopping off the fingers of the people who cling on. He may write me a brutal letter tomorrow. Still, that evening was satisfying. I did want to see Jay once again before life was over.

Wednesday, March 13, 1935

Bought a spring coat . . . from exhaustion.

Too many people, and I got up too early, and the coat was too expensive. What makes me do things like that? Sheer weakness of character in front of sales girls and that ugly misfit person in all the other coats. "If she is so hard to fit she can't be so choosy." You'd better take this one—at least it looks "all right" on you! Also lunch with the B.'s always makes me feel shoddily dressed.

Realize I've done too much and am too tired. Too many people,

Anne Lindbergh
with Jon
at Next Day Hill,
1934

Charles Lindbergh
and Jon
at Deacon Brown's Point,
July, 1934

PHOTO ANNE LINDBERGH

*Aerial view
of Next Day Hill,
Englewood, New Jersey*
COURTESY AMHERST COLLEGE

*The Lindberghs
take delivery of
their new plane
at Lambert Field,
Saint Louis,
September, 1934*
WIDE WORLD PHOTOS

*Plane being pulled by a team of horses from a furrowed field
after the forced landing near Woodward, Oklahoma,
September, 1934. Anne Lindbergh under wing*
PHOTO CHARLES LINDBERGH

RIGHT:
*Anne Lindbergh, Jon,
Thor, and Skean
in garden at
Next Day Hill,
fall, 1934*
PHOTO CHARLES LINDBERGH

*Anne Lindbergh about to testify
at the trial in Flemington,
New Jersey, January 3, 1935*

*Anne Lindbergh, Jon, Thor,
and Skean, at
Next Day Hill*
PHOTO CHARLES LINDBERGH

PHOTO CHARLES AND ANNE LINDBERGH

View of North Haven and the mainland taken above island of Vinal Haven, looking northwest

Anne Lindbergh with Jon in the cockpit of the plane before flying over North Haven, summer, 1935
PHOTO CHARLES LINDBERGH

Deacon Brown's Point, the Morrows' summer home at North Haven, Maine

PHOTO CHARLES AND ANNE LINDBERGH

*Jon and his father
on the rocks
at North Haven*

PHOTO ANNE LINDBERGH

*Anne Lindbergh, Jon, Thor,
and Skean at North Haven*

PHOTO CHARLES LINDBERGH

PHOTO CHARLES LINDBERGH

*Anne Lindbergh and her sister Constance,
sailing off the coast of North Haven*

*Anne Lindbergh and Margot Loines
on the* Astrea, *North Haven*

PHOTO CHARLES LINDBERGH

Anne Lindbergh at her desk, Deacon Brown's Point

PHOTO CHARLES LINDBERGH

Jon at the swimming pool, Deacon Brown's Point

PHOTO CHARLES AND ANNE LINDBERGH

Charles Lindbergh's boyhood home on the west bank of the Mississippi River, near Little Falls, Minnesota. The property had recently become a state park

UNITED PRESS INTERNATIONAL PHOTO

The Lindberghs were constantly harassed by press photographers

*The Lindbergh family arriving in Liverpool, England,
December 31, 1935*

UNITED PRESS INTERNATIONAL PHOTO

and the rest of the week is irretrievably full. Nothing to be done about it. Very angry at myself.

Sunday, March 17, 1935 [Elisabeth's birthday]

A tearing wind, but still bright. I put flowers on Elisabeth's grave —not that she would want it particularly, but Mother would. I do not and cannot think of that copper vault as holding Elisabeth. The flowers, though, look like her, freesia, tulips, iris, mimosa, daffodils—very gay—and I pick some pale blue crocuses from the garden. The vase holds them erect and they blow in the wind.

At night Connie [Chilton] comes up. We look over old photographs of Elisabeth and talk of old birthdays. I had so few with her, I feel, at least in the end.

Jon loves to look at the stars, so I put him up on the window ledge tonight, but there were not many out. Jon: "We must wait till the wind blows the stars out (pause). If the wind blew one down here I'd catch it in my hand." I said only, "Would you, Jon?" but was delighted and ran to tell C. (at night), who looked mock-alarmed and said quickly, "Well, we certainly must get ideas like that out of his head. You must tell him the wind doesn't blow stars around—it blows clouds!"

Tuesday, March 19, 1935

Lunch at the Cosmopolitan Club to hear Betty[1] read. She read so beautifully that I forgot all about my cringe-feeling at being at the speakers' table, up on a stage and in the middle. She read first "Thomas the Rhymer," and then "Innisfree." I wanted to cry through "Innisfree" and then "The Stolen Child." She intoned perfectly, beautifully; one sailed off quietly on those rising notes until one was in another world. The transition from speech to music was so gradual that it was not artificial but like going to sleep, or leaving the ground, flying. I could hardly listen to "We who are old . . ." for Elisabeth's sake, but the last one,

[1] Betty Van Dusen, wife of Henry P. Van Dusen and friend of the Morrows.

> "And never was piping so sad
> And never was piping so gay . . ."
> [W. B. YEATS]

Again, the Irish understanding of the complete contradiction in life—a contradiction that finds animate form in the fairies, who are "old and gay," beautiful and hideous, small and powerful, cruel and kind. They understand that love has nothing to do with happiness, and marriage very little to do with love.

[*Englewood*] *Wednesday, March 20, 1935*

Harold Nicolson came out for lunch today, also Jo and Arthur Graeme and Miss Shiff:[1] It was not so bad meeting H. N. (Why is it such agony to meet people—at least sensitive people?) Such embarrassment that all you can do is to hold some phrase in your hands as you go up to them to bridge that gap—a buffer to take the shock, like the ones you use for boats coming up to docks. After the first bump it's all right. Then there is saying good-by, though of course you've got your past conversation to hang on to there, like a life rope. But still to have a meeting and a good-by all in one day—awful! I walked up holding out: "You look quite brown." It is easier without Mother, strangely enough, for a certain amount of responsibility makes me strengthen.

H. N. talked all through lunch, was amusing and entertaining (that's the word, that's what the British are—"entertaining"). It baffles me like sitting in a theater and looking always at a beautifully painted curtain. I keep waiting and waiting for the curtain to rise and show the real play. After lunch we all went down on the sun porch and sat and listened some more. Then gradually they left and H. N. sat and talked to me, keeping carefully to the book.

Mostly he wants to use me (quite properly, diplomatically) as a buffer between him and some of the critical family. He wants

[1] Mrs. Cecil Graeme and her son; Madelon Shiff, secretary to Harold Nicolson.

to find out what they think, to be reassured, to take the temperature of the house, for he knows I'm sensitive to it and also because I'm indiscreet and often drop out things he didn't know—not gossip, but reactions.

The curtain was hardly raised at all, although it did not seem so heavy and gaudy. For of course he is sincere about his work. I like listening to him when he talks like that. Even though he is not talking to me but always to someone else, over my shoulder. Strangely enough, I am not talking to him either, but always to someone else, over *his* shoulder, so that we never meet.

The curtain was partly raised at the end. "Will you be in North Haven in July?"—"Are you going to North Haven?"—"Yes, for the proofreading."—"I *do* hope we're there some of the time. I love it more than any place in the world, but I don't know . . . We've been quiet so long, I feel we may go off on a trip. I think Charles needs to get away from my family." We talked a little—or I did. "He needs a feeling of freedom."—"Yes, but *where* can you get it?"

Then as we were both standing up to go: "Well, if you *do* go you must keep a record. You must write about it and let yourself go more."

"No, I think I've let myself go too much in the things I've been writing lately." (Here at least I *have* to be honest.)

"No, you should let yourself go more, there is nothing more wonderful than the sensitive person leading an adventurous life. Lawrence . . ."

I said something about people who stand on the outside of adventures and write of them (thinking of myself, not Lawrence) and then tried to explain:

"The people who really do things, really have adventures, can't see them, and to the other people they *aren't adventures*. That is, it was much more thrilling watching the Greenlanders dance than going over the icecap, where you could only think about your feet being cold."

"Well, I think you keep yourself in watertight compartments."

"But I think that's the only way to live. Besides, flying, I can't afford to do anything else. I can't afford to be imaginative. I would be terrified. I've got to control it. I've got to think about cold feet over the icecap, otherwise I'd be afraid. That's what's wonderful about Charles: he has imagination but he controls it, he controls his fear."

"Yes. If only one weren't afraid . . . If I could have *one* wish, if I could ask one thing of my fairy godmother and had my life to live over again, I'd wish to be born without fear."

And then of course he had to add,

"And I don't think I'm more timid than other men."

"Well, I hope you have a good trip."

I was grateful, anyway, for one or two seconds of pure honesty, on my part as well as his.

Monday, April 8 1935

I have been much happier lately, with a kind of artificial activity: Elsie's leaving, getting a new nurse, spring clothes. The children [Constance and Dwight] down for vacation. Mother back, Aubrey and Margot. The house buzzing. Now I again realize, I have accomplished nothing, written nothing.

Sunday, April 21, 1935

Guests for lunch—and that complete numbness trying to talk to people you don't know and care about. It becomes increasingly difficult to talk to the people with whom I cannot be completely honest. It is exhausting to do it, as if you were pushing great weights—to talk, to smile, to move an arm—to listen, even. You are weighed down as in a dream. All actions are difficult and take incredible effort, as though you were under water.

Monday, April 22, 1935

We all have colds; Jon cannot go to school. Read the life of Daddy all day—it is quieting and helpful.

Mother's strength behind Daddy: her selflessness, her courage, the force of her love behind him—a great power, evident all through the book.

Mother gave a speech today, met people afterwards, spent the evening correcting the book with zest! Where does she get the strength from?

Friday, April 26, 1935

Into town, lunch with Margot. We talked about the theory of having everything "emotionally real," "mean something." I think it is a rather silly theory. All relationships have to have commonplace bases. In marriage one can get it in something physical—not the physical act of marriage, but simply the peace and security that comes from touch, rather like that of sitting on your mother's lap as a child. A rest and a security so complete and real and simple. As though one said, "This is real, because I can touch it." Relationships between women get the commonplace from those trivial feminine things they have in common: hats and brassière straps and children's problems, tomato juice and Haliver oil. I don't know what men get it from—all that business of smoking, drinking, and cussing the government. But I don't think relationships can be emotionally real all the time. It is like Emily Dickinson's

"Nature, like Us is sometimes caught without her Diadem."

Falaise, Saturday, April 27, 1935

Woke up to find it very warm and still and the sea spreading still and soft and blue way out the window in front of us. I wanted to glide out the window, with my arms spread, out into the sea. Went down and walked by the sea wall and sat for a long time—watching the horizontal ripples of the waves on the sand, thinking of all the horizontal things that give me peace and have always—waves, and long wave-marks on the sand, and flat beech branches, and tiers of pine branches, and lines of clouds in a late afternoon sky—horizons, and steps. I tried to think of any perpendicular things that gave peace: great pines close together stretching up cool and dark in a forest, and yet they don't give me peace. They pull you up, stretch you, make you grow. And then I realized what my feeling came from. Perpendicular is man erect: awake, active, growing. Horizontal is man lying down: asleep, resting. | This line is power and —— this line is peace.

I thought of Elisabeth too, peacefully, happily. I must go to Maine and Nassau and be quiet there. Then I will find her, not in Englewood, where one can't be quiet except at night, but in Maine. I want to be quiet for a long time.

Tuesday, April 30, 1935

I went down to Harcourt, Brace with *North to the Orient*. I was pretty trembly about it and before I went I did a stupid thing. I counted the number of words. It was 42,000 something. I was in a panic. It was much too short and I was already committed to talk to them.

I stop in front of the directory, people are bustling back and forth, people who go every day to Harcourt, Brace. No one knows who I am or what my business. I feel as though I were carrying a bomb. The chaste sign. The telephone girl. "Yes, I have an appointment— Mr. Sloan."—"Who is it?"—"Mrs. Lindbergh."— "What Mrs. Lindbergh?"—"Mrs. Charles Lindbergh." He came out—a nice face. In past all those desks, those people. Mr. Harcourt at the end. "So you have a book under your coat! Well, well. Sit down." "No, thank you—I don't smoke."—"I rather thought you might be bringing us a book because when Mr. Nicolson was in here he said (something nice) about the things you wrote for him about your father." I said nothing, because I was pleased.

Then about the book. I told them it was too short ("How long is a piece of string?" said Mr. Harcourt) and that it was too *old* —three years or so. Mr. Harcourt (twirling cigarettes he was making out of a white cotton bag of tobacco and thin little pieces of paper): "You mean it isn't *news*. . . . I wouldn't take a book that wouldn't have just as much value in five years' time," or words to that effect. I felt very humble, but I said it was an interesting story in itself—the trip—and that I thought one or two chapters were good and I wanted their advice on it. I told them that I came to them because I felt they published more on value than ballyhoo and I'd like them to be honest about it.

Mr. Harcourt said he was just as anxious as I to avoid the criticism: "He took that book just because Anne Lindbergh wrote it." They wanted to see it. I said it would take a week. Mr. Sloan said he would honestly tell me what he thought of it, and I believe him. I liked them both, and went out, still trembly, but happy.

Later I began to have misgivings. Why did I say so much about it? I knew what it was really like: two or three good chapters, several poor ones. The rest mediocre. I had acted as though I had "a book," as though I thought I could *write*. Why not just admit it was interesting as the story of an interesting trip—no more? Flax into gold, again, and no fairy-story elves to help.

A week of work—very hard work—at first discouraging. C. on the Preface: it should have been smoothed out before. "If I read this first paragraph I wouldn't go any further." Very discouraged. "Why did you let me go down if you think it's as bad as all that?" No, it's my fault—I had illusions of grandeur. Then just typing, rewriting, words, phrases, looking things up in the dictionary. C. going over chapter by chapter painstakingly and then with me, changing small words, phrases. I work on two or three bad places. Someone is typing in the office, running up and down with newly corrected chapters. The joy at clipping them in, all clean and neat.

Wednesday Mr. Sloan comes out. The apologies don't do any good. He wants to look at the manuscript. He says, a little cautiously, that he will really tell me what he thinks of it. That will suit them best as well as me, and we can go over it on Monday—perhaps make corrections—then he goes off. The day suddenly spreads wide and empty in front of me. I am taking care of Jon. (They won't let me know until Monday. But if it were good . . . ?) At one or two I think now he has read it. They're not excited about it, or they'd call up. I don't think it's good, so why the excitement, and what justifies letting it go out under C.'s name?

I feel that if I don't get this out and find out one way or another about writing I will burst, or just die quietly inside. I've got to find out whether or not I can and want to write, whether it is worth it. Perhaps I could throw myself into children, or a home. That is really most important anyway. Jon is most important, and if I could have another child . . . Why worry about the things that are not fundamental? If writing helped those fundamental things, so much to the good; otherwise, don't break your heart over it. It was out of proportion.

For I felt that I would more or less let their comments decide. That is, if they said it needed rewriting, etc., I would perhaps get this one out for C. but never write another. I felt convinced they would be honest, or at least that I could sift the real from the exaggerated and tell what they thought. I would meet the issue now and not go on pretending any longer that I had hidden talents that I didn't dare test for fear they might not turn out to be true. I would be honest about it and give up longing and dreaming foolishly.

Six o'clock and no word. It would be till Monday then. I did not feel exactly disappointed—just tired. It was what I expected.

At about quarter of seven, the baby in bed, I went out to walk in the garden when Banks met me: "Mr. Harcourt . . . publishing house." I rushed in, breathless. "Mrs. Lindbergh" (from out in Greenwich somewhere), "Mr. Sloan brought in your manuscript this morning and I've just finished it. I couldn't put it down. It's splendid. I would take it if it were written by Jane Smith. It's a good story, it's moving, it's well constructed, and parts of it border on poetry." By this time I was quite ga-ga and showed it—how pleased I was. Then he told me about various things to change. Wants to close deal and see Charles and me tomorrow. "You've written a book, my dear." And closing, "I have quite a little glow I don't often get." I said I'd call back.

Then I went and stood looking out the window, completely happy. They like it—and my happiness was pure and tangible and right there. It's true—I have it, then. It's here. Tasting one of those long-waited-for, on-a-pedestal moments, I almost shouted for C. I wanted so to tell him and he didn't come and didn't come.

I went out and walked in the garden, counting up the other moments like it—moments of personal triumph. Not happiness exactly, something fiercer, and probably not a very praiseworthy emotion, and yet it wasn't pure ambition, for other things entered into it—other moments of joy. The Jordan Prize announcement in chapel, but also my first proposal, and my first kiss, and then C. asking me to marry him, and my first child and my second. And soloing a plane, and that moment off Africa when I got WSL. And H. N., after reading the Geographic [article], telling me I should write. They are moments of power and fitness. They are personal, but they are more than that: "I fit into this world. There is a place for me. There is some reason for my living. I can hold my head up." It is that feeling.

C. came home and said I looked as if I had swallowed the canary. When I told him he *beamed* with pride. He was terribly, childishly proud.

We called back Mr. Harcourt to tell him I could come in, but C. not, perhaps. There was a decided droop in his voice and doubt assailed me. He wants to see Charles and not me. He didn't *really* say it was *well written,* but he just is a good businessman and knows the psychological value of . . . etc.

Very hard to sleep.

Friday, May 8th

We go over the business of the book. I think publishers are like obstetricians. There is the same fuss of making you feel what a wonderful little woman you are, and then getting down to the facts about the head size, pelvic bones, etc. They have a decided bedside manner. After all, though, they are right, you must get over the feeling that you are accomplishing God's mission,

"doing something beaut'ful
merely by being fruitful"
[OGDEN NASH]

However, I feel embarrassed talking of clothing my book, just as though the doctors were talking about an unborn child. "You don't *really* mean to say it's going to walk around on two feet like other children?"

At night, to the theater with Neilsons. I am so tired and dizzy from excitement I can't talk, I am buried down somewhere in myself, the way you are when you're in love, and can only say over and over to myself the things they had said in the office.

We send a wire to H. N. asking him if he has any objection to date of publication.[1]

Saturday

A grand letter in the morning from Mr. Sloan about the book. Very happy—just what I wanted to know. It really pleased me more than Mr. Harcourt's compliments.

Dita calls me to tell me of Aunt Hattie's death. She wants me to tell Uncle Jay.[2] Mother and I go together. It is awful walking up that quiet walk. I felt we were going to shatter it all with our news—as though we were going to kill Uncle Jay. He is at the golf club. It is a still and blooming day, ripe and lovely. We meet him walking up the hill. He sees our faces and knows. It is unbearable seeing all Mother's sorrows breaking in her, against that wall that is her strength. And Uncle Jay saying grimly with tears in his eyes, "There will be no cemetery plot for people to visit . . . we had an understanding; the ashes were to be thrown over the Gatun Spillway. There's where I did my best work and that's where we were happiest."

[1] A. M. L. did not want the date of publication of her book to conflict with that of the publication of Nicolson's biography of her father.

[2] Brigadier General J. J. Morrow, brother of D. W. M., Governor of Panama Canal Zone, 1919–24; his wife, Hattie, died while on a visit to her adopted daughter, Dita.

He seemed to have almost a return of youth, or romance, in his devotion, in his sorrow, in his energy and care about each detail of the service.

The service is quite wonderful—everyone trying to help, everyone caring about Uncle Jay. He is so pleased by the messages, the flowers, and people. (C. went down Sunday and shook his hand. Mother said, "C. is like a very beautiful woman who lends grace just by *being* present. He doesn't have to say anything or do anything—just be there.") Uncle Jay sits in his own chair, frightfully natural. Mother with those waves of sorrow breaking inside of her. I watch her throat and head thrust up—it is so gallant and beautiful, that gesture—and wonder if she can hold it all, without cracking.

The whole family is there, and friends and flowers. Aunt Hattie would have loved it: people dressed up, the low murmur of appreciative conversation, the flowers, and the spirit of helpfulness.

The walls are covered with pictures of people now dead . . . of another life. Daddy—Elisabeth—Dita's husband—little Charles —Aunt Hattie—Grandma and Grandpa Morrow.

Uncle Edwin's[1] voice: "One star differeth from another star in *glory*," and Ruth[2] singing—just the kind of family party she would have liked.

Uncle Jay, like a soldier, going out and watching the coffin go off . . . running out with a branch of lilac . . . and his sisters in the window watching.

Monday and no telegram from Harold Nicolson. I tell Harcourt, Brace I don't want to do anything until we get word back. Mr. Harcourt says H. N. won't answer and that I don't know the English! Then I come back to find the cable. Very relieved.

[1] Reverend Edwin McIlvaine, husband of Hilda Morrow, D. W. M.'s sister.

[2] Ruth McIlvaine Voorhees, his daughter.

Now everything is all right. We signed the contracts—"Author signs here →"!!! Harcourt, Brace say they sent me a letter after the *Geographic* article asking for a book. Also, that they prefer Anne *Morrow* Lindbergh. Very pleased. I call up Miss Hughes[1] to tell her about the book and she says, "Oh, how happy Mrs. Aubrey would have been!" It was sudden and personal and warm like the touch of Elisabeth's hand.

May 14th

Wednesday was a lovely day with Jon. I could really enjoy him and show him so. Suddenly smile at him, for no reason, and he smiles back, mischievous understanding. We talk about rabbits while he eats his asparagus. He with excitement: "An' if I ran after him could I catch him—an' could I walk down the street with him an' could I take him by the hand?"

He likes to go up the stairs entirely alone, with me neither before nor after him. If I step on the lowest step it spoils the whole thing and he must start over again. I can remember myself those rites, those dreadful rites that seemed so important and whose sacredness no one understood. The stairs are an entity, a whole and complete experience. It is just as much Jon's accomplishment as a house of blocks he might build himself and would not allow me to put one block on. Climbing the stairs is something he is creating, and I must not touch it.

Thursday, May 16, 1935

Work hard all day, analyze *North to the Orient* and [the chapter] "Paper and String." I cannot change it much. The whole thing is true to itself and me three years ago.

Uncle Jay comes up for supper. In a strange way he seems better than before she died. Of course he is physically hit, but mentally and spiritually it seems to me that he has been jogged out of a rut. He is reinstated by the affection, the attention, the telegrams and letters, all from a former, more successful

[1] Laura Hughes, secretary to E. R. M. M. while she was in California.

part of his life. The Canal Zone period seems the important thing, and with memories returning, he feels himself that man again and it restores his youth and confidence.

He stayed and listened to Mother and Mrs. Rublee discussing the [D.W.M.] book and Mr. Nicolson's comments. He held my hand or had his arm on my shoulder the whole time. It seemed to comfort him. Daddy used to do it, unthinking. It used to anger me. I didn't like to be just a lump of flesh that wasn't worth talking to, or even looking at, but nice to stroke, like a spaniel's ear. I wanted to be a real person, and respected as such. It seemed a little cheap to have to give happiness that way instead of through conversation or action, as Elisabeth or Mother gave it.

But I do not mind now. Because I know how those ordinary things help—inconceivably. They are bigger than I thought. They are the security of that rhythmic pat your Mother gave you rocking you in her lap. They are the safety, the infinite safety and deliverance from terror, that you got as a child, lying in bed afraid of the dark and just touching, ever so lightly, with an elbow or a knee, the older person sleeping with you. They are C.'s shoulder to lean against in a car, and Jon's rhythmic breathing, slightly moving the covers as I go in to see him at night, and his damp curls. They are trivial on-the-surface things that indicate great wells of security and faith and peace and the whole unconscious, hardly noticed, but infinitely precious structure of life.

Sunday, May 19, 1935

Sneezed all morning. Hay fever. Tired out and apathetic. I give in to it and sit in a window in the sun and listen to the Ninth Symphony. Music is the only thing that really makes me stop fearing death and age and all the other things. "There is always this," I think. It restores everything to you—everything that really matters. A touchstone.

Cannot touch the book.

I am beginning to respect the apathetic days. Perhaps they're a necessary pause: better to give in to them than to fight them at your desk hopelessly; then you lose both the day and your self-respect. Treat them as physical phenomena—casually—and obey them.

Monday, June 3, 1935

The Book goes—

Saturday, June 8, 1935

Harold Nicolson has left after four hectic days. I am glad. His being here seems to exaggerate for me the worst faults of this house. All the things that have dominion over me break out like a disease, just hidden under the surface. It has been dreadful, fighting all my worst enemies at once, my worst faults—shyness and self-consciousness—absolutely shackling, like a rheumatism. It takes the grace out of life. Every movement is painful.

Then my frightful feeling of inadequacy, especially as regards Mother. I get paler and more exhausted and less a person as she gets more energetic. I become Mother's little girl under his influence. Anything real in me is lost. I want to put my word in as I have not wanted to since I was seventeen and shy and miserable and unattractive. I have to fight all the things I fought then: shyness, selfishness, jealousy.

Sunday, June 9, 1935

C.: "Jon, would you rather be a bumblebee or a turtle?"
Jon: "I'd rather be a rabbit."
C.: "Would you rather be a turtle or a bullfrog?"
Jon: "I'd rather be a rabbit."
C.: "Would you rather be a bullfrog or a . . ."
Jon: "I'd rather be a rabbit."
However, he admits he does not want *me* to be a rabbit—wants to be a rabbit by himself.

Later—

C.: "Jon, whom do you like best—your father or your mother?"
Jon (very slowly): "I like better . . . (pause) *rabbits!*"

Monday, June 17, 1935

It was a very strange day—on the platform in those robes.[1] I
was Mrs. Charles Lindbergh. "I know—I am getting this as
C.'s wife—really for C., but still—yes—I take it as that. It is
all right." And then suddenly, President Neilson called my
name, Anne Morrow Lindbergh (the *Lindbergh* was a strange
shock!) and began to read the citation. And I felt that he was
speaking right to me, way down into me, like an omniscient
father or one's old idea of God. He was praising me not for
what the newspapers and what the world saw, but for those
inner struggles inside of me. He saw. He understood. He knew
what life had been and what had been hard for me. It didn't
look like much achievement—for anyone else—but for me,
yes. He knew. He understood. It was unbelievably thrilling.
"Say not the struggle naught availeth, The labour and the
wounds are vain."

Con carrying off all the honors![2] I can hear Elisabeth saying,
"Little *Con!*"—just the inflection and the tone—that expression
of pride and half-humor and surprise. "She just *would*—she
would. Little *Con*—Wouldn't you know it!"

An extraordinarily nice relationship, that of Con and President Neilson: intellectual understanding, using the same symbols and values and language, so that just a word or two suffices
for the exchange of thought. A practical, working relationship
there, and reservoirs of affection and trust behind it, like that
between father and daughter.

[1] A. M. L. was given an honorary degree at Smith College.

[2] C. C. M. graduated *summa cum laude* from Smith College.

[North Haven] Friday, June 21, 1935

Today it came out in the paper about C.'s pump[1] to keep organs alive. It is thrilling to me—the accurate, bare account in the *Times*. I am glad to have it known, and glad, in a way, for the publicity on this thing. Not publicity in itself, but as though the right values were being set, even for his other achievements. Every act of his is not a fluke, not chance, not charm and youth and simplicity and boyishness but the expression of a great mind that can turn its searchlight in more than one direction.

North Haven. Elisabeth is not here either. I thought somehow I would find something of her here. Perhaps I will when I am accustomed to it; now I just feel restless and far away from her. Except in that wonderful book of Peter Rabbit: Mrs. Flopsy setting off across the wide lawn on a hazy morning to find her children. The blue apron, the erectness of the rabbit, the expanse of lawn—it is all our childhood and Elisabeth in that figure.

Monday, July 1, 1935

Left Long Island Aviation Country Club at 4:23. Landed North Haven via Matinicus 7:34.

That delicious feeling of setting off over Long Island Sound —what is it? Boundless, smooth, blue, like a child's idea of summer, endless, bright, stretching out ahead—"the world is mine" feeling.

Seeing right down into the water, into channels and watercourses, harbors and reefs, so plainly defined. You wondered why those silly little buoys were needed up on top to show the boats where it was safe to go when it was so plain from above. Flying is like X ray, letting you see through to the bones of the earth.

[1] C. A. L. had designed and constructed an apparatus in which living organs could, for the first time, be perfused for long periods at controllable pulse rates and pressures, and without the entrance of infection.

Jon is up to see us. "I seed it on the ground. Did you hear the big noise?"

Tuesday, July 2, 1935

We sail in the *Mouette* to Matinicus. A happy day, C. and I, alone, steering the boat. I feel young and just married, as on our first trip. The Camden Hills from Matinicus are small, withered, flattened out, and indescribably *wrong*. I have a childish feeling of disillusion, to have my eternal landmarks move, change, dwarf, as though some eternal truths were being shaken. "*You* aren't secure either," I feel like saying, "or everlasting."

It was like the feeling of shock at seeing your parents helpless the first time, and realizing that they weren't all-powerful and that they too were forced by outward things and suffered.

We think we will build on Matinicus. It is a calm day— delicious and smooth. C. wishes it were rough. He says with a glint in his eye, "I bet there are terrific waves here in a storm." I think only: Yes, I can live here.

Wednesday, July 3, 1935

I read over my old diaries last night: last year at college, the summer before I was married. I have changed so little. All the faults just the same: self-centered, worrying about my sins; daydreaming, running away from the people I like best. And all the things I wanted to do—the writing—the same, only it has taken me about six years to get back there again. I am the same, only the things that were simply indications have hardened. As though the thing that is I had passed through the fire of C. and all that C. has meant in my life. A kind of change has taken place. The shape is the same but the metal has changed. And yet it gave me a feeling of great confidence at recognizing myself— finding again the straight stick inside of me, that is I. I must keep it.

Thursday, July 4, 1935

Charles thinks perhaps we can live here, build a little home on a near point. We both love it. I have roots here. It is convenient and accessible.

It makes me so happy, I can hardly take it, as though a kind of security was mine forever—this place and all it gives back to me. It is too good to be true. I can't believe it and even object to it. I must not persuade him. I want it so much that I must only take it if he wants to in spite of all objections.

We walk over the points. I feel tired. We have been doing things every moment since we arrived: Matinicus, the sea-raft, sailing, Jon in the pool, walking. I want to sit still a long, long time and let everything pour back into me—Elisabeth and my old self and the sense of being alone.

Friday, July 5, 1935

A beautiful day. I get all my books and papers, downstairs in the study. A grass-cutter motor starts outside my window, back and forth, back and forth, steadily insistent, getting farther away and then a roar nearby. I writhe and wait for the recurring roar. I hope he finishes before C. comes.

C. comes up, tight-lipped. "It's getting to be a Long Island estate—noise worse than an airplane factory." I agree but feel terribly depressed. We walk out to the point; a mowing machine has thrashed down all the daisies. They are spread out withered in the sun. Over to the little house, a van of furniture has just moved up to the door. They are unloading it. C. clicks on his heel and turns away.

TO E. L. L. L.   *North Haven, July 7, 1935*

Dear "Farmor,"[1]

It is a rainy day and I am at my desk. Jon is sitting at a little table next to me, drawing pictures and then cutting them out.

---

[1] Swedish for father's mother.

I have been dreadful about letters, I think because writing has meant work this winter. Here it is different, and the book is all done—proofs, maps, *everything*. It is off. I will never see it again. It comes out August 15th.

I have not written you about C.'s exploits, which you understand much better than I. I really was so happy about them. He would do as well in anything he turned his mind to. It is genius. I really think it is and it has been recognized by those scientists. People have said that his work—enabling science to keep alive organs outside of the body—opens a new field, just the way the microscope opened a new field for work, endless possibilities. C. is very happy about it.

He has been working hard this spring, on that project, on writing it up, on my book, on getting Elsie off to England (she has arrived safely, we just heard) and on a second report. C. is working on the proofs now. It is entirely on the apparatus, and highly technical. These first days here in North Haven he has spent in active sports—swimming, sailing, aquaplaning off the end of the *Mouette* (C. is very good at it). He has been a great deal with Jon, taking him every day to the pool and throwing him in! He has got Jon to swim the length of the pool and back in a life preserver and partway in water wings (much less buoyant). He says he has given Jon quite rough treatment (I cannot bear to watch, I am so soft-hearted), but Jon seems to thrive under it and C. says, "He certainly is a game little youngster." Jon says he likes his father best now and me next!

Here is one of Jon's conversations with Aubrey Morgan (who was here a week).

Jon is looking for wild strawberries and putting them in a basket.

Aubrey: "Jon, come and help me look for golf balls."

Jon: "Dun't want to look for golf balls; want to look for strawberries."

Aubrey: "Oh, come on, Jon, and help me look for golf balls."

Jon: "Can't eat golf balls."

Doesn't that sound like Charles!

We are working over ideas for a home of our own next winter.

North Haven [*July 7*]

Darling Con,

Sleepers Awake is my song! It is the *chorale* in the very end, the next to last record. It is simply heavenly. And I have been singing it only slightly wrong for seven years! It is all lovely—the first cantata too, a wonderful present. Con, dear, I do appreciate it. Did you play it—or was it just a lucky try?

Speaking of presents—the evening dress is a present, most of it anyway.

We are still in the preparation stage here—you know, a load full of furniture going over to the Little House. One of the Grant nephews walking slowly back and forth in front of the house with a huge lawn mower chugging along like a tractor, Chester Dyer upstairs sawing on a door that sticks, Mother hanging pictures, and C. and I moving furniture. The two aunts (Alice and Agnes)[1] are here, and Auntie Paul and cousin Francis came over today for the day! C. and six women! I tremble at every lawn-cutter and blow of a hammer—and C. saying it is "just like Englewood." I think each time, "We will never come again—this will finish it."

Of course there always *were* those days at North Haven—weeks, when we waited breathless, and said staunchly, this is the last batch of visitors, or this is the last noisy week. After this, no more moving or hammering—"a war to end wars" kind of talk. Next week, it will be the quiet, blissful, fruitful, full-of-work North Haven we dream of. I suppose it is rather a dream. Or perhaps we had more escape when there were more young people. I am more conscious of it now because I am feeling two people's annoyance. I want so much to have C. like it—and how I hate perpetually making excuses, explain-

---

[1] Alice Morrow and Agnes Morrow Scandrett, sisters of D. W. M.

ing, saying, "This will be the last." "So and So is coming, but you know *her*."

Besides, if you were here I would rather enjoy kicking about the interruptions. There was fun even in that—in escaping.

Monday Thelma comes, which will be such fun, and an antidote for the subduing effect of H. N. and son, Mr. and Mrs. Rublee and Chester and Amey (not that I don't like them—but so *many*, all together!). "A very nice group," Mother says patly. "I think it always goes better when you have a lot of people." I don't agree except for a definite "party" when you want to be slightly artificial anyway—and a lot of people create that atmosphere.

As a matter of fact I shall rather enjoy watching them interact. But C. won't. If only Aubrey were here. Dwight will be a help, but I'm afraid he is going to summer school.

We have had some nice sails. The sailing is very satisfying.

I feel that Elisabeth is here somewhere—if we could just stop talking about her and could be quiet long enough.

I *love* my record—music is *the* complete escape.

DIARY   *Monday, July 8, 1935*

I did not sleep last night for sheer excitement and weariness, after correcting C.'s article. I read it out loud. Such frightful language—I understand none of it. We correct all morning. I think it was a help for C. I felt happy doing it.

Harold Nicolson and son arrive. Not as bad as meeting people generally is. Thor was a help, running out to bark so that I had to hold him back. Son looks *just* like her. That proud and beautiful face, the half-closed-blinds look to the dark eyes. He is quick and perceptive and sensitive and shy (though English people never show a thing under their masks). I like him. H. N. is much more natural here, and very nice. We play hard tennis, I with the boy, who plays well—strokes like swallows.

Tuesday, July 9, 1935

A lovely day—swimming and tennis—a breathless day. Then, in the evening, driving around the island, and singing, at last, all the intensity that I don't know what to do with . . . singing it out. At last being completely natural in the dark in the back seat alone.

And still quite unable to go to sleep. The feeling that sleep enters my eyes and is trying to pour down my whole body, but it can't get by that place in my chest that isn't a pain exactly but a throbbing tightness.

Friday, July 12, 1935

Harold Nicolson talking to his son about choice of career. He wants to be a painter but he really doesn't think he can, or can afford to waste a year finding out. I know exactly how he feels: "What is there to justify my taking myself so seriously!"

H. N. talks about writing and how if you want terribly to do a thing you probably have it in you. "I can! I can!" pounds inside of me, so loud that I feel it is bursting out of me, and yet I feel I must not show it because it is unproved and untried. Caring about writing and not having proved anything is like being in love and not being able to show it. And all the time it is pushing inside of you—that giant.

Saturday, July 13, 1935

Perhaps if one has complete understanding and complete expression writing is unnecessary.

Off on the boat with Jon, in the evening. Jon is very good and still and happy, looking at the gulls and the houses on shore and the sailboat in the distance. He eats cornflakes and milk happily.

Sunday, July 14, 1935

Thelma has left. She makes me feel free and that it is possible to remain myself and yet make something quite wonderful out of marriage. Those moments of being completely aware of life are marvelous, but not necessary to have every day. One cannot live so dangerously aware all the time. One cannot walk a tightrope, and look down at one's feet walking, with abysses on each side. She makes me free for a moment and it seems easier now to take up life again—the old role. I have not written anything since she was here. It wasn't necessary—but writing is my flywheel and I need it, even very trivial private writing.

Monday, July 15, 1935

I feel marvelously released this morning, calm and controlled with the day stretching out ahead. The mist has come in, shutting me in, thrusting me back on myself. The mist is cooling too. To have the world drenched in it is a relief. It coincides with the feeling in my mind, as though my mind had been plunged into cold water.

It was a lovely day. I wrote about a shy girl. I thought I would try to do it quickly, make myself finish it, like those swift water colors, one right after another, as fast as possible. It was satisfying, anyway, and perhaps good practice.

Then at night I felt suddenly free, unself-conscious, happy and in control of myself, so that my words and actions *did* seem to proceed from me and I could say almost anything.

Tuesday

Some typing and some golf. Mother home: her annoyance at the house not going as well as it should, my feeling it's my fault. Her energy behind the pantry door, adjusting small details. ("Did you get the two pitchers—the two yellow pitchers?")

Cannot write—feel my general inadequacy next to Mother. She carries action and life into whatever room she walks. I carry shyness and silence and inaction. It spreads in pools around me wherever I go....

At night C. talks to me—beautifully, so beautifully: that I can do anything I want to do, write anything, do anything I set my mind to. His faith is thrilling although I cannot believe him—what proof is there? But even his faith makes me feel better.

Friday, July 19, 1935

The Rublees. Mrs. Rublee asks questions about Italy, Abyssinia, and the League. Harold Nicolson is very interesting answering them. And I enjoy it. I like hearing him talk about disarmament and the hope, or no hope, for peace. He believes about the relationships between countries all the things I believe about relationships between people.

Saturday, July 20th

Playing golf on the little course—walking down that hill of green on the second hole, swinging at daisies, the wind blowing through me, and feeling perfectly happy. Then through the cut at the bottom—the wet path, with the ferns on either side and the sea ahead. The lighthouse and the sea and the island suddenly rushing in on me, through that cut. Then up the hill, the wind blowing up my arms, through my sleeves, my skirt flapping against my legs—the sea and all of life blowing up the hill to me.

Sunday, July 21st

Jon swims alone. C. has been making him go out first with the life preserver, then water wings, then one wing, and then nothing. The Rublees go, and H. N. Mother and I take H. N. to the boat. I mind that we will not see him again. I wish people did not mean so much to me.

Monday, July 22, 1935

Amey talks to me this morning, first about keeping a diary. She feels that it is a mistake to write constantly, to force out "half-baked ideas" instead of just letting them grow inside until they come out inevitably. She talks about all philosophies and all religion—the best in any spiritual thinking—preaching self-negation: *get rid of self.*

It is probably true, and yet I don't think I can get rid of self by stamping on it. I've tried that and it just rears its head more terribly than ever. You must throw yourself into something else.

Your daily emotions are not important enough to warrant being written down, Amey thinks. Everyone has them, everyone goes through them, do not give so much weight to them. I think she is right . . . and yet I still think I must write out what I feel, otherwise there is too much stopped up in me. They become more important *not* written.

The Puritan in me tells me she is right. Myself always comes first, and that is the trouble. Keep up the fight always, like the Sunday School precepts; keep on trying to kill it, forget happiness and those selfish longings and try to throw yourself into C. and Jon, Mother and other people. Jon seems to be the easiest, only *there* do I really wish I could suffer for him—suffer fear and hardship, anything. I suppose that is selfish, too.

C. and I have a lovely talk on the point. He is security and peace. We decide that really Jon is the object of life—giving to him what we have learned, so the next generation is better. What is "better"? We talk about people. C. is sick of people and silly talk and useless dinner conversation. I get something even from that—I like it. And as I look over the people who have been here, I am glad for all of them and they all give me something. It is none of it wasted. Aunt Alice with her staunch loyalty and Aunt Agnes, who seems absolutely selfless, who never intrudes. And Thelma—quick, lightning understanding.

To see the way different people have worked out marriage is wonderful. As though each one had been given a block of wood to make something of. For some it is easy and seems all ready-made. For others, very very difficult—some people give up. Many of us think it should be given to us ready-made, all carved, and then throw it away to pick up a new one, expecting *that* to be all carved. I don't think you ever get a perfect marriage given to you. It is like your face, or your body, or your circumstances, or your life. It's given to you to make something out of. I think of Daddy's life that way, what he was given and what the limitations were, and what he made of it. It is wonderful. The book has given me that. Not only has it given back to me a sense of what he was and what he did, but it has given me a great sense of strength in myself.

I suddenly feel my heritage, feel him in me. It is mine. "He bore transplanting into common ground." It is in me, *some* of that strength and tolerance and vision, and the ability to make something out of my life, my marriage, my work. I am challenged by it, and I feel a great wall of strength behind. My mind is challenged when Harold Nicolson talks, about peacemaking, about governments, about history. Something of my father rises in me, is pulled by it, finds itself fascinated, finds it can understand and grasp and wants more!

Thursday, July 25, 1935

There is so little waste about C. I was thinking about it at the [Long Island Aviation] Country Club. He ran into the Department of Commerce Inspector during lunch. C. talks to him, finds out about the new tailless plane. The inspector, for his part, finds out about monocoupes. No small talk, no chaff, no waste!

To Cleveland.

Flying again. Intensely clarifying, satisfying, and soothing. I feel freed to think over everything, released and older. There seems to be so much I want to do, to read, to write. "One can't afford to waste an inch of mind." Will I have time to do what I want with my life, carve out marriage and keep wanting to write, like this? I want to keep this reborn feeling I had in college, that my mind was an able tool and that life was not long enough for all the things I wanted to read and think and see and analyze and write.

The radio weather report. That monotone that is somehow so exciting: "Sunbury—Sunbury—overcast—scattered clouds—ceiling estimated four hundred feet." (Not too good to Washington.) Out of the dry report [further west] that wonderful word, like a window opening: "unlimited."

Take off. The low gray curtain is down on all sides but light underneath. A storm toward Sandy Hook, purple with pink spots, like a bruise. Storm over Newark, sea and sky merged, intense purple. Muddy sky ahead.

One thousand feet. Storm to our left, light to our right. Suddenly the Delaware—green islands in its arms.

Storms into Cleveland—and my terror. The beauty of them —veils of rain like brooms sweeping the ground. Flying gives a healthy awe of the elements, like farming and the sea.

July 26th

Take off at Chagrin Falls for Cleveland airport. C. goes in our plane and Dave Ingalls[1] takes me in his. That strange feeling of seeing C.'s head out of the window of a plane, me on the outside, as it used to be, before I was his.

[Leaving] Cleveland hot, unlimited, except for a ground haze, the second-horizon look. We follow the lake, which goes off into haze, as though the water reached a higher level in the sky. The lake is green, dappled with blue shadows of clouds.

There is no way to describe clouds, the peace, the exaltation of flying through them. It is being transported to another realm, like one's early idea of heaven—the pearly gates, the

[1] Naval aviator and World War I ace, Assistant Secretary of the Navy for Aeronautics, 1929–32. The Lindberghs had landed at Chagrin Falls, Ohio, to visit their friends David and Louise Ingalls.

gleaming towers, colors too dazzling, pure, iridescent for earth; shapes too fantastic, and the earth lying so flat and drab below. A giant growth—a jack-and-the-beanstalk land.

Iowa, southern Minnesota, very flat, beautiful crops. Those minute piles of grain in the fields—an ant's store. The Mississippi coming in, a long shadow to our right, a gap of blue. The towers of Minneapolis, surrounded by lakes and rivers. The young Mississippi—early manhood. The dark band of trees skirting the river, the gleam from some roofs—Saint Cloud. Following the river around a bend Little Falls.[1]

Friday, July 26, 1935

This has been a strange four days. I must write at once and hope I can remember. I feel terribly grateful for Little Falls and seeing C.'s aunts and talking to C. about it. It has made me understand so much, in him, in his father, in his mother, in marriage—in me.

As we approached Little Falls, it got frightfully hot. C. pointed things out: a village they used to drive through; the river, full of logs; the spires of Little Falls, a water tower, a mill, the dam; and on the river, above an island, "The Farm." We circled it: a wooden strip, pines, a creek lost in the trees; fields behind, that C. used to plow, and the roof of the house, backing on the river.

We landed at Fort Ripley, a modern army camp outside of Little Falls.

Drive into town. The sign on a water tower: "Charles A. Lindbergh's home town welcomes you." Little Falls is just like hundreds of other small towns in the West: the brick buildings on a main street, the drugstores, the nondescript hotel, the gas stations, the plate-glass store-front windows. Not one building stands out in my mind; not one different from another

[1] Little Falls was C. A. L.'s home town during boyhood and early youth. The Lindbergh family farm lay on the west bank of the Mississippi River, about a mile southward.

or hundreds like it in the West for me to remember. Yes, the post office was rather a nice brick building apart from the others, in grass and shrubs.

A hot wind and dust and hair flicking in my eyes. We cross the bridge to the "West Side" and stop in front of an old building with dowdy store windows on the ground floor—not dirty, not run-down, but nothing to attract the eye or to distinguish it from other stores. Just plate-glass windows with Coca-Cola posters and magazines.

C. went in, and came out followed by a short man, unshaven and sleeves up, a farmer's rough look about him, but a nice face, honest, kind, and dependable—Mr. Engstrom.[1] He welcomed us and said he could put us up. I jumped out. Mrs. Engstrom stood at the door. She was pretty and delicate-looking, with that incredible smooth, soft complexion some women have, and beautifully waved auburn hair; a little shy. She has a sense of what she is and what she isn't, what she has and what she hasn't, that he has not got. He was perfectly frank, unembarrassed, natural, and self-respecting. Another woman, "Lottie," behind the soda fountain (gray hair and a cheerful face, not self-conscious: "Well, Charles, how are you?" "Well, Charles"!

We mopped our faces, had a glass of water from the soda fountain, and started right out to see "The Farm," Mrs. Engstrom driving along a dusty road ("very little changed") past shacks and small farms with now and then a glimpse of the river. Into the woods: pine, birch, poplar, and oak. The Farm:[2] a big anchor fence around the grounds; a round driveway now

---

[1] Martin Engstrom, an old friend of Charles Lindbergh, who owned the West Side hardware store and soft-drink parlor.

[2] The farm and buildings were given by the Lindbergh family to the State of Minnesota in 1931, for a park. The house has now been restored and much of the original furniture returned under the direction of the Minnesota Historical Society.

overgrown; a good-sized house, clapboard, of no particular form or style. There were several tourists wandering about and a boy in a scout hat watching them.

We went up the stoop into the kitchen and met a large old stove and boiler from which the screws and handles had been wrenched off by tourists. The rooms were bare, dark, varnished woodwork doors and sills, light-colored walls; only a few scattered things left, as though a family had just moved out and deserted it: a tumble-down icebox, some old bedsprings, a bulky dusty bookcase that turned on a swivel.

An old man showed us around. Mrs. Engstrom remarked on the lovely living room. It had a bay window and was quite big. The screened porch was deliciously cool and right in the trees, looking down over a steep bank to the river. Here, C. said, they lived most of the time. Upstairs, the old man rattled keys and opened the closet doors. The attic had some old trunks, falling-to-pieces furniture, sofas, and crates. C. found an incubator he had made. It was stifling. We went down into the basement which was cool. An old broken-down car—a Saxon —the one C. took out west. "Hello Lindy" was scribbled on the walls.

Outside again, we walked over the place and saw where the fire burned the trees long ago, the seared marks where the bark curled away, like unhealed scars. Down by the river it was cool, a breeze and the sound of it in the poplars.

The moo-pond,[1] and across the road to the creek—very hot and windless. We walk and walk, C. eager to find the old places. The old trees—some beautiful big pines; white-pine needles, the silver-green color of the sea. The creek, where C. swam, has dried up. We find the spring and the big pine where they had picnics. C. plunges ahead with Engstrom, zeal on his face.

I know—I have felt it, too, revisiting North Haven and

---

[1] A small concrete pond C. A. L. made for his ducks.

Northampton, that longing to find something that pushes you on. I couldn't complain, I must see it Charles's way, I must try and feel it with him.

Mrs. Engstrom and I stagger along behind, she in high-heel shoes and I in ones already wet (from slipping in the creek), waving handkerchiefs round our necks and stamping our feet to keep the mosquitoes off. Finally we reach the car and start back for supper (C. forgot that in his eagerness). We stop and see two Swedish families. A Mrs. "Yonson"[1] comes out of the door, a wisp of a woman, thin, but with a young girl's figure. She has pale, wispy hair drawn up in irregular strands on her baldish head; a scrawny face, thin, colorless, and lined. She peers at C. suspiciously and then capitulates, girlish, smiling, shy, and sweet. It is intensely moving. She has the beauty of a young girl in love when she smiles and a lovely musical Swedish voice that ripples: "So! I cou'n tink it was Mr. Leenberg. So!" I could not keep my eyes off her. This, I feel, is the first thing that has *really* touched me.

Then, seeing more people, and a dusty drive home, dead tired. It is terribly hot. Mrs. Engstrom gives her room to us— the front room which has the breeze. She will sleep in the back room in a double bed with Mr. Engstrom. I cannot think of such discomfort—our room is hot enough. We cannot open the second window: no screen. A large double bed, dark woodwork, high ceiling. On the wall, Mr. Engstrom's Hardware Diploma, a picture of a beautiful lady, a cut-out parrot, a spray of painted yellow poppies, a framed poem of Edgar Guest on the bureau, lace covers on the tables, a heavy red crocheted cover on the bed box, a large leather rocking chair, shell and bead caps for the lights.

I try to help with supper. The dining room is in a small hall between the parlor and kitchen: a Grand Rapids glass

[1] The Johnsons were farm neighbors of the Lindberghs and their children playmates of C. A. L.

cabinet, a table, and pictures of Glacier National Park, and "Welcome gifts" (a water color of apples, grapes, and a bunch of violets); also the old war cartoon of the doughboy saying good-by to his dog. A good supper: potato salad, meat and egg cooked together, a heavy frozen pudding, and bread and butter. We wash dishes and go off again, stopped by the Bolanders,[1] downstairs to meet us—she, effusive; he, taciturn. "*Such* good friends of Mr. Lindbergh."

Back to our room. I cannot write in my diary—too tired, hot, and discouraged. It's no use, I couldn't possibly write, read, or even think in this environment. There are noises all night —trains and street noises. I am so tired I only dimly hear them, but one thing seemed to recur regularly, and I had the impression that it was an engine simply roaring in the window and over the bed, running me down! C. woke up once and said dimly, "I can get used to everything . . . except that!"

Sunday, July 28, 1935

Drive to Melrose—talk with C. about his family.

Monday, July 29, 1935

Aunt June[2] for supper. Wonderful talk about C.'s grandmother. Louisa Carlin was the second wife of August Lindbergh, thirty years' difference. He was about fifty; she, twenty. They homesteaded in 1860 on Sauk River. The first house was a log cabin. It was hard farming. She milked the cows in her silk dresses, because calico was expensive (a dollar a yard) after the Civil War and she had silk dresses from Sweden. Also lots of little bonnets, worn over the back of the hair, with flowers or ribbons on top and a ribbon under the chin—a bonnet for each dress. (Aunt June remembers especially a little gray bonnet.)

---

[1] Carl Bolander, real-estate dealer, at one time partner of C. A. L.'s father.
[2] Mrs. William A. Butler, younger sister of C. A. L.'s father.

She was very homesick—cried and cried. The cow died and she sold her gold watch (from Sweden) to buy a new one.

Louisa had a white silk parasol, with a carved white filigree handle. It was borrowed by neighbors if anyone was going to Sauk Center. The family photograph was a great occasion—all drove in an oxcart to Sauk Center.

Louisa had the first sewing machine in the community. People would come for miles around, bring a big basket of sewing and stay all day.

Tuesday, July 30, 1935

To Detroit.

Thursday, August 1, 1935

Detroit to North Haven. A clear day. Under the cup of a very blue sky lies a layer of white clouds. In the distance—the sun on them—clouds are flowerlike, with the iridescent quality of narcissus or lilies. They seem floating on depths of water—water lilies, their stems hidden in the dark water below.

The Adirondacks are past at Lake Placid. The Green Mountains over at the Connecticut. Only the White Mountains (the highest) to pass. One half-hour to the border of Maine. We are about eight thousand feet, clouds at six thousand. Mount Washington, a little over six thousand, is simply a dark brunt of a peak in a circle of clouds.

The coast—a dim demarcation in the blue haze to our right. The fretted bays of Portland.

[North Haven], Sunday, August 4, 1935

One of those days when, as Amey says, "the black drop" is in me. It is partly reaction from the last week—or two weeks, almost, of traveling. A completely wasted day because I tried not to waste it. Instead of lying out in the sun I tried to sit at my desk and write.

The trip out west was a success. I think I gave in understanding and appreciation and delight, for I did *relish* it so. You can't simulate that. But now, coming back, I am tired. The apathetic days are so many, the energetic so *rare*.

Friday, August 9, 1935

Laura and I get started talking about apathy and its cause. I say it is the natural reaction of forcing yourself into things you don't want to do. Forcing yourself only makes it worse. The only help is to give in to it. It is like sailing, I think. You can't force a boat to go further into the wind than it can, and by trying to, you lose speed and control. The only thing to do is to give it its head. It will swing and swing and then suddenly catch the wind, bite into it, and go—find speed and control again. Then of course you're out of position and have to tack back. But you get there quicker that way.

We talked about the dead periods in anything—do they mean growth? Or does apathy come from trying to do what the other person or circumstances want (because living is easier that way), pushing and pushing until the spark inside of you is dead?

How to get the spark back? By giving in to the apathy? Or must someone from the outside give it to you? Harold Nicolson gave it to me while he was here. Now it has melted away. Elisabeth, of course, gave it to me. And today Laura gave it by being there ahead of me with her understanding. She seems always to be there ahead of me. So funny: I have been looking at her all winter and saying, "How *can* she do it—how *can* she?"

I told Laura this, and she has been looking at me and thinking *I* was succeeding because I was keeping the spark alive! *At what price,* I say, *and to what good?* "For this," said Laura: "helping me, like this."

Today was a nice day, for I had Jon—most of it. He was very good, chewing on a chop-bone lunch. After his nap we went down with a basket to the tennis court to pick raspberries.

As we approached, Jon said, "Now you go play tennis." He was perfectly happy for an hour. I could see him—his curls among the raspberry brambles, his yellow sweater and brown pants. Finally he went up and sat on the top of a hill on a rock. I came up after tennis. He was putting raspberries into "dishes" (shells). "What a lovely place this is for Jon," I said, "with a stump and a hole to hide things in (under the stump), and a little pine tree." Jon repeated it after me and added, "And a raspberry bush just behind." We hid the shells in the hole and decided to take the raspberries back to Daddy Bee [E. C. M.]. "They're just a little bit squashed, just a very little bit squashed," said Jon, picking them up from the dirt.

Friday, August 16

Will Rogers, killed in plane crash at Barrow.[1] The day is knocked out and down to some other level. Mrs. Rogers—how dreadful to have her fears justified. So unnecessary—so unanswerable and so *terrifying*.

C. is telephoning all day, suddenly electrified into steely usefulness (no waste about him—everything counts)—and a deep understanding and respect for Mrs. Rogers' grief.

TO E. L. L. L.   *North Haven, August 17*
Dear Farmor,
Yesterday Jon had his birthday cake with three candles. Nancy and Dwight Scandrett (age three and one-half and eighteen months) were visiting us. I took some pictures. I had three balloons tied to the chairs. (Two broke before the ceremony was over!) Jon has used his big ball for a football, and is very pleased with it. He has also read the paint-book—not colored it yet. The sand machine was almost torn to pieces by Nancy and Dwight and had to be rescued. We will try it again quietly, as it has possibilities!

[1] Will Rogers and Wiley Post, his pilot, were killed when their seaplane crashed while taking off from a lagoon near Point Barrow, Alaska.

Jon was not a very good host. When the children appeared he took his balloon and said, "I'm going upstairs now"! And he was completely oblivious to Nancy's sweetly sung "Happy birthday to yooo," crawling under the bench after a ball the whole time. C. (sticking his head out the window, at the scene below) said tersely, "Just his father's reaction!"

He repeated that he was three ("free") years old—and, when questioned, said he liked his birthday.

C. is proud of his swimming. He swims about eight feet (under water) and can pull the big water mattress out of the pool by himself.

DIARY   *Tuesday, August 20, 1935*

Jon has a cough.

C. talks to me all morning about what I will write next. He is wise and sweet about it. But the morning is gone and I have not had any time alone and I have not written anything.

Wednesday, August 21, 1935

C. wants me to go back to Minnesota with him—tomorrow to New York? I dread it.

[North Haven to Long Island], Thursday, August 22, 1935

I gave in to it today and it was much better. C. was an angel. He understood. I tried to explain that I felt the summer had been a complete failure—as wife, as mother, in trying to write and even just in trying to get strong. He was a comfort and said it had not been a wasted summer for him—the Institute article and Minnesota—and that he felt much better than when he came up. He said the book let me off for a long time—"sit back on it, don't try to write"—that we needed a home and we would get it. He is not worried about Jon. It was a great relief. I am going with him to Long Island and undoubtedly Minnesota.

A terrifying trip down [to Long Island]: rain, fog, and

thunderstorms. As usual, I think we're going to be killed and think of Wiley Post. Physical terror, though, and proximity to death (even though just apparent) give one a wonderfully tenacious appreciation of life when they are over. After we finally landed in a driving rain at Long Island (the field was silvered with pools, a sheet of water over *all* of it), everything was so beautiful: water dripping slowly off the roof, wet grass and puddles, the trees on the way to Harry's,[1] and the sky, still and streaked with gold after the storm.

Sunday, August 25, 1935

C. and I walk over the place.[2] The fire to "clear out" brush has burned some of the trees. C. is cross about it and takes me over there. Incredibly stupid—he'd fire the man who did it— he points out each scarred tree. "See here, they laid the wood right on the roots. That tree will never come back. Some of our best trees are ruined," etc.

[Falaise], Tuesday, August 27, 1935

"Zero—zero" over the mountains. Low blurred horizon. We cannot go till tomorrow.

I walk down the sea wall in the evening. It is delicious. I feel happy and released in walking and feeling the air through my clothes, and in watching the gulls duck into the water for snails and sail just over the mirrored surface, then arch their wings and flutter up perpendicularly, braking themselves (use of "flaps") to land. Then all the gulls sit on the smooth wave and glide out with the tide. Gulls take off *into the wind,* and turn if they want to go oppositely.

And the startled stillness of rabbits. I feel I have done a great thing if I can get by one without frightening it away. I wait

---

[1] Falaise, the Guggenheim home at Port Washington.

[2] The Lindberghs were considering buying a plot of land from the Guggenheims at Port Washington.

and watch one nibble the grass, its whole face twitching, for I can't bear to frighten it. I love sea grass, swept and combed in one direction like wavy hair, and haws of wild roses. I love that long point tapering out into the bay in the distance, yearning out to sea. I am so happy I do not want anything or anyone, as though someone I loved were walking with me and I was satisfied.

Long Island to Detroit, August 28th

Weather report: "Clear and unlimited" to Columbus. Heat and threat of thunderstorms here. We cut to the right of George Washington Bridge. The river is dark gray—darker than the sky. But beyond the Palisades we can see, under a rolling curtain of rain clouds blowing past us, blue sky and clouds very high above.

Down at Rochester. The threatening roar of a wind around the plane. In suspense, you hear it rising. You wait for it to crash around you like a wave, and the plane shakes—a dog worrying a rat.

Rochester to Detroit under the clouds—a low rolling gray curtain, scalloped, billowing. The ground is uninteresting robbed of sunlight—no emphasis, no shadows. The sun breaking through onto the lake is lovely again, like patches of sunlight on a wood floor. In the evening, looking west, the streaks of gold on Lake Saint Clair might be streaks in the western sky. We circle the house at Detroit.

Mrs. Lindbergh is pleased (and worried) to have us arrive unexpectedly and see the house in disorder. I don't know why she should mind. In the first place, I am untidy myself and a poor housekeeper—don't care about it. She has a very tidy mind, far more than mine, accurate, scientific, clear. Besides, what good does it do to hide your "faults" from people—at least that kind of outward fault that doesn't hurt anyone? Do I do it? I suppose I do, but it seems to me I am more apt to do the opposite, to tell them my "faults" immediately (that is, if I like them and want them to like me). I don't want to be liked on false pretenses, I don't want their friendship built on something shaky. They might discover my fault later and the whole thing tumble down.

Thursday, August 29, 1935
Detroit—Duluth—Red Lake Falls

Mrs. Lindbergh, her hand raised to wave us good-by as we leave—dignity, courage, faith, and restraint.

Scattered clouds. Fly just under a low even-ribbed curtain. Approaching the Straits of Mackinac—water on all sides—I can see Lake Huron on our right, Lake Michigan on our left. The geographical sense—of being able to see islands and waterways spread out below you. They look a little different from the map —pulled out of shape—but that makes them fun to recognize.

How humanity brightens the look of the landscape. The touch of man anywhere has a brightness to it seen from the air, as though it burned with the spark of life—houses, grain stacks, roads, cows, boats, fields even. The eye picks it up quickly. Is that because it has significance to me? Or does it stand out in such contrast to untouched nature, or, as I feel, does it actually sparkle?

Under the curtain again, skirting Lake Michigan, rain clouds around us.

Lake Superior coming in—a blue line on our right horizon, a little bluer than the blue land, a widening strip of blue.

I am flying while C. sketches, keeping the o on the line, watching altitude—a secure feeling when you are flying; bumps do not mean anything. You are a part of it. The country is like the North—pine trees, lakes, and those flat yellowish marshy places. On the whole, though, one of those days when the sky is more interesting than the land and you measure time and distance by it.

Flying through rain, a gray wall dead ahead, keeping your eye and your faith on that clear strip of horizon on the right,

like walking through a dark room, your hand on the wall to
guide you. How much faith there is to flying!

We land in a little cornfield at Red Lake Falls, after dragging
the field. A bumpy landing! Wing goes down and up. Stop
quickly, before we get to the stack, turn around, and go
toward the road. "There they are." (C.'s half-sister and family.)[1]
I look around for an older woman; there is none. A young slim
woman who looks about C.'s coloring and age, very pretty; a
daughter like her, but the son is dark, about ten, angley, wistful-
faced. We drive through the town to their stucco house—comfortable, simple. I think, first: she is pretty and young-looking;
second, she is honest and frank; third, she has taste. The house
is nicely done, quiet colors, not overcrowded, livable, cheerful
and attractive. The guest room has maple furniture and a
bright and dainty bathroom. I enjoy watching them. The
husband is intelligent and perceptive, runs the newspaper. She
is gay, witty, lots of pep. The girl is sensitive, with a rather
unusual taste for words.

Friday, August 30, 1935

C. flies off to Little Falls. Eva [Christie] arranges a drive to
Itasca Park, headwaters of the Mississippi. I think she has
managed her life very well. She is happily married, has brought
up two nice children, and has an attractive home. She keeps
busy in social welfare work. She is sensible, has no pretensions,
is intelligent and cheerful and independent. I think she's extraordinarily young and attractive-looking. I like studying her face:
high cheekbones, fresh fair complexion like C., a dimple in the
chin like C. (quite a strong chin). But the line of eye, nostril,
and mouth is sharper and more pointed—French.

She says about Uncle Frank's[2] divorce, "We don't have many

---

[1] Mr. and Mrs. George W. Christie, their son George, Jr., and their
daughter Lillian.

[2] Younger brother of C. A. L.'s father.

ing calm in danger may help Jon eternally. I hope so that he grows up like C.

A lovely day. Ideas bursting this morning. First I go out with Jon and pick flowers. Jon holds the basket. "You aren't going to pick them all?" he says, discouraged. Then back and arrange them. Get terribly absorbed and angry at them. Why won't they compose? The zinnias are easy, their leaves help. The bushy daisies fall to the outside and the spindly scabiosa string together in the center—terrible. Then the daisy bushes catch as you try to pull them out. I want the daisies as a kind of mist, permeating the dark spots of the scabiosa on all sides. Finally I do it. Thoroughly pleased—a sense of accomplishment. I think arranging flowers is a wonderful way to start the day: it gives you a sense of something concrete created.

Then to work, bursting with ideas—too fast to write them down. Also I played good hard tennis.

At night C. and I take blankets out on the point and lie down under the stars, under the pine. Very cold, the wind and the sea roaring. Lying flat on the hard earth, I feel rooted like a tree, or perhaps dead, buried, and attached to the earth forever. A wonderful feeling of security—to hear the wind and the sea and not be afraid of them, rooted and part of the earth, unshakable. . . . The Milky Way, Vega, and the Dipper spread out above us, flattening us out, pushing us down with their magnitude and heaviness and wide expanse. The black branches above shake in the wind, hiding temporarily some of the stars. This is eternal.

Then back to the house and get the eleven o'clock news— very gloomy. Italy is communicating to Hitler. Germany is neutral but veering toward Italy—eager to recapture her colonies. Germany plus Italy—that *will* mean war.

Saturday, October 5, 1935

Article in *Vanity Fair:* "The Lindberghs, a Love Story." Rather strange picture to me—idyl of the air. "Whatever they do, they do—together. . . . They remain unchanged." Looking back on this year, on any year, it seems so odd. Do I really present an unchanged front to the world?

North Haven, October 5, 1935

Dear Mother,

Aubrey arrived this morning. It was quite cold and we have had a nice day: tennis and target practice at rocks and much talk, rather gloomy, about the war. Both Charles and Aubrey gave Jon a "ride" in the (wood basket) "airplane" tonight, whirling around the room. Jon holds tight to the handle and goes, "Brrrr-r-r" for the engine.

Sunday

I had a nice letter from H. N. about the book (mine). It did *not* say, "How like *you* it is!" or that "You *reveal*, Mrs. L., the charming personality of your husband and yourself." It pleased me very much although I had the feeling he was talking about someone else's book. I think it was extremely nice of him to write me about it, as somebody's travel book cannot seem important in times like these.

Aubrey, C. and I talk European war constantly and listen to the radio. Trying to get a news talk this morning, we hit the relayed British program of a Tennyson anniversary meeting, with H. N. and several other people speaking. You could hear them well, though I couldn't, as Aubrey and Charles (both vitally interested in Tennyson!) were talking. And the poems were terribly mouthed by someone, "R-Ring Out Wild Bells" and "Break Break Break." "Ring out that program," C. finally shouted and, in amazement and some masculine disdain at the affected voice, "Is *that* Harold Nicolson?!" It wasn't.

DIARY   *Thursday*

C. came home in the evening. We went up [flying] to see the
sunset. It had already set in a low cloud bank but, climbing,
we made it rise again, a red crack at a time. Then it disappeared
and we tried to catch it again. Climbing against the sunset!
Finally we swung back ("Can't quite make it"). We turned back
to darkness and the world below, spiraling down. I had never
seen it in that light before—a drowsy world, the islands spread
out gray-blue in a gray-blue sea as though under veils of lavender
or covered with one wash of paint. And floating over them,
strings of soft white clouds—not really white—all colors were
dimmed in the half light. Between the horizon and the darkening blue sky was a band of pale blue, misty like the colors in
a rainbow. And as we turned and went back, the moon—full
and now quite bright—riding over the land swiftly, touching,
startlingly, the coves of Vinal Haven, and then the lake (filling it with moon!), and then The Thoroughfare. We spiraled
down into darkness as we had climbed into light. I, trying to
remember it, to grasp it, could think of nothing but "Drowsy
world, lovely drowsy world."

North Haven, Tuesday, October 8, 1935

Dear Mother,

I think we leave on Saturday or Sunday. I hate to break it
up. Everything is going so smoothly. I like the little house and
arranging flowers before I start the day's program in the morning. (Charles and Aubrey are away playing tennis, so the house
is alone and quiet.) In the afternoon, talk and tea and the
papers, and then Jon and I pasting a book—mostly ships and
planes—and perhaps music and letters.

Yesterday was *very* cold. A strong north wind roaring across
the bay from the Belfast Harbor direction, a rough gray sea,
whitecaps and spray on the rocks by the point, and the tops
of the pines shaking. It was winter, clearly cut from summer—
a wild North Haven. I thought of Matinicus and

"There in the autumn when the men go forth,
With slapping skirts the island women stand
In gardens stripped and scattered, peering north,
With dahlia tubers dripping from the hand. . . ."

[EDNA ST. VINCENT MILLAY]

But today it has bloomed again into a lovely day, the bay
stretching out still on all sides. Everything still and warm.
It seems very precious, because I know yesterday was the real
thing. We won't have this much longer.

DIARY [*Englewood*], *Tuesday, October 22, 1935*
Today I walked out into the woods, very much tangled up. I had
to get "outside the Russian enclosure." I had to go by George
and some men. I knew that I ought to "break through" somehow—I should say to them, "Nice pumpkins, there"—but I
couldn't. I felt so vulnerable and looked down and walked
out. Then I sat on a stump for a long time, looking at the
browns of many folds of leaves and the bare branches and a
few yellow leaves and pale gold grass. I felt soothed, and all those
things that had burst their compartments I could sort out and
put back neatly. I walked out of the gate again and passed
George still loading up the cart and they smiled at me and I
said easily, "You have a lot of nice pumpkins there!"

[*Englewood*], *Tuesday, October 29, 1935*
Today is frightful. The Birth Control meeting in the afternoon.
At nine the chairs come; all the doors are open downstairs;
women arrive to arrange chairs. Even upstairs I can hear them,
directing. There is a constant sound of chairs collapsing and
rumbling on top of each other, the stacks being taken in, un-
wrapped, set up, and people running back and forth, and cars.
I sit in the little [upstairs] study, having moved all my books,
papers, pictures out of the desk in the big room downstairs. The
desk upstairs is piled with last year's papers. C.'s desk is a pile of

papers and envelopes. The only comfortable chair is piled with this year's books. I put my bag of diary on the other chair. Another bag of unanswered mail is on the floor.

My unanswered invitations, mail, requests, business telephone messages overwhelm me. If people would just leave me alone— all alone. If only I were faceless. I feel so trapped and bound by those letters. I cannot write, diary or anything, and despise myself for not being able to overcome my environment. It is so infantile not to be able to manage your face-to-the-world. And I must see those people this afternoon. I get in the car. It is a physical relief to get away. I try to remember: this is the way C. feels *all the time* here. He comes home to find people just leaving and somebody coming to supper. He feels suffocated and must go out.

Wednesday [*October 30th*]

The trustees of Elisabeth's school for lunch. I dread the effort, then am stimulated, pulled by the objective quality of the men's minds and talk on education, the different factors influencing the quality of work, limitations in surroundings, quality of professors. I am sitting on the edge of my chair to make my mind grasp, feel it pulled, realize how seldom I talk to first-class minds. As usual, I am astounded at C.'s mind and how, as always, it goes directly and swiftly to the fundamental points, in every field. The joy of seeing one first-class mind challenge and meet the steel of another! We should meet more people like that.

Thursday

Mrs. Neilson:[1] "Marriage is the saddest thing I know." She is wise and brilliant and charming and has a wonderful husband and they are happily married. She laughs, of course—but she says it. "And it could be so wonderful." She showed me so

[1] Wife of William Allan Neilson, President of Smith College.

much—much more than she *knew* she was showing me, or than I could possibly tell her: what were the real things in my life and what the unreal, the escape mechanisms. Then, too, of "justifying one's existence" being really at root a Puritan attempt to separate matter and spirit. Practically, too, she helped me: I must get strong, have children, have a home of my own. And then that fundamental truth that "when one is young, one loves the things that are oneself, or like one, but when one is older one loves things objectively for *themselves.*" It is really, she said, the difference between the classical and the romantic.

I thought of what I had discovered about reading this summer, why I like to read history. She said, yes, that one must have a "core" that one was working at, and that everything related to, as she had Rilke. But as long as one knew it was there inside, it was not necessary to work at it all the time. She said too what I have learned lately, that when one is "vegetating" one is growing.

I said I thought marriage should be "further apart." She said she thought it should be closer. I: "But I think that is impossible." (An impossible ideal.) "One is just as difficult as the other," she answered. She is right. And it is better to try for the "closer" ideal than the "further apart" compromise.

Saturday

C. unhappy, restless—must-get-away-from-Englewood walk.

We go out for supper. Neither of us wanted very much to go but both felt it would be "*good*" for us." I wash my hair and fix it myself. It won't look as well, but whom am I looking well for anyway? At night my hair *does* look well! Great feeling of success. New dress; slight party terror, driving in. Haven't been out like this for so long. My party self is so stiff, it creaks. Panicky feeling going up in the elevator—powder on the nose, stockings the wrong color, hair is falling down. C. looks handsome and distant in a tux. Put the powder back quickly.

That girl at the door . . . coat off awkwardly . . . that first shyness, and then, "This is easy." It was surprisingly nice —not in that private individual way when I find someone that I feel I can and *must* talk to. Or even in the trustee-meeting way, when I felt my mind stretched onto unaccustomed subjects. Or exciting in C.'s way when I go to listen, to see C. showing his special strength and I can be faceless and sit back and appreciate it as no one else in the company can. No, this night was a purely social pleasure, a conventional pleasure, like "playing lady" as a child. We were playing "nice young married couple." Because that was the picture we presented to them, we were far more conscious of our "married quality" than we are when alone.

"That very good-looking man across the table with that dazzlingly intent look when he talks—he's my husband." I was delighted to see how C. invariably impresses people, how they listen to him, and he was proud of me. I felt pretty and charming in a light-hearted way!

C. teasing me on the way home (secretly delighted) at the way I "work" people. And I laughing and also delighted, though we both know it really isn't true and doesn't matter. The evening restored our party faces to us and we were surprised at how nice they were.

Sunday, November 3, 1935

A wonderful day: Mrs. Hand,[1] talking about Greek acceptance and Oriental acceptance. I give her Rilke. I *long* to talk to her—not about myself, either. I don't want sympathy or understanding of my life or help but *just* to talk about those ideas. Acceptance—did the Greeks do it more sanguinely than the Oriental? *Must* read about the Greeks! She gives me lists of books.

[1] Mrs. Learned Hand, wife of Judge Learned Hand, old friends of the Morrows.

But C. had a dreadful day—oh dear—because there were too many people and we were talking *all* day. An hour's talk is enough for him, he is so economical—so little waste—and he does not need "stimulus" from the outside. He has enough of his *own,* inside, and it needs expression only in action.

Monday, November 25

That argument at night over Pericles' speech about the Spartans ruling by force, the Athenians by the spirit of freedom. C. says freedom cannot exist without force to protect it. I argue bitterly and passionately, as though my whole life rested on it—as it does —and it hurt me way down inside to be beaten at it . . . as I always am.

Friday, November 29, 1935

I have been working on the apartment[1] for weeks now, and all the active excitement of getting out one's own things, seeing them shape around you, gradually forming warmth, familiarity, security, peace—and a sense of *you.* A dog turning around and around in the grass before he settles down, doing it even when it isn't necessary, in a drawing room, from habit. So I am going round and round now—I cannot sit down.

I have pushed everything away in this busyness—not only writing and thinking and awareness but letters, obligations, people, all pushed away until I get settled. I feel now as though I never would.

[Englewood], November 29

My darling Con,

It was good to get you in that letter, which struck such familiar chords. How well I know it all. It brought back the fever of those first few months in Mexico, after I had finished college.

---

[1] A. M. L. had taken a small one-room apartment for the winter as a place to write.

Elisabeth was not there and I was also completely mixed up about C. But it was still very much what you describe. That rush—the overpowering flood of laughter, gaiety, social life, sunshine, and color, with not one moment of nice cool dark mist, of being really alone, except (for me) on those early morning rides with Sue.[1] The perpetual *"feuille tremblante"* feeling. Do you remember *"L'extrême félicité à peine séparée par une feuille tremblante de l'extrême désespoir, n'est-ce pas ça la vie?"*[2] (Sainte-Beuve)? I found that quote down there and it does describe one's feelings in Mexico perfectly.

Also the personal complications: people pulling in different directions, just like Englewood, in a place *much* smaller and airtight. Gracious—how frightfully difficult for those who realize and try to bridge it. Perhaps it is better not to try. I am glad I am not there, as I should be pulled in every direction to no purpose. Much better to stand stolidly pat, pretending you are stupid and don't see the other person's point of view. Did I tell you about Mrs. Neilson's saying to me, "I feel like a tired bridge"? I think it is wonderful—my whole life. "And then, when the bridge is tired, no one walks on it. If only it were walked on it would not be so difficult!"

I have led such an active life lately, getting the apartment and winter clothes for Jon—running, running, running—that I've had no time to think or write. You know I do get somehow terribly bottled up if I don't write even letters or diary, and I haven't done either.

The apartment looks heavenly to me now. It really is very pretty, with *the* perfect place for a desk. The pictures are hung. I am putting the big *black* Orozco over the mantel. It isn't right there. I really want a Cézanne—pine trees, and the

[1] Susanna Beck Vaillant, A. M. L.'s friend from the Mexican years, later Mrs. Robert Hatt.

[2] Extreme happiness barely separated by a trembling leaf from extreme despair—is not this life?

valleys seen through them—but I don't think there are any good reproductions. I have had no chance to sit and read or write there—not yet. I hope, I do hope, it will work out.

DIARY   *Tuesday, December 3, 1935*
Day Elisabeth died.

All day I have been thinking, saying, "Three things survive mortality. They are courage, memory, and love."

I wrote Mother from the apartment. It was quiet and still and I could think about Elisabeth.

But she is so dreadfully far away. I keep wondering why I have pushed her so far away. Do all my selfish longings do it, or just practical busynesses and the need to keep clear of too much emotion, and there has been so much this last year. I wanted last winter to soak myself in Elisabeth, her letters, her diary—remembering her, writing about her, her friends, pictures, memories—re-create Elisabeth. Then I pushed it off because I could not afford to, emotionally; I had to keep clear. The Trial, C., everything—I couldn't afford to give way to that emotion. Is it that I am afraid now of the bigness of the emotion that I avoid it, or am I afraid of failing in the re-creation and then realizing her death, more than I ever have?

I think about her in a hundred little ways every day—all day alongside of me—but that intense glowing picture is gone. Mother seems to have it, and E. N., sitting here tonight, talking with conviction and assurance about a person I never knew. Where is *my* Elisabeth?

Englewood, Saturday, December 7, 1935

Mother Darling,

I have just had your letter. It sounds lovely as though you were really getting a rest and something more out of Cuernavaca. Isn't it wonderful to have it there to go back to—like the mountains in Maine, restoring one's faith perpetually in the permanency of some spiritual realities. I am glad you were there during those weeks which are so dreadful to remember.

I went down to see Mrs. Loomis the other day. She greeted me as always with "I'm *not* resigned at *all* to being old and deaf!" But I had a nice time. We talked about you. I don't think she was peeved at you—just indignant at your doing too much. She said she was worried about you the last time she saw you. I said you had been carrying much too much and that I thought it was that New England conscience we all have. You always feel that you must be doing things for other people. "Here I have this big room . . . here I have this house. It should be put to *use*—should be used for some *good*." She was under the impression that all those meetings were "social affairs." I was bound to blast *that* idea. I think she understands now.

We talked about the Greek and Christian idea of life (through an ear trumpet!) and she said she'd been brought up on the Christian one but she didn't know but what the Greek one was more sensible. Oh, what a grand old lady!

I had lunch with Mrs. Hand and the three graces (Mary, Frances and Connie)[1] yesterday. I talked too much as usual when I am shy, for the three graces have always had so much of their father's keen quick irony and humor that I am a little afraid of them. But it was fun watching them, all expressing themselves in flashes of wit, humor, half-allusions, half-stated jokes—the flicker of a smile, the flash of an eye—a little understated and yet complete understanding, depths of affection, and joy and confidence in the solidity of their relationship.

It made me terribly hungry for the thing we had as a family held together by that web of understanding, humor, and affection that shuts outsiders out. And oh, Mother, they were so *secure* in it—they took it so for granted. The *security* in their attitude separated me the most from them. A world we can never get back to. But perhaps it is best not to have it any more (the secure feeling). I trembled for them. I mean I had a kind of

[1] Daughters of Judge and Mrs. Learned Hand.

breathless feeling watching them, as you do watching the arrogantly young.

I have got to the it-must-be-perfect stage in the apartment. I cannot work or read or think about anything except "I need a small high bookcase there" and *"Why* doesn't the man come for the wood-box?" But every day when I unlock the door and step in I get a wave of happiness—and security.

DIARY   *Wednesday—With Jon*

Monte[1] helps me today. I talk to her about Elisabeth and this dreadful feeling that I have shirked the thing I was left alive for: to be conscious of her, to remember her, re-create her. Monte says it would have been bad and morbid to soak in it last winter and Elisabeth would have hated it and that I must *live* Elisabeth, not just collect memories and photographs of her. I must *live* her, in the blood and in the bones, and perhaps when I have lived and am quite old and have long hours then it will be all right to sit and collect memories and write of her. She says I must not feel I have "shirked," for that makes Elisabeth a "duty." How could Elisabeth be a duty? I think she is right and I never saw it that way.

I felt the day not a failure because at night perhaps I kept Jon from one fear; he said he didn't want me to turn the light out, that he didn't like the dark. I thought in that second of my long fight against fear of the dark, as a child, and tried to think of something nice to say to him. "Don't you like the dark, Jon? It's like a big blanket over you—like the blanket of leaves and grass over the flowers in the garden we saw this afternoon, so the flowers can sleep all covered up in the dark."

Jon smiled, relenting: "I like the dark." And after I'd gone out and turned off the light and shut the door, I heard him calling out to me, "I like the dark!" I called back, "Yes, darling!"

---

[1] Margaret Bartlett Millar, friend of Amelia Earhart and the Lindberghs and part-time secretary this winter.

Saturday, December 7, 1935

C. thinks we may go abroad to England or Sweden for the winter, or longer.[1] "Be ready to go by the end of the week— at twenty-four hours' notice."

I am thrown in a turmoil, and yet, isn't it just another one of those times when life seems to be so exciting that it is impossible to get "down to business," *my real* business? (I can't even find out what it is!) Perhaps it is just this: being able to jump into anything, with C., at any moment. (We take Jon, so there is no tug-of-war.)

But the apartment, "my own room," and the world of Greek books and Mrs. Hand, and writing—Bathurst, Greenland—and finding Elisabeth, all pushed aside again.

You should be able to carry that with you anywhere. Yes, I can, but it takes time and peace, so much time and getting acclimatized and not being excited. It takes a settled feeling.

I make lists all evening—hard to get to sleep—clothes, books, baggage, Jon.

All my life seems to be trying to "get settled" and C. shaking me out of it. But you like it? Yes.

Thursday, December 19, 1935

Aubrey to my apartment. He liked it and "saw" it. Now it is more real. He spoke about possessions, how beautiful possessions like silver, pictures, furniture, were tangible expressions of spiritual values you believed in. In a sense, then, they are creation, too. He understood how I felt about tearing it down. I feel worse about leaving what I created there and what I hoped for from it than anything else—except Thor! Like preparing the ground, and then leaving it again; like "warming

---

[1] Newspaper publicity became so intense and threatening letters arrived so frequently that an armed guard had to be kept day and night at Next Day Hill. Colonel Lindbergh decided to take his family abroad for security and in order to live normal lives.

the teapot" (Katherine Mansfield) and "There ain't going to be no tea!"

TO E. L. L. L.   *Saturday evening, December 21*

Dear M.

This is just a line—we are leaving in an hour. I wish so much we could have seen you before we left. I planned for it so happily. I should like to have talked over this move with you. I do feel that we are doing the right thing and will find safety where we go and security during a difficult time, for Jon, and for us all.

Jon is in fine shape. I took him to the doctor's and he sees great improvement and says that a peaceful winter in England will be good for him (those are our tentative plans now). C. and I are taking him alone. The boat is slow—ten days—but I have plenty of warm things for him, and your warm blanket, which I shall put on him tonight.

Our first address—after the news gets out, of course, for we are trying to get away quietly—is care of Morgan, Grenfell & Co., London, England. We go to Liverpool and then perhaps to Aubrey Morgan's family's home, till we get oriented. It is quiet and peaceful, in the country in Wales. Then I will write you.

I have thought often of you lately. C. showed me a letter you wrote him, before he went across [in 1927], that he found in his old trunk of valuables. It was such a beautiful letter—courageous and understanding and generous and unselfish, in accepting whatever life was bringing—that I felt quite humble reading it. I wanted to tell you how much I felt.

DIARY   *Saturday, December 21, 1935*

Sail for England.

Jon—silent, absorbed, watchful—sunk in the voluminosity of his town clothes in the dark corner of the car.

Into the silent dock—deserted—up the gangplank of the forward deck (like emigrants, I feel) through dark halls. Very comfortable rooms, a little crib for Jon. Jon's voice: "When I get too big for that crib, where will I sleep?" and "Can I open a package now?"

The beaming officials; smell of paint.

Put Jon to bed. It is very hot, steam heat. We do not sail for hours; noise of docks and ships.

Sleep badly. Dream vividly of Elisabeth again.

Sunday, December 22, 1935

Sunny and warm; sit on deck. There is a kitten on board to delight Jon.

We have meals, the three of us, in the little cabin room. A nice white-haired steward (English—erect, military, and respectful), has served in two wars—Boer and World War. "And we're getting trimmed for another one, sir."—"Think so?"— "Oh yes, sir, to settle the question.—Chop for the baby."

Jon (sitting up on two pillows), very hurt: "Are *I* a baby?"

Jon cries at night. "I don't like it very much. Will we go back to Englewood? I don't mind, I don't mind, but will we go back to Englewood, will I see Daddy Bee?"

Monday, December 23, 1935

Find Mother's note—in a pocket of my coat! How wonderful she is—how close we all are.

Bad weather: snow, wind, damp....

Cables begin to come in. Rather shocking, the amount of attention, the splash, so to speak.

Christmas Day, 1935
On board S.S. American Importer

Mother Darling,

I am just going to bed, next to Jon's little crib in his stateroom, but I simply must write a good night to you. I have not been able to write a line before this, *not* because it is hectic. It is peaceful, quiet, and easy, taking care of Jon, for there are no interruptions. But it is *so* absorbing. I am with him every minute and adapt my schedule to his: sleep when he sleeps, eat when he eats, even take a nap when he does. We are on deck a good deal of the day. It has *not* been smooth but not *very* rough and quite mild. But I cannot write on deck—too windy—and I must watch Jon every minute. It gives me countless hours in which simply to think letters.

I found your letter in the coat the second day when I opened the trunk to get it out. It was completely unexpected and miraculous. We so far away, separated by the sea, the quiet, the endless sound of waves—and then suddenly you bridging it, exactly like *touch,* in that pocket, and the old handkerchief of Daddy's, so comforting. "Wisdom, strength, and love" seem to express you.

I shall write about Jon later, and the Christmas presents. I sat here on the bed alone in my cabin opening them tonight, from my precious family, thinking, "How like them! How wonderful they are!"

I longed to send a wire today but we did not know what the circumstances are at home. I gather from the radiograms that the pressure is great and that, as always, we are being watched for shreds of news. So I sent nothing, though I wanted to. Anyway, my heart is with you!

DIARY   *Thursday, December 26, 1935*

I am terribly tired. I do not know exactly why. It is not as difficult taking care of Jon as I thought, much easier than at home—no interruptions. The routine goes well and easily: orange juice at 7:30. Jon sits on my suitcase and talks *all* through breakfast. Then up on deck, for an hour or two. This is peaceful. I generally sit while Jon pulls his boat down the deck or plays with the kitten; and we walk around.

Lunch, then out on deck, then down, wash for supper. Alone without C. (C. eats with the Captain). I am terribly anxious for

Jon—to eat, sleep, have his exercise properly. The eating is the worst. Also the sheer physical exhaustion of dressing and undressing, against the movement of a rough boat. One seems always to be trying desperately to get a shoe on, while child, boat, sea, gravity are pulling against you. And waiting with the greatest suspense for that slow spoonful of peas to get actually *into* the mouth.

I cannot write in my diary, or write Con or Margot. For there is not enough time alone to gather myself together, except in bed at night, when I lie awake and think and try to prepare for the future—try to pry out its secrets. What will I meet? I must be prepared for disappointment, for difficulty. I must look at it sanely and not excitedly.

Sunday, December 29, 1935

Very rough sea. Storm at night. Jon seasick all afternoon and evening—so miserable. I want so much to comfort him. I think of Elisabeth—something in his pale face. Once he put his arm around me, silently drawing down my head to his, with no explanation—he did not want me to go away. I am worried about Jon, feel he is the only thing that matters. How could I ever have worried about anything else, longed for anything else? Let me get him safely there.

A wave crashes through the window. The terror of it, the force, impersonality, hopelessness of any chance against the sea. It floods the room, soaks Jon and me. I grab him up and run with him into the next room, leave him on the floor, rush back and shut the window (I couldn't budge it fifteen minutes before). Ring for the steward—*everything* is soaking wet. At last, mopped up, we succumb to bed. I cannot sleep—tossed all night by storm and crashes outside the window.

A clear blue day, though rough. The coast of Ireland "off port."
A land smell.

The sea is beautiful, buoyant, and we all feel fresh, renewed.

> "It cannot be
> that I am he
> on whom Thy tempests fell all night."
> [GEORGE HERBERT]

Pack at night; excited. No sleep, but quieter. I think the trip
has accomplished so much, won back such joy with Jon, such
understanding and happiness. Also placed the whole year on
a better basis. I think I am clearer about C. and the future.

Night. We are in Liverpool. A strange day, early rising and
long wait. Jon is an angel, playing with toys as we wait. The
Customs men. The shock of the papers: quotes from New York
editorials.

C. carries Jon through the gauntlet of cameras down the
gangplank. The drive through the streets—trams, buses, chimneypots, red-cheeked children, women with shawls, nursemaids
wheeling prams, brick houses, raincoats, drably dressed women
—and a wave of feeling, "How *terribly* English," and then,
"How long till I see *mine*—my 'Americanisms' again?"

Extras calling in the streets: "Lindbergh in Liverpool!"

INDEX

235–36, 240, 248, 249; in Labrador, 51–60; in London, 129–31; Minnesota trips of, 288–95, 298, 300–6; monoplane of, 193 and *n.*, 194, 195, 200; 1927 flight of, 131 and *n.*; in Norway, 121–23; in Paris, 134–38; as a pilot, 26–37 *passim*, 47, 48, 56–57, 64, 72, 76, 77, 87, 97, 132, 133–34, 139–41, 142, 143–44, 148, 153 and *n.*, 154, 158, 163, 165–73, 176–77, 178–79, 199, 201, 266, 303, 311; perfusion pump of, 278 and *n.*, 281; in Portugal, 144–51; in Praia, 158–63; and press and publicity, *xx*, 15 and *n.*, 19, 95, 99, 101–2, 105, 116, 136–37, 146, 240, 331; received Roumanian decoration, 5 and *n.*; at Rockefeller Institute, *xvi*, 15, 137, 209, 244, 252; Roswell trip of, 312 and *n.*; in Russia, 116–20; and security for family, *xx*, 331 and *n.*; in South America, 173–79; on survey flight for Atlantic air route, *xiii, xiv, xvii–xix*, 40 and *n.*, 42–43, 46–182; on survey flight to Canada and Alaska, *xiv, xxv;* on survey flight to South America, *xiv;* in

Sweden, 108–14; and war, 317, 320
Lindbergh, Charles A., Jr., *xiv, xv, xviii, xx,* 3, 4, 12–14, 15, 17, 19, 23, 32, 33, 44, 57, 94, 178, 215, 247, 273. *See also* Kidnapping case and trial
Lindbergh, Evangeline Lodge Land (E.L.L.L.), 21–22, 25, 40, 41–43, 48, 89, 111, 183, 290, 300–1, 303, 305; letters to, 14, 18, 39–41, 70, 94, 110, 187, 191–92, 194, 202, 235, 280, 297, 332
Lindbergh, Frank (uncle of C.A.L.), 302 and *n.*, 303, 304
Lindbergh, Mrs. Frank (Ruth; aunt of C.A.L.), 303 and *n.*, 304
Lindbergh, Jon Morrow (son), *xiv, xvii, xviii, xix, xxii, xxiv,* 5, 6, 8, 14–15, 16, 18, 23, 33, 38, 40, 41, 42–43, 44, 47–48, 54, 57, 59–60, 71, 89, 94, 110, 127, 128, 153, 174, 183, 187–97 *passim*, 203, 208–9, 211–12, 214, 215, 216, 225, 229, 230, 235, 238, 241, 242, 244, 246, 249, 251, 252–53, 258, 263, 266, 269, 270, 274, 275, 276–77, 279–87 *passim*, 296–98, 306–10 *passim*, 313–21 *passim*, 327, 330, 331, 332–36; security for, *xv, xvi, xx–*

Falaise –

Woke up to find it very warm & still – & the
sea spreading still & soft & blue way out the
window in front of us – I wanted to glide out
the window – with my arms spread – out into
the sea – went down & walked by the sea wall
& sat for a long time – watching its horizontal
ripples of the waves on the sand – thinking of
all the horizontal things that give me peace & have
always – waves – & long wave-marks on the
sand – & flat beach branches – & trees &
pine-branches – & lines of clouds – in a
late afternoon sky – horizons – and ships
I tried to think of any perpendicular things
that gave peace – & great pines close together stretch
up so cool & dark in a forest – and yet they
don't give me peace – they pull you up – stretch
you – make you grow – and then I realized
that that was what the fundamental of my
feeling came from. Perpendicular is man
erect – awake – active – growing. Horizontal
is man lying down – asleep – resting.
| this line is power and —— this line is
peace.

I thought of E. too, peacefully – happily. I must
go to Maine & Nassau – & its quiet there – then I
will just be – not at Englewood – where one can't be